The Art & Craft of Case Writing

Julia M. Christensen Hughes

Univ. of Guelph

The Art
& Craft of
Case Writing

William Naumes
Margaret J. Naumes

 SAGE Publications
International Educational and Professional Publisher
Thousand Oaks   London   New Delhi

For information:

SAGE Publications, Inc.
2455 Teller Road
Thousand Oaks, California 91320
E-mail: order@sagepub.com

SAGE Publications Ltd.
6 Bonhill Street
London EC2A 4PU
United Kingdom

SAGE Publications India Pvt. Ltd.
M-32 Market
Greater Kailash I
New Delhi 110 048 India

Printed in the United States of America

Library of Congress Cataloging-in-Publication Data

Naumes, William.
    The art and craft of case writing / by William Naumes and Margaret J. Naumes .
    p. cm.
    Includes bibliographical references and index.
    ISBN 0-7619-1724-1 (cloth)
    ISBN 0-7619-1725-X (pbk.)
    1. Case method. 2. Textbooks—Authorship. I. Naumes, Margaret J. II. Title.
    LB1029.C37 N38 1999
    371.39—dc21   99-6230

99 00 01 02 03 10 9 8 7 6 5 4 3 2 1

Acquiring Editor:	Harry Briggs
Editorial Assistant:	MaryAnn Vail
Production Editor:	Diana E. Axelsen
Editorial Assistant:	Nevair Kabakain
Typesetter/Designer:	Danielle Dillahunt
Indexer:	Paul Corrington
Cover Designer:	Candice Harman

Contents

■

Preface

■

This book is intended for case writers, present and future. Its purpose is to help you develop effective cases, particularly those intended for teaching. If you have never written a case before, we will help you take an idea and develop it into a document that you can use in class. If you have written only a few cases, this book can help you to refine your cases, create the accompanying Instructor's Manuals, and share them with others, perhaps even publish them. Even an experienced case writer may find some ideas of value, just as we continue to learn from other participants every time we attend a case-writing workshop.

Let us introduce ourselves.

Bill Naumes, the senior author, has been writing cases for virtually his entire career. Trained in strategic management at Stanford, he has taught with cases for nearly 30 years. His case-writing skills were developed with the assistance of the ICCH Case Workshops. His cases have been published in a number of texts, including five of his own. They have also been published in refereed journals. He is coauthor of a case that won the prestigious Curtis E. Tate, Jr. Case Writing award. He was editor of the *Case Research Journal* and was President of the North American Case Research Association. Bill has lost count of exactly how many cases he has written.

Peggy Naumes learned to write cases by helping Bill with the Instructor's Manuals for his textbooks, starting with the case summaries and working up to the questions, suggested responses, and finally, cases themselves. Originally an economist trained at Stanford, she enjoyed the real-world stories that cases tell and has used the case method of teaching extensively in a variety of management courses. Some of her favorite case ideas have been suggested by class projects in which her students have researched and written cases for their class.

Collectively, we have written a wide variety of cases. Many have been lengthy and complex, to help students develop their decision-making skills in courses in strategic management and entrepreneurship. Others have been very short end-of-chapter cases, only a page or so, which are intended for students to use to apply concepts from the material that they have just read. Many have been field researched, through extensive interviews and on-site visits. Others, particularly on ethical questions, have been "library cases" written from published sources. We have learned that different purposes require different styles of cases. We've practiced these skills at workshops at regional and national professional meetings throughout the United States and in Europe. We've taught and worked with faculty in Europe and Indonesia, as well as the United States. This book grows out of our experiences in case writing and case teaching, our case-writing seminars, and the many questions that we have been asked over the years.

The outline of this book leads you through the process of writing a case, in a series of stages. The first chapters ask you to explore your reasons for wanting to write a case and help you to decide what type of case to write. The next step is to gather your information, and Chapter 3 offers advice on making contacts, obtaining releases, gathering information, and finding additional sources for data. Chapter 4 discusses cases that are written primarily for research; their style and format, and even the types of information they require are quite different from a teaching case.

The remainder of the book focuses on cases that are designed for teaching. Whereas many beginning authors write the case first and then an instructor's manual to go with it, we believe that case writing is an iterative process in which the instructor's manual and the case are written together. In order to begin writing, the case author must have already determined his or her reasons for creating a case; these objectives, key issues, and basic pedagogy that form the first part of the instructor's manual are covered in Chapter 5. The writer must then organize a multitude of data into a coherent, readable case, the subject of Chapter 6. Once drafted, the case must be class tested and refined, as described in Chapter 7. The instructor's manual can then be expanded to include specific information for other users, based on the input from actually teaching the case, and expanded to include materials that will make the case more user-friendly (Chapter 8). Chapter 9 covers industry notes, case series, and other supplemental materials that can create a more in-depth learning environment. Last, Chapter 10 describes cases created with emerging technology—video, multimedia, and the Internet.

Throughout the book, we have provided extensive examples and stories of our case-writing experiences. We have also provided a complete example: the first draft of a case and its instructor's note, found in Appendixes 1 and 2. We will end many of the chapters with an analysis of these drafts, including an evaluation based on the ideas in that chapter and what the drafts need for improvement. We hope that you will use the chapters and the outlines and checklists that are included as tables in Chapters 5, 7, and 8 to evaluate the drafts and refine your diagnostic skills. The final published version of the case and its accompanying instructor's manual are included as Appendixes 3 and 4.

There are a number of people who have contributed to this book in a variety of ways. We offer heartfelt thanks to our editor, Harry Briggs, who believed in and pushed for this project. Thank you to the editorial and production staff of Sage Publications. We also received assistance from Todd DeMitchell, Department of Education, University of New Hampshire, and from Achilles Armenakis and his students Phil Chansler, Bill Schaninger, Lori Muse, Jifu Wang, Laura Russell, and Matt Rutherford of Auburn University. We owe a special debt of thanks to Peter Rainsford, John Seeger, and Jeff Harper whose thoughtful comments made our manuscript much better. John is also our inspiration for the "bad" case and note.

The opportunities provided by the Prasetiya Mulya Foundation of Jakarta, Indonesia, and the University of Odense of Denmark gave us the opportunity to articulate and refine our vision of the case-writing process. We have also learned from the participants in many years of workshops and seminars, and their input and questions have also contributed to our knowledge. Last, we thank our relatives, particularly Andrew Oyaas, who confirmed that every-one has at least one story to tell, and Joanna and James Naumes who put up with years of "work talk" at home but turned out OK anyway—we love you, and thanks!

Prologue

Long ago, people gathered around campfires or in the hall of the clan chief, to listen to legends and stories. These might be told by a minstrel or a bard or by the shaman or wise woman of the tribe; they might be spoken or sung; they might be new or almost known by heart. But in whatever form, these stories drew listeners, so much so that many are known today. Schoolchildren of today study native American tales and, later, Greek and Roman mythology. The exploits of the ancient Scandinavian gods and of Beowulf's battle with Grendel are still known, more than a millennium later. Above all, the epic tales of Homer, *The Iliad* and *The Odyssey,* are still read, and fresh translations made, nearly three thousand years after they were composed.

What do myths and storytelling, or Homer's *Odyssey,* have to do with case writing? A great deal! Writing a case *is* telling a story, the story of a company or an institution or a situation. Like any story, it has a beginning and an end. It has sufficient detail to enable the reader to picture what is being described, whether events or people or relationships. A case, like a good story, also has a theme or a message, something for the listener or reader to take away and continue to think about, once the story has ended. Like stories also, some cases are "better" than others. They are more memorable. When this occurs because the message is more useful or thought provoking, not just because of the vividness of the details, the writer has created a truly effective and powerful case.

There are several reasons for the power of storytelling. The specifics of the story itself, the details, draw in the listener or reader and make the scenes vivid and the characters live. There is power also in the story's message or theme, if it explains our world or teaches us something about ourselves. In the oral tradition, there is power in the telling itself. The best storytellers know how to weave spells with words, through rhythm and repetition. All three of these aspects—message, details, and style—work together to create a memorable experience for the listener. All three are also necessary for a successful case. It is the intent of this book to assist the case writer, novice or experienced, with development of a stronger case, more appropriately targeted in its message, abundant but not obscurant in its details, and clearly written. But case writing, like storytelling, has elements of art. It must be experienced and practiced. We can provide techniques, and editors can provide grammar, but each author will provide his or her own unique style.

MESSAGE

Part of the power of storytelling lies in the theme or message of the story. In preliterate societies, these tales played an important role in the transmission of the group's history and culture from one generation to another. From the legends, one learned many lessons: how the world was created, humankind's relationship with other species, what makes one's own clan different from (and superior to?) all others. Natural phenomena could be explained: lightning as Zeus's or Thor's thunderbolts or how the curious coyote let loose the sun and moon from chests stolen by the eagle from the kachinas, as told in a Zuni story (Hulpach, 1965). In addition to its primary story, *The Odyssey* contains many examples of good (and bad) behavior, most notably the faithfulness of the hero's wife, Penelope, in spite of 20 years of separation and the demands of a host of suitors that she remarry. Stories could also serve as oral history. Many of the places described in *The Odyssey* have been found thousands of years later by archaeologists, and bards in medieval Europe carried news as well as legends.

Storytelling appears to be as old as humankind or at least older than any written language. People still read tales that were told in ancient Egypt, Sumeria, and Israel, from India and China two millennia ago. African tales were told by the griot and passed down long before their languages were written. Although the stories themselves might differ (and in fact, there are many similar tales in diverse cultures), they served the same human needs:

"Curiosity about the past, the search for an understanding of beginnings, the need for entertainment and the desire to keep alive a heroic past" (Baker & Green, 1987, p. 1). Over time, some of these stories became tales to be told in their own right, valued for their entertainment. But even Pecos Bill and Paul Bunyan tell us something about our own culture. They are larger-than-life American folk heroes, native to America, and their exploits illustrated the untamed nature and the possibilities of the American frontiers.

Some stories are more obvious in their messages than others. Aesop's *Fables* were short vignettes. The characters were animals—a fox trying to reach a bunch of grapes, a tortoise, a hare—but their activities were very human. The rabbit knew that he could win a foot race with very little effort, so he allowed himself to become distracted. The tortoise knew that a race would be very difficult to win, so he concentrated on achieving his goal. After trying repeatedly to reach the grapes, high over his head, the fox decided that they weren't worth pursuing and were probably sour anyway. Aesop made sure that the reader-listener would not miss the point, however, by providing the lesson or "moral" at the end of the tale. The listener would indeed be left with a message, but she or he would not have to work for it. Legal cases are frequently of this type. They are rich in the essential details of the case, including all key evidence on both sides, but the lesson is spelled out for the reader by the judge's verdict.

The legend of King Midas, whose greed was so intense that he wished for and was granted the power to turn everything he touched into gold, is longer than Aesop's short stories, but its messages are almost as obvious. The king's "gift" backfired when he touched his daughter, whom he loved but who was turned into a golden statue, regardless of his feelings. Two lessons that can easily be drawn are "People are more important than riches" and "Be careful what you wish for." However, the listener or reader can't simply jump to the end to find the "right answer" but must learn it from the details of the story.

The story of Persephone is more complex. In Greek myth, Persephone was the daughter of Demeter, the goddess of corn and the harvest. Persephone was snatched by the lord of the underworld to be his bride. Her mother mourned for her and refused to let the crops grows until Zeus, king of the gods, arranged a compromise that allowed Persephone to spend two thirds of the year with her mother. The story can be enjoyed simply as an adventure, with love and loss, conflict and mystery—where has she gone and how does her mother get her back? On another level, the resulting compromise offered an explanation for the regular and orderly change of seasons, when the earth's rotation around the sun was not yet understood. On still another level, the characters illustrated basic human desires and behaviors, even when attrib-uted to the gods, thus reassuring the hearer about human nature. Most listeners would be able to recall the plot, and many would remember the explanation of the seasons. Different people might take away varying inter-pretations of the characters, however, and would probably not consciously think about this aspect unless questioned. These responses represent different levels of analysis and learning from the same story. A well-written integrative teaching case often displays these same characteristics. It allows students to identify issues and important relationships for themselves and to draw their own conclusions but is rich enough in detail to allow for more than one interpretation or depth of analysis.

The Odyssey represents the most complex example of all. It contains many shorter stories, each describing a set of characters and events, all of which are connected together by the passage of time, the years following the end of the Trojan War, and an underlying common theme, Odysseus's desire to regain his home, despite all obstacles. In contemporary case writing, this is analogous to the medical case history of an individual or to a study of the same business enterprise as it responds to a variety of situations over a period of time.

DETAILS

The specific details included by the case writer or storyteller also contribute to the power of the story. They give it life, vividness, memorability. When a griot described Anansi the spider, a frequent subject of West African stories, as a "trickster," this gives the audience a glimpse into the character and prepares them to understand why he acts in a particular way. The cliche of "a dark and rainy night" creates a mental image of a foreboding and threat-ening atmosphere. When the Great Spirit underbakes or overbakes the clay figures, we gain a vivid and lasting picture of how a Native American tribe saw itself ("just right") compared with other races.

The details also affect both the message itself and how it will be perceived or learned. The storyteller decides how much description to include. The choice may depend on the time or space available, on the format, and on the audience. A myth that explains the seasons or a fable with a moral would be relatively short and concise. In keeping with the strong theme or focus, the fewer the details, the more obvious the point. A story for children would be shorter and have less detail than one for adults, who have longer attention spans and more experience in building mental pictures. The more abundant and varied the description, the more complex the listening or reading be-comes, and the more possibility there is for people to combine and select those details that they feel are most important. Too much detail, however, can confuse listeners and cause them to lose track of the story's point, whereas too little detail can make the point or plot obvious and boring. Thus, the amount of detail and description is an important choice that the storyteller must make.

The storyteller also has the power to chose what specific details to include. Not all descriptions are equally relevant. Without the description, the reader might well assume that Paul Bunyan's blue ox, Babe, was brown or some other color that is normal for cattle. However, knowing that Paul wore brown boots does not add to his uniqueness and is probably unnecessary. The baking details, in the story of the Great Spirit making humans out of clay, are necessary to understand the point of the story, whereas details about cooking time would be irrelevant in many other settings. A detailed description of how children are disciplined or conditioned to follow the group's rules would be very important in understanding a society's values. However, the story of Peter Rabbit contains only one sentence telling the reader that Mrs. Rabbit made Peter Rabbit go without his supper when he disobeyed. In a story or case about a corporation, it may be necessary to include details concerning how its product is made, even though the main focus is on competition, so that the reader can better understand the capabilities and limitations of that company.

In addition, real situations take place in a world that is so complex and rich in details that it would not be possible to include them all. Thus, every storyteller must make choices as to which to include and what to leave out. Some are essential, or the story will not make sense and the message will not be understood. The storyteller may choose, however, to stick only to the essentials or to incorporate information that is not absolutely necessary but that will add to the vividness, the memorability, of her or his word pictures. Sometimes, he or she may not be sure how much detail is enough or exactly what pieces of information each listener-reader will find useful. He or she may also choose to include details that are irrelevant, designed to create false trails ("red herrings," in the language of mystery stories). In cases designed for educational use, this gives the student an opportunity to evaluate and assess the details and determine which ones *are* in fact most useful. The fewer the details, the clearer the relationships will inevitably be. More, even too much, information forces the readers to identify these linkages for themselves.

STYLE

What can we say about style? Every person has his or her own. No two people will tell a story the same way. As evidence, consider family accounts of the same event, such as a vacation or a "disaster." Each person will have a slightly different point of view and will include different details. The result will be two, or three, or more stories that are similar but not the same. A person's recounting may even change with each telling, depending on memory and the receptiveness of the audience.

Although style is individual, there are some guidelines that make writing, or storytelling, more effective. One noted storyteller described the importance of the pace of the tale:

Put your mind to it and you will see how definitely certain stories call for a marked timing. Some stories, heroic ones, march from beginning to end. Other stories go quickly, on light feet; they call for the suggested rhythm, the delicacy of touch of a Strauss waltz. (Sawyer, 1962, pp. 145-146)

Her mentor described the impact of a pause:

With children it means an unconscious curiosity that expresses itself in a sudden muscular tension. There is just time during that instant's pause to *feel*, though not to *formulate*, the question: "What is standing at the door?" (Shedlock, 1951, p. 34)

Some stories use repetition or rhyme as a key ingredient. Think of the Three Little Pigs and the refrain-dialog: "Little Pig, little pig, let me come in." "Not by the hair on my chinny-chin-chin." "Then I'll huff and I'll puff and I'll blow your house in!"

The line of the story is also important:

Action unfolds through word pictures, maintains suspense, and quickly builds to a climax. Each incident must be related in such a way that it makes a vivid and clear-cut image in the listener's mind. One event must lead logically and without interruption to the next. (Baker & Green, 1987, p. 20)

Younger, less experienced listeners in particular need a clear structure to the tale. So, too, with cases. For novice learners, a more structured, more focused style is necessary, whereas more mature case users can cope with more detail and more complexity of meaning.

CASES

Cases represent a particular type of storytelling. They are written, rather than spoken. They are intended primarily as teaching tools to provide students a realistic look at their world and an opportunity to practice their skills in an environment with few consequences. They should also be concretely based on facts, rather than imagination. Whereas style may seem less important in a fact-based case than in fiction, there are still some conventions that should be observed. Even if a case is being written as its situation occurs, it should be written in the past tense—because, to its future readers, it will take place "once upon a time." It should have real people who, like the characters in a story, are allowed to speak in their own words, whose actions are described. The amount and vividness of detail will vary, depending on the needs of the story or the case, as we have already discussed. But for each type of case, each purpose, some formats will be more effective than others. Our intention is to help the writers of these written stories, these cases, to be as effective as the storytellers of old.

1

What Is a Case, and Why Write One?

Case studies form an important pedagogical tool in many fields of study. The use of case studies allows students to actively participate in the learning process. To be able to use the case method in our courses, we must have a continuous source of fresh case studies to maintain the interest of our students. These cases must provide value to the learning process, as well. Ideas for case studies can come from a wide variety of sources.

Case studies are more than teaching tools, however. Using these examples from real experiences, we can show the links between theory and actual occurrences and can bring our research into the class room. Cases also provide the data for in-depth traditional research and are particularly useful for exploring causality and other linkages behind survey data. Both teaching cases and research cases can be submitted to refereed journals (though still, for the most part, different journals).

There must be an objective in developing a case study for it to make sense. Many times, there is a gap in our knowledge or understanding of some concept that should be analyzed and explored. There are also gaps in the range of suitable materials available for student learning. Bringing your own work into class can be very rewarding. Students build on your obvious interest in the topic. Locally based cases not only catch students' interest but also help to involve them in the regional economy—and, on occasion, may enable them to meet the characters from their readings. One of our motivations is always curiosity; we want to know more about how each case's organization really operates. For all of these reasons, we write cases.

DEFINITION OF A CASE

A case is a factual description of events that actually happened at some point in the past. Although fictional stories may meet some pedagogical objectives, they do not have the intellectual rigor of a case based in factual research. The case is designed to meet specific pedagogical or research objectives of the case writer. As such, the case must provide sufficient material concerning the situation and the environment surrounding it to meet those objectives.

The case method has been used in a variety of forms as a pedagogical tool for quite some time. It has been used in medicine, psychology, sociology, and law since the 1800s. In these fields, the vehicle used is a case history of an event, individual, group, or decision. It includes the results of the actions, as well as the actions themselves. Based on the use of case studies in those fields, the method was adapted for use in the study and teaching of managerial decision making. Cases were first used for this purpose at the Harvard Business School in the early part of the 1900s. The school developed a series of case studies based on field research and used them to study decisions in all of the functional areas of a typical business program. From there, the method spread to the point that it is used not only in most business programs but also in other fields including, agriculture, education, political science, nursing, and others.

A case study is designed to elicit discussion and analysis of a particular situation. A case may first be used to allow students to learn how to evaluate a situation or identify problems in a variety of settings. In teaching, as in research, cases can be used to explore the relationships within a setting or organization or to observe changes over a period of time.

Cases are also designed to provide the basis for analysis of the decision-making process under a variety of conditions. Students can develop their ability to determine appropriate criteria by which alternative solution sets can be measured. The students can then develop those alternatives and perform the analysis to develop an appropriate solution. Last, the case can be used to help our students develop an understanding of the problems involved in implementing the selected solution. In this manner, the case can be used to follow the entire decision process from analysis through to implementation.

Case studies provide a means by which readers can learn through the discussion of actual situations and circumstances, by following the actions and analyzing the thoughts and decision process of real people, faced with real problems, in real settings. This is true for heuristic decisions where there may be no one "best answer," as well as for algorithmic models that are designed to provide an optimal solution. Students are often uncomfortable with cases' ambiguity, the lack of a single "right" answer. With cases, understanding how to evaluate a situation or make a decision is often as important a student outcome as the specifics of her or his discussion. From the analyses of a series of such cases, our students can develop the ability to apply these processes and extrapolate their understanding of the underlying concepts and theories to situations they encounter in the future.

The case method is an active pedagogical process, as opposed to the passive process that ensues from lectures. Students, therefore, learn by performing all the various analyses and activities themselves, instead of being told how it is done. For most students, learning by doing provides far better and more lasting results than learning through lectures.

■ How Students Learn

The goal of any instructional material was defined by the Association for Supervision and Curriculum Development in this way: "To stimulate and nourish students' own mental elaborations of knowledge and to help them grow in their capacity to monitor and guide their own learning and thinking" (Resnick & Klopfer, 1989, p. 4). As will be discussed in the next chapter, cases lend themselves to this process. A case is a form of teaching in which the student *must* involve himself or herself in order to learn. What is taught is not just a set of facts about a specific situation but also a process of thinking, of analysis, of problem solving, even of evaluation and judgment. Students learn these skills by practicing them in a "real" situation, the case, thus developing the thinking tools that will be needed when their experiences call for real decisions.

One approach to teaching students how to think is to embed "thinking" in the regular content of a course. Many instructors explicitly outline the process of how to approach a problem (or a case), then give students the opportunity to practice that process. Cases provide a rich environment for this type of learning. Each case presents a different set of details, yet students may apply a similar type of analysis. Once mastered, they are ready to move on to more complex skills, as well as more advanced course concepts.

Many educational researchers are coming to favor an immersion approach to the development of thinking. Although there is no precise definition of this approach, Prawat (1991) summarizes its main arguments:

There is general support, for instance, for the view that ideas, as opposed to skills and processes, should be assigned the highest priority in promoting thought and understanding in the classroom. There is also general agreement that discourse plays a key role in this regard. (p. 8)

It is based on the concept that students learn best when they derive the underlying ideas for themselves, out of the material presented. They are learning how to think by thinking, rather than being told how to approach the subject. Cases are among the educational materials best adapted to allow students this active a role in their own learning.

Cases are also versatile in their adaptability to the ways in which different students learn. Most people have a preferred learning style or way in which they approach experiences and develop meaning from them. There are a number of models of this process. For illustration, we will use the model developed by David Kolb and associates (Kolb, Osland, & Rubin, 1995), which identifies four basic learning style types: *converger, diverger, assimilator,* and *accommodator.* A converger relies most heavily on abstract conceptualization, which is an analytical, logical approach, and on active experimentation. His or her strength is the practical application of ideas. The diverger prefers concrete experience, which looks at every situation as unique and tends to judgments based on personal feelings, and reflective observation that takes an "objective observer" approach. She or he is likely to be strong in imaginative ability and to be able to see a situation from many perspectives. The assimilator relies on abstract conceptualization, like the converger, and reflective observation, like the diverger. His or her strength is the ability to create patterns out of discrete observations or facts and is likely not be particularly interested in applications. An accommodator prefers concrete experience and active experimentation. She or he likes to learn by doing, and is likely to solve problems by trial and error, rather than through logical reasoning.

Cases work in a variety of ways that make them adaptable to more than one learning style. A converger could apply theories or concepts to the facts in the case, to bring order and meaning to the situation described. A diverger is likely to be intrigued by the multiple details and viewpoints in the case. The assimilator can look for patterns in the data of the case and develop her or his own hypotheses about what has led to this point and what will happen next. The accommodator is most likely to appreciate the "real world" aspects and the opportunity to practice his or her decision-making skills. It may not be possible to use each case to involve all of these learning styles. However, cases can be used effectively for a wide range of educational objectives, as will be discussed in Chapter 2.

■ Case Types

Essentially, a case is a research study with a sample of one. The "one *n*" sample is the particular event, situation, organization, or selection of individuals that is presented in written or other forms. It provides readers with a vehicle to discuss, analyze, and develop criteria and potential solutions for the problems presented in the case.

There are many ways to categorize cases: factual versus fictional (which, as already noted, we would argue are not cases at all), field researched versus library researched versus personal experience, teaching versus research, evaluative versus decision focus. Cases also come in a wide variety of lengths and complexities, from one- or two-paragraph stories found at the end of textbook chapters, to 20-page (or more) descriptions of an entire corporation's strategic decision making, to a series of cases that explore events over time or in different aspects of the organization.

In disciplines such as anthropology or medicine, cases are written after extensive personal observation in the field. Many business cases are also based on interviews and personal observation of an organization. In some fields, where the focus is on objective data, or where members of the organization are willing to talk "on the record," or where there are significant ethical or legal issues that create issues of confidentiality, research may be done primarily through published or public sources. Cases can also be written from the author's own personal experience, although it may be difficult to present the material objectively. Issues of data collection will be discussed in Chapter 3.

As already noted, there are many potential objectives in writing a case. The greatest difference is between cases written primarily as vehicles for research and those that are written primarily for the classroom. Research cases, discussed in more detail in Chapter 4, are intended to develop or test a hypothesis. They present both the data on an organization and the analysis of those data, including linkages to the relevant theories or hypotheses. Teaching cases, which are the primary focus of this book, present only the direct observations and facts, serving as vehicles for students to apply their skills in analysis and decision making. However, the author of a teaching case is expected to provide a detailed analysis in the form of an Instructor's Manual, which includes both pedagogy and theory. The organization and content of cases and their supplements (such as industry notes and case series) will be covered in Chapters 6, 7, and 9. Instructors' Manuals will be developed in Chapters 5 and 8. The match of length, data, organization, and objectives will be explored in detail in Chapter 2.

A major pedagogical distinction may be made between *evaluative* and *decision focus* cases. A case may be designed primarily as a description of events and decisions that have occurred in the past, with the intent of having the readers learn lessons from the results of those actions. This is often referred to as an evaluative case, because the major, or even sole purpose is to have readers analyze and evaluate the events described in the case. This is the analog of using case studies to replicate previous research or to test previously proposed hypotheses.

An alternative, and usually more valuable form of a case study is one where the readers are expected not only to analyze and evaluate past events but also to develop criteria and decisions for future actions by the principals presented in the case. This is often referred to as a decision focus case. This is the analog of using case studies to develop hypotheses and theories.

All of these types of cases have many factors in common, however. They are all descriptions of real events and situations. Moreover, a case presents the events and situation in a factual manner, much in the same way that a reporter describes an event for a newspaper. In a teaching case, value-laden judgments and statements are left to the Instructor's Note, much as newspapers leave this approach to the editorial page. In a research case, however, the value judgments are essentially analysis of the facts to prove or develop hypotheses and may be interwoven with the factual content, as will be discussed in Chapter 4.

■ A Real Situation

Using the definition of the North American Case Research Association and many other groups of case writers, including the authors of this book, a case is a description of a *real* situation. Although the case may disguise some or most of the facts, the basic situation is neither changed nor invented. Case studies are a form of research, whether intended for teaching or developing or testing hypotheses. In no legitimate form of research do we invent or mask material such that it does not match what actually happened.

Case studies are meant to involve the readers in the decision process. To do that, the situations must be realistic. It is rare that fiction actually seems truly real to the reader. We read fiction, more often than not, to escape from reality.

We once used some fictitious cases in a course because they seemed to meet the specific needs of the points we were trying to present. The students saw through the fiction in the cases and stated, almost unanimously, that the cases simply lacked realism. They ended up spending as much time analyzing what was unreal about the cases as they spent studying the situations and applying the concepts from the text and readings to the cases.

■ Facts, Not Opinion

Case studies are a presentation of facts. Not only are the facts as presented real, they are as close to what actually occurred as is possible, given the reporting process. You, as the case writer, are not expected to interpret the actions or events that have occurred. As noted earlier, you are to act as a reporter, describing as closely as possible what has occurred. However, you typically have to rely on the recollection of other people, who were either party to the events or at least witnessed them. As a result, there may be bias in the way they remember the incidents or situations. The way to overcome this is to follow the same procedures used by reputable reporters. That is, you should try to find corroborating evidence concerning the events discussed in the case. This usually requires the supporting statements of one or more people other than that of the person providing the principal account of the situation.

The material describing the incident usually comes from interviews, either primary or secondary, of people involved in the situation. There is another danger in reporting this information. That is, that you will paraphrase the material in writing the case. In doing so, you may inadvertently introduce bias into the description. It is always best to let the words of the people providing the information speak for themselves. In this way, you are letting the readers provide the interpretation of those words. The incident, described in the words of the people who actually lived it, typically has far greater impact than when restated by the case writer. By presenting the case in this manner, you are adhering more to the principle of reporting facts, instead of interpreting the events.

■ Research as Anthropology

Case research is much like that presented by anthropologists. Case writers are preserving situations, actions, or decisions as histories of events that have occurred. Much like the anthropologist, you are saving the description of the events so that others may learn what occurred. Because the purpose of the case method is to provide a realistic means by which readers can learn through analysis, discussion, and providing solutions from actual events, you should be attempting to present a variety of such events from which we can learn. It is by exposure to similar events in an assortment of backgrounds and environments that readers can apply the concepts and theories widely.

Anthropologists look at different societies and try to extrapolate how they, and other cultures, developed. From this, they then try to determine the impact of various cultural and environmental factors on that development. Similarly, we analyze a variety of events and try to determine the common themes that led to the actions, decisions, and results produced from those situations.

As the environment affecting our disciplines changes, we find it necessary to study new events. These new situations become the case studies from which we develop and refine our perceptions of the theories and concepts defining our disciplines. Essentially, we are analyzing and explaining the cultural development of our fields. By then presenting these cases to our students, we help them to learn the field's theories and concepts. From the analyses of these different cases, our students gain an understanding of the complexity and changes facing people in our various fields.

REASONS FOR WRITING A CASE

As was noted at the beginning of this chapter, there are many reasons why you might decide to write a case, ranging from "because it was an interesting situation" to "I had access to the data" to "I want (or my Dean wants me) to publish." Any pretext that gives you the incentive to put pen to paper or fingers to keyboard is worthwhile. New case writers often start either because they can't find a case to fit a particular topic or because an abundant supply of information on an interesting situation was available.

■ Gap Analysis

We often find that there are gaps in the supply of case studies as we prepare our class syllabus. We find that there is no suitable case to present a particular aspect of the theories or concepts in our courses. This is especially true as we widen our knowledge of our respective fields. New concepts and theories require the development of new case studies. This is even more true for research cases, which are typically written to expand knowledge of a new area by studying the "why" behind the data or to develop new theories.

We want our students to be able to learn from the experience of those who have been faced with the environmental factors that help to define and explain these theories and concepts. Therefore, we need to close the gap between theory and pedagogy.

One way to close these gaps is to search out and develop case studies based on relevant situations appropriate for that analysis. This is a form of research that provides us with a better understanding of how the theories and concepts we develop are applied in the real world. They help us to better explain these concepts and theories to our students. We are also able to help our students learn directly, as well as indirectly, from these newly described experiences. In this manner, we are able to close the circle between theory, research, and teaching through the development of case studies based on actual occurrences. We consciously seek out these new case incidents to close the gaps in our pedagogical and research activities.

One of the authors was teaching a course in strategic management during the mid-1970s. At that time, the conglomerate business structure necessitated a new approach to strategic management. Unfortunately, there were few case studies dealing with this organizational form that also explored the interaction of managerial values and corporate objectives. The author decided that, to teach that segment of the course effectively, it would be necessary to write a case study that incorporated those factors. An analysis of the conglomerates at the time led to the selection of Gulf & Western Industries (G & W) as an appropriate subject for a case study. Fortunately, and this entered into the decision, the Chief Executive Officer of G & W, Charles Bludhorn, liked to talk to the business press. It was a rather easy task, therefore, to develop an effective case study of the company from published sources. Of equal importance was the fact that the company was considering two acquisitions that fit the education objectives of the course. The author was able to write a case study that included all the major components needed to teach students about the conglomerate form, including strategic objectives and the importance of managerial values on the decisions made by the people within the firm (Naumes, 1982b). The case was subsequently published in other writers' texts. It turned out that others also saw the need for such a case study and used this case to meet those objectives. In this situation, a gap in the teaching literature was determined, and a case study was written to fill that gap.

■ Serendipity

Sometimes, we write case studies simply because we are presented with them by fate. For whatever reason, a situation presents itself that seems too good to pass up. We start to develop the case simply because it appeals to us as a good teaching vehicle for presenting a particular idea, even if there are other case studies that already present that idea.

Often, these are the result of discussions with colleagues, friends, students, and managers. Colleagues, comparing notes and talking shop, may describe interesting experiences that they have used to fill in the gaps. Friends and former students have, typically, been introduced to the case method in classes or through other sources. They describe events that have occurred to them at some time in the past. Sometimes, the events are current. That is, the people are currently involved in the situation and the decisions that are needed or are being made. This often takes the form of an attempt at free consultation, much the way we might describe a current illness when we start talking to a physician at a party or talk about a legal problem when we run into a lawyer. The people, once they discover what we do, describe the situation in hopes that we might be able to provide some guidance to them. When this happens to the authors, we often ask them if they would be willing to have a case study written describing the events. Although we do not offer the free consultation that they desire, we do note that simply seeing the situation in written form often helps to better understand the decisions that have to be made. On occasion, this does even lead to a consulting engagement. But the case study is always in the backs of our minds, whatever the outcome of the discussion.

SUMMARY AND CONCLUSIONS

A case study is a description of a real event. The purpose of developing a teaching case is to enhance the pedagogical experience for our students. Case studies are used to involve our students in the learning process. By becoming an active participant, our students are more likely to retain what they have learned.

Students with a variety of learning styles can be included in case discussions through various means and still gain from the experience. Moreover, case studies need not have a decision point for the students to learn from them. Even evaluative cases can provide valuable lessons, as will be shown in the next chapter.

Case studies are descriptions of real events. They are the equivalent of anthropological studies. They are, in essence, a research study with a sample of one. They allow the researcher to explore a situation in depth, looking at such issues as linkages and causality. By exposing our students to these studies, they are able to see the link between theory and practice. This provides a sense of reality to the theories and concepts that we present in our class rooms.

Case studies are written from the perspective of a disinterested observer. They should be factual accounts of what happened, with the provision of corroborative evidence to support the facts as presented. We save our perceptions of the meaning of these facts for the Instructor's Manual.

A case study frequently comes from our need to fill a gap in our teaching needs. We find a subject or topic where there is no effective case study designed to analyze that topic. We then seek out a situation that would help us to study that set of issues when presented as a case study. On occasion, a situation presents itself that is simply too good to pass up. We write this situation up as a case study, simply because the opportunity presents itself, not necessarily because we set out to meet a particular pedagogical objective.

Case writing can lead to a satisfying experience for the case writer, the teacher, and the students. You, as the case writer, have the opportunity to investigate and learn. The real situation that you are studying adds to your understanding of your field. If you can write up both the case and your experiences with it, it becomes an effective tool that can be used by other teachers. Students are able to become involved and interested by a real situation to which they can bring the tools and theories that they have learned from text and lecture. Effective case studies meet the needs of all those involved in the teaching process.

2

■

Objectives

Key to the Case

■

Once you have an idea for a case, your next big challenges are to find and collect the necessary information and to organize it into a meaningful format. But how do you know what information is necessary? There is often a wealth of details, of data, about a situation. The case would be the length of a book if everything were included. Whether the case is for research or teaching, it is important to select all of the appropriate information if you are to accomplish your purpose. This means that you must have a clear concept of what that purpose is.

Even if your reason for embarking on the case-writing process is to fill a gap in the materials available for your course, you still will need to consider what you want that case to accomplish. You will have to consider both the specific knowledge that students should take away from the class discussion and the types of intellectual processes that they will be developing. Your choice of objectives, particularly in terms of the analytical tools that students will use, will have a strong impact on the facts, and even the organization, of the case. If the case idea came to you through serendipity, because an opportunity to do research presented itself, then it is even more important to focus first on your case's potential objectives as a means of focusing and organizing the information. In a research case, the objectives will, of course, relate to the hypotheses that you are testing or to the phenomenon you are investigating, if you are engaged in theory building.

In later chapters, we will talk about how to locate and collect information for your case, how to establish the specific ideas and key issues that the case will illustrate, and give guidelines for organizing your material. This chapter focuses on the process of choosing your objectives, the fundamental purposes for which you are writing the case. These are rooted in your pedagogical (or research) goals. They, in turn, will shape the case's length, its complexity, and even to some extent, its style.

WHAT SKILLS OR THEORIES DO YOU WANT TO DEVELOP?

Before discussing the types of objectives that are appropriate for different types of cases, it is helpful to have an understanding of how a person's thinking process is developed, from basic knowledge to complex analytical skills. There have been many writers in the fields of education and psychology who have studied this process, with differing approaches. We will give you a brief introduction to two of these approaches as background to the discussion of choosing your case's objectives.

■ Marzano: The Thinking Process

One approach looks at the processes involved when we learn to think about a new subject or discipline. This process of thinking is composed of two parts: acquiring knowledge and producing or applying knowledge. Marzano et al. (1988) consider knowledge acquisition as the basis for learning any discipline. They identify three components of knowledge acquisition: *concept formation, principle formation,* and *comprehension.* Concept formation is integrally involved with learning the vocabulary that describes the key ideas of a discipline. Once a student knows the basic concepts, she or he can go on to form in her or his mind the principles or rules that explain the relationships among those concepts. Comprehension, the final aspect of knowledge acquisition, is collecting and understanding specific information and its meaning in the context of that discipline.

However, Marzano et al. (1988) emphasize that the acquisition of knowledge is only useful if it can be used, either to apply to a real situation or problem or to produce new knowledge (pp. 64-65). The important processes in knowledge production or application are *composing, problem solving, decision making,* and *research.* Each of these takes basic information, concepts, and relationships and uses them to achieve a new outcome—or at least one that is new for the student. Composing is, essentially, the reinterpretation or rearrangement of ideas into a new format, whether written or artistic. An example might be a summary of the important facts of a case. Problem solving involves more than plugging the right facts into an existing formula, although that may be a stage in this process. More advanced students learn to identify and define the problem from a poorly organized set of information and to select a strategy for reaching a solution. Decision making requires the student to choose between two or more solutions to the same problem. An important component of this process is the development of criteria against which to compare the alternatives. Research, the fourth process, is the act of finding explanations and making predictions by creating hypotheses and testing them. Although this is usually associated with the sciences or social sciences, students in subjects such as literature often create mental models of how characters will interact or what certain images represent. In history classes, students may theorize about the underlying forces that caused important events. Cases as an instructional tool are very well adapted to foster students' thinking processes, in particular, those relating to knowledge application or production.

A final thinking process, which can be used to learn all of the other processes, both knowledge acquisition and knowledge application, is *oral discourse* or dialogue. By interacting with other students and with the teacher, the student collects information, sees how it relates to what he or she already knows, is able to form and test ideas about these relationships, and learns to come up with solutions and explain or defend them. An instructor who teaches with cases relies on class discussion to stimulate students' learning, from the case and from each other. Although they may or may not retain specific facts about the situation or company in the case, they are developing thinking processes that will help them not just in school but also in the real world.

As Marzano et al. (1988) state,

> Thinking processes often begin with an unresolved problem, a need, or an indeterminate situation. . . . The teacher's challenge is to see opportunities for using thinking processes to enhance student learning in any content area, teaching the component thinking skills as necessary. (p. 67)

The thinking processes are goal related; students learn to compose, to solve a problem, to conceptualize. Thinking skills, on the other hand, are means to achieving those goals. Marzano et al. identify 21 core thinking skills, which they group into eight categories: (a) focusing skills (defining problems and setting goals), (b) information gathering skills (observing and formulating questions), (c) remembering skills (encoding and recalling information), (d) organizing skills (comparing, classifying, ordering, and representing), (e) analyzing skills (identifying attributes and components, identifying relationships and patterns, identifying main ideas, and identifying errors), (f) generating skills (inferring, predicting, and elaborating), (g) integrating skills (summarizing and restructuring), and (h) evaluating skills (establishing criteria and verifying; p. 69). Although there is a rough progression from focusing through evaluation, any of these skills may be used and combined in the various thinking processes.

■ Bloom's Taxonomies

A more hierarchical approach is exemplified by Benjamin Bloom's taxonomy of educational objectives (Bloom, Hastings, & Madaus, 1971). He defines "the art of teaching" as "the analysis of a complex final product into the components that must be attained separately and in some sequence" (p. 13). His taxonomy is a classification system for educational objectives, in which "each category is assumed to include behavior more complex, abstract, or internalized than the previous category" (p. 39). There are, in fact, two hierarchies: one (the cognitive domain) classifying levels of intellectual objectives and the other (the affective domain) describing levels of feeling, emotion, or acceptance of key values. (For a brief summary of both aspects of the taxonomy of educational objectives, see the Appendix to Part 1 of Bloom et al., 1971, pp. 271-277. A more detailed explanation may be found in Chapters 7-10 of the same book.)

The taxonomy of the cognitive domain begins with objectives related to *knowledge.* Here, knowledge is defined as the ability to remember. It could be simply recalling specific facts or could extend to abstract principles or even knowledge of ways to organize and work with other information. However, *comprehension,* or understanding what is being communicated, represents a higher level of skill. The third level is *application,* in which the student begins to be able to move from the specific material to general principles or abstractions. *Analysis* is one step higher, because it involves working with the information. This could involve breaking it into components, to clarify the relationships among the ideas, or delving into the organization or structure of the material being learned. *Synthesis,* the fifth level, involves building on the analysis to create a new whole. This could be a summary of the important points, or a reaction to them, or the development of a plan or a new set of abstract relationships. The final level is *evaluation,* in which the student learns to make judgments about the material. These can be quantitative or qualitative, based on internal consistency or external factors, measured against others' standards or against criteria that the student develops for herself or himself.

The case method of teaching assumes that students are competent in knowledge and comprehension. It is particularly well suited for analysis, synthesis, and evaluation. A case typically presents a depth of material that must be assessed for its significance and understood in terms of its relationships. Students must use their analysis to identify problems and synthesize plans to deal with them. Because there is often more than one potential solution, students must also learn evaluation skills.

Objectives in Bloom's affective domain involve emotional responses rather than intellectual skills and are arranged in order of increasing power for the individual. The first level is *receiving,* in other words, indicating that the student is willing to pay attention to the material. *Responding* is the next level, where the student is sufficiently involved with the material to do something with it. *Valuing* is the third level. The student herself or himself determines that the material is important, as are the values or attitudes that it represents. Initially, he or she may simply accept these values; however, some values come to be preferred to others and may even be internalized and actively defended. When the student encounters multiple values that could apply in the same situation, he or she learns to categorize them, to form a value system. This is the *organization* level. The highest level is *characterization* by a value or value complex. The individual has learned to act according to that value system and to extend it to new situations. As it expands, she or he is developing a philosophy of life, an internally consistent view of the world. In most disciplines, there is a set of beliefs or attitudes about what is important and how to approach new information. For a student to be a fully accepted and productive member of the field, he or she must learn these values. Cases present the opportunity to discuss not only specific situations but also the attitudes and reasoning, the values of the individuals involved. As students' skills improve in intellectual objectives, they also learn to identify their own attitudes, and in the process of discussing and explaining, they develop and clarify their value systems and their own unique world views.

CASE CHARACTERISTICS AND EDUCATIONAL OBJECTIVES

Bloom's taxonomy (Bloom et al., 1971) and similar hierarchies of educational objectives can be adapted for a discussion of cases as an educational tool. One such adaptation is provided by John Reynolds (1978). His framework related a hierarchy of educational objectives to its implications for other aspects of a case, including length and complexity, the quantity and types of data, the appropriate analytical methods, and the value system that is appropriate to the case. His model is given in Table 2.1. We will use Reynolds's basic framework as the organizing principle as we discuss how your choice of educational objectives affects the type of case that would be most effective.

■ Educational Objectives

The first column, "Educational Objective," begins with Category II rather than Category I. This is because the first category is the equivalent of Bloom's *knowledge*—the ability to remember—in the cognitive hierarchy and *receiving,* the lowest level in his affective hierarchy. Category I could include recall of abstract principles and learning key vocabulary definitions for the field, Marzano's *knowledge acquisition.* All of these are essential components in the learning process, but it is not necessary to use a case to accomplish them. In fact, a case is an inefficient way to transmit facts and definitions, if this is its sole purpose.

Cases are much better suited to the next level in Bloom's taxonomy, *comprehension* and understanding, in which the facts serve as the basis for illustrating a concept. This is Category II of the educational objectives in Table 2.1. Many text chapters have brief examples that lay out how a theory applies in a real situation. Category III, "Understanding Techniques," includes ways to work with basic facts and concepts. The short case (one page or less) at the end of a text chapter usually falls into this group. It does not clearly match the chapter's content with the real situation described in the case but provides questions to direct the student. In both of these categories, the student's role would still be primarily knowledge acquisition, according to Marzano.

The remaining categories, IV through VIII, correspond to the knowledge production or application processes in Marzano's schema and build through a hierarchy similar to Bloom's. In Categories IV and V, students learn to apply techniques to new situations, at first with their choices guided and then with the choice of techniques based on their own analysis. These correspond to Bloom's stages of *application* and *analysis.* Category VI calls for students to build on their analyses to develop an action plan or otherwise synthesize or create something that is new to them. The final two categories help students learn to evaluate (in Bloom's cognitive terms). They gradually

TABLE 2.1   Case Characteristics and Educational Objectives

Category	Educational Objective	Case Description	Data Dimensions	Analytical Methods	Value Dimensions
II	Develop concepts	Exposition of problem in business	Facts clustered to highlight cause-and-effect relationships	"Worked-out example"	Objective function made explicit
III	Understand techniques	Problemette			
IV	Acquire skill in use of techniques	Short, realistic business problem, structured	Facts "selected" for relevance but not clustered to attach meaning	Method signaled but not worked out	Value system clear (usually profit oriented), but objective function open for choice by student
V	Acquire skill in analysis of business problems	Complex, unstructured slice of life	More facts added, mainly within one value system, but amenable to more than one analytical method	No clear signals regarding methods; analytical techniques open to students' choice, including mixed and sequential analysis	
VI	Acquire skill in synthesis of action plans	Problem with clear emphasis on action			
VII	Develop useful attitudes	V, VI, VII with emphasis on key executives	Still more facts (often including seemingly irrelevant facts) related to more than one value system; heavy use of opinions of case characters	No known satisfactory technique	Choice of value systems left open to student
VIII	Develop mature judgment, wisdom	Complex, realistic, unstructured problem			

SOURCE: Reynolds (1978, p. 130). Reprinted with permission of Academy of Management, P.O. Box 3020, Briar Cliff Manor, NY 10510-8020. *There's Method in Cases* (Table), John I. Reynolds, Academy of Management Review, Vol. 3, No. 1. Reproduced by permission of the publisher via Copyright Clearance Center, Inc.

develop their own internal value systems (the highest levels in Bloom's affective hierarchy) by dealing with situations that are complex and that may have more than one possible "right" answer, learning to create and use criteria to make these choices. Cases with an ethical component could fall into these categories.

■ **Case Description**

One of the choices that you, the case writer, must make is determining the type of skills that your students will need to use in reading and analyzing your case. In an introductory course, your objectives might be simple: to introduce students to the important vocabulary and principles and the techniques that will be needed. As they build this basic understanding, they will be ready to begin to perform their own analyses, looking at the data and deciding which facts are important and how to interpret them. At the end of the course or in more advanced courses, the students will be ready to solve problems, as well as to identify them. As they progress, the problems and the decisions will become increasingly complex. Their decisions will depend on choices that they make, based on their understanding of which factors are most important. Each of these types of learning has its own needs, in terms of the complexity and organization of the case. The case corresponding to each level is described in the second column of Table 2.1.

■ **Data Dimensions, Analytical Methods, and Value Dimensions**

The remaining columns in Table 2.1 describe different aspects of a potential case. "Data Dimensions" concerns both the quantity of information and how it is organized. The next column, "Analytical Methods," discusses the role of theory or models in the case and whether students are given or must pick the techniques or analysis to use. The final column, "Value Dimensions," describes the criteria that students will use to analyze the case. In lower categories, it will be clear how they are to interpret the case's information, what point of view they are to use, and what they are to do. As they become more familiar with the field of study and more skilled in the use of cases, they will learn to identify the point of the case for themselves. Ultimately, they will be faced with multiple points of view and a diversity of values held by the people in the case. At this point, the students will have to choose among these values or build their own on which to base their decisions.

DESCRIPTIVE CASES AND OTHER STORY PROBLEMS

The combination of the type and quantity of information, the amount of guidance given to the student, and the degree to which the student should acquiesce to or decide what is important determine the characteristics of an effective case for each category. At the level of developing concepts (Category II), this is more of an illustration, because the concept is explained or worked out in the case. The facts are chosen because they relate to the example, and they are arranged to make it easy for the students to see the relationships.

Category III, "Understanding Techniques," is similar in its degree of structure and information but asks the students to make the application, instead of working it out for them. This is still essentially an illustration or *problemette*, as it is called on the chart. Its length will vary, depending on the field and on the complexity of the concept. However, it is still essentially descriptive. It is useful for transmitting knowledge, particularly how a concept or theory might be applied in the real world, but does not ask students to take a very active role in their own learning. The case at the end of a chapter in a text is often of this type. Although the questions may ask the student to explain how the facts in a case apply to various theories, she or he knows which theories to apply and how to structure the analysis by looking back into that (and only that) chapter.

EVALUATIVE CASES

The next levels of educational objectives require students to begin to apply theories or concepts for themselves. In Category IV cases, it may still be relatively clear which concepts should be applied, but the choice is left up to the student. The relationship between the case's information and more abstract concepts or theories is not as clear as in Category III cases. The facts are not necessarily told in the order needed; they are grouped by topic, such as "marketing," or "agricultural products of the region," or often, in the order in which they occurred. The dominant question is: "What's happening here? Can you explain it, in terms of theories or concepts?" The focus is on evaluating the situation.

Evaluative cases can be very simple and short. They can also be quite long and complex. An example of the latter would be a case on the grounding of the Exxon Valdez and the oil spill and environmental damage that it caused. Many issues are involved and must be described, ranging from personnel questions (who was really on the bridge at the time of the accident? Had the captain been drinking on duty?); the geology of the region (including the shape of the harbor and the distance of the oil fields from their primary markets); environmentalists' pressures and the political and business reactions to them; economic pressures, including the demand for oil-based products, and perhaps even technology (because building tankers with double hulls had been discussed as a way to control potential damage from collisions).

An evaluative case is a good way to learn to apply theories (Category IV). Students must look over the information in the case and mentally sort it, to choose what technique or concept seems to be the most relevant. Evaluative cases are also a good way to develop skills in analysis (Category V). Not all of the information is equally important, so students must begin to weigh and interpret what they read. An evaluative case may even give the student some opportunity to exercise his or her own values, by asking "Do you agree or disagree, and why?" But the event has already happened; the important decisions have already been made. An evaluative case is therefore limited in its usefulness in developing higher orders of learning.

DECISION-FOCUS CASES

One important outcome of education is the ability to deal with new or unfamiliar experiences. We must understand the new situation, and that involves using analytical abilities, such as those already discussed. It is not enough, however, simply to understand what is happening. The analysis serves as the basis for actions. Using the facts and concepts that we know, we make decisions and create plans. We also recognize that not all decisions are equally effective; we learn to evaluate them and make judgments.

Just as cases provide a rich environment for students to learn and practice their analytical skills, these analyses become the basis for learning to make good decisions. A case that is intended to teach decision-making skills must be at least as rich as an evaluative case, because the student will need to perform her or his own analysis of the situation. At this level, Category VI, the problem has not yet been solved and may even remain to be identified. The student must move beyond analysis, to make predictions about what will happen, then to develop the sequence of actions needed to affect the outcome. He or she will soon discover that there is often more than one possible plan. The more difficult task may be to choose among the alternatives. This is hard to teach, because each situation presents its own unique set of alternatives.

Cases in Categories VII and VIII are designed to give the student practice in making these decisions. They contain even more facts of varying importance that could support a variety of plans—and even some information that may be of little use. If there is a decision maker in the case, the student must begin to put herself or himself in that person's shoes. This means considering what factors are most important to the decision maker and using them to weigh the alternative plans. Ultimately, students may be placed in the role of the decision maker. They must each determine for themselves what the most important issues are and evaluate how different alternatives would accomplish those goals. No one answer is necessarily correct, because each student may see the issues and the decisions differently. The important point is for each student to experience this process for himself or herself, to develop the power to evaluate and judge.

If your intent is to write a Category VI case, with the educational objective of helping students to acquire skill in developing an action plan, your case should include more than the minimum amount of data. The extra information will give students practice in the analysis and problem identification that they have already learned. It will also allow them to pick and choose among facts, to support their ideas. The information shouldn't be structured to lead the students to a particular plan, because there is no single correct plan. However, it should still be relatively clear what the constraints are and what types of solutions would (or would not) be acceptable. The case should be told primarily from one point of view, generally that of the person who has to decide what to do.

To learn to evaluate and choose between alternatives, students will need even more information. The case begins to represent the complexity that students would encounter in making a decision in the real world. This includes information that is not immediately useful or that may seem more important than it really is. In a case written by one of the authors of this book, the decision maker's immediate concern appears to be an ethical issue of how to deal with a competitor who was engaged in an illegal action. However, careful reading of the case reveals that the decision maker's most pressing concern should be survival of his company, because it will be out of money within a month, even if the unfair competition can be eliminated. A Category VII case may also include more of a focus on individuals, in addition to the organization or the situation. The human dimension not only makes the case more interesting by giving students someone to identify with but also helps them to visualize the decision maker's thought process and what is important to him or her. Students have to explicitly consider the values that underlie the decision process and evaluate (the highest level in Bloom's taxonomy) the acceptability of various alternatives.

The highest category in Table 2.1 has, as its objective, to "develop mature judgment and wisdom." What is acceptable to one person may not be to another, even within the same organization. The real world is a very complex, often contradictory place, and a case written with this objective should reflect that lack of clarity and structure. It could also include more individuals and their opinions, creating multiple value systems that may have to be considered. This type of case makes the heaviest demands on the students, not only because of its complexity and (often) length, but also because they must weigh all data and all points of view. They must come up with a reasoned plan based on intangibles, as well as on the facts. In short, they must exercise their good judgment.

Decision focus cases are often fun to write. There is a problem to be solved or an issue to be dealt with around which to organize the data, but the information need not be tightly structured or limited to only what is immediately useful. The situation often includes important people, whose personalities may be revealed through quotes. However, a decision case may also be difficult to write. Because it encourages multiple alternative decisions, it must have the information to support them. But not everyone will agree on what information is necessary, and it is difficult to avoid leaving out some key fact. It may be necessary to test and rewrite the case several times before it can achieve the educational and knowledge objectives you have set for it.

RESEARCH CASES

In a research case, the choice of objectives is even more important than in a teaching case. Marzano et al. (1988) considered *research* to be one of their key thinking processes. In Bloom's terms, the writer or researcher is engaged in *synthesis* through the development of hypotheses and in *evaluation* when assessing the results. Although research cases are not included in the categories in Table 2.1, they do have their own educational purpose. Their role is to stretch the boundaries of current knowledge in the field for the writer and hopefully also for other readers.

A research case is generally written for one of two reasons. First, it allows the researcher to test hypotheses. Cases are effective for a different type of hypothesis than other forms of research, such as surveys. A case allows an in-depth look at a single organization, individual, or situation. Although this does not create "significance" in a statistical sense, it provides the opportunity to study a single sample in great detail. The researcher collects and sets down a multitude of facts about that specific sample of one. Moreover, he or she is able to collect the data interactively, asking additional questions to clarify the important facts and relationships. The case contains the raw material on which the hypotheses are being tested and describes the results of that testing process.

The second reason for writing a research case is to develop hypotheses. The researcher may have noticed, based on observation, survey research, or the field's literature, that there appears to be a relationship between certain variables. Sometimes, it is possible to proceed directly to hypotheses about causality. Other situations, however, may be sufficiently complex that simple explanations may not be possible. A given set of medical symptoms may be influenced by many different factors in a patient's lifestyle, for example. The failure of a new product may not be due to poor market research, if there are changes in other aspects of the company's environment. Here, a classic example is the Edsel automobile, which was developed in the 1950s after extensive research into the features Americans said they would like in a midsized, medium-priced car. However, the car took several years to develop (a factor inside the company), during which competitors moved quickly into the market by adding features or offering stripped-down models of their current automobile lines. Other potential problems were the car's unusual grill design and its name. Case research allows the researcher to look at the interactions among these and any other facts, to understand the relationships. Based on that understanding, she or he develops hypotheses that can then be tested by further case research or even by survey or other "large *n*" means.

The choice of objectives is the crucial starting point in a research case. Without an objective, the researcher does not know what type of organization or situation to study. If he or she wants to test hypotheses, he or she must carefully select the subject of the case so as to be able to collect the relevant information. If the purpose is to develop hypotheses, she or he must look for a situation that is sufficiently rich in information. The researcher must also look for a cooperative subject, one willing to share in-depth information and open to follow-up questions. Although it is possible to write a research case based on published sources, it is difficult to find information in this depth

PRACTICE SESSION

Many of the chapters will include a section that gives you, the reader, an opportunity to practice the aspects of case writing that have just been described. Appendixes 1 and 2 are the drafts of an actual case and its instructor's manual, and the final (published) versions appear in Appendixes 3 and 4. Read the case in Appendix 1 (pp. 185-186, this volume) and ask yourself, If I were a student, would I know what I was expected to do with this case? There are a variety of potential issues. It starts like a case in Human Resource Management, with issues relating to recruiting and hiring a new employee. Because Mr. Adams has already been hired, this implies that students will be asked to evaluate some aspect of the recruiting or hiring process, although, because no purpose is stated, the case would probably be classed as Category V. The second paragraph raises questions of employee behavior and motivation. Students could analyze Mr. Adams's behavior, but again, no decision is needed. Neither of these is the issue that is raised at the end of the case, however, when the partners are trying to decide how to respond to his leaving the firm and trying to take clients with him. This could give students the opportunity to make recommendations of their own, using skills in Category VI. Although the partners' concern is with maintaining customers, students might also raise questions of whether Mr. Adams's behavior is ethical, demonstrating their development of useful attitudes or even mature judgment. However, according to Table 2.1, a case in levels VI, VII and VIII ordinarily would include a variety of facts that are not selected or clustered to direct the students, and levels VII or VIII would also require an emphasis on the key decision makers. The case characteristics don't match with the author's probable objectives.

The instructor's manual (Appendix 2, pp. 187-189) does not make the author's objectives any clearer. The opening paragraph talks in general terms about "studying the interactions," which might imply analysis as the educational objective. The discussion questions range from application of techniques (the stakeholder model referred to in Question 2), to analysis (Question 1), to development of an action plan (Questions 4 and 5), to the useful attitudes practiced in the consideration of ethical issues (Question 3). It is often pedagogically useful to start class discussion with lower-level skills and build up to the more challenging objectives. However, because the case itself does not give the student guidance, you would have to provide more explicit direction in advance or lead the discussion through the various topics.

The later versions of the case (in Appendix 3, pp. 191-198) and instructor's manual (in Appendix 4, pp. 199-210) have much clearer educational objectives. At the end of the case's introduction, Mr. Morrison asks, "What do we do now?" The student knows that he or she is being asked to develop an action plan for the partners. The case then moves back in time to show how the situation developed and ends with the phone call that began the case. This gives the student a variety of facts, but the chronological presentation requires her or him to select those aspects of the case that are most significant. Although still relatively brief, the case now has the complexity that is appropriate to higher-level educational objectives. These objectives are also stated much more explicitly in the revised instructor's manual, particularly in the "Purpose" section. The questions are the same as in the draft, but they are now accompanied by a section on "Teaching Methods," which describes how the case could be used in different courses or to achieve different objectives.

SUMMARY AND CONCLUSIONS

The idea for the case leads to the first decisions that you, the case writer, will have to make: the choice of objectives. Every teaching case has two purposes: the specific knowledge that students should take away and the educational objectives, in terms of more generalizeable skills and abilities that they are developing. Although there are many ways to present specific knowledge to students, cases enable students to stretch their thinking and judgment skills. Your choice of educational objective will have a strong influence over many characteristics of the case, including the amount of information you present, how it is organized, and whether to include more than one point of view. These will be among the topics discussed in the next chapters.

The objectives are even more important in research cases; without them, the case writer doesn't have a clear picture of what to research. The choice of objectives determines the choice of research subject, as well as the types and quantity of information, data, to include. The particular advantages and demands of research cases will be discussed in Chapter 4.

3
■

Finding a Case Site and Gathering Data

■

Coming up with an idea for a new case is often the least difficult aspect of the case-writing process. Ideas frequently come from frustrations in not being able to present a particular topic, issue, theory, or concept in a course setting. More difficult, however, is finding an appropriate example or setting capable of fulfilling the case objective. This becomes still more difficult when the case writer wants to use direct observation or field research for this purpose. Although field research tends to be more effective than library-based research in developing the objective, it is also more difficult to implement. There are also issues involved with gathering your information, once an initial contact has been made.

IDENTIFYING POTENTIAL CASE SITES

Field research involves interviewing the people who were actively involved in the situation being investigated. This includes the ability to visit and describe the sites involved, because these environmental aspects can have a critical impact on how, when, and why a situation developed or a decision was made. As an example, describing a cluttered and overused manufacturing site where inefficient procedures are obvious can help to lead readers to either make a decision about the manufacturing process or to understand why a decision to change the process was made. Also, visiting the site and interviewing the people who were involved in the decision helps to give life to the written word. Readers can now feel a sense of being a part of the decision process, as opposed to simply hearing about the results of the decision. This process, therefore, presents particular problems in bringing the case to a point where it can be widely disseminated. The first of these is simply finding an appropriate site for the case. We have found that there are a wide variety of sources for case sites.

■ Students as Resources

Students frequently make excellent sources for finding case sites. First, they are intimately familiar with cases through their course work. Often, they have developed an innate feel for what might constitute an appropriate case. Although they may not be able to verbalize what those factors are that constitute an effective site, they may provide an example from personal experience of situations that exemplify some of the concepts or issues that are being presented in class. These situations may come from personal experiences they have encountered during their own work experiences. Alternatively, the students may offer examples they have either heard or seen directly or indirectly through family or friends. An undergraduate student provided the inspiration for the Meyers & Morrison case, which was published in a refereed journal and a text and is included in this book as Appendix 3.

Students provide several advantages when seeking access to case sites. First, as noted, they already have an understanding of what constitutes a case study. This means that any suggestions or leads that they provide are more likely to be useable, because they understand the types of materials needed to write an effective case. Second, the student's connection can make it easier to contact the appropriate individuals to be involved in the case. Third, the students can often provide initial insight into the environment in which the case writer will be soon finding him- or herself. This can help to save valuable time and effort during the case-writing process. One must be cautioned, however, to realize that students often misunderstand the true dynamics that are occurring within the organization that is to be studied. Their statements need to be taken with a degree of skepticism. Last, the student helps to give credibility to the case writer, because it becomes clear to the individuals being interviewed that the case writer has both a degree of professional standing, as well as some form of expertise in use of case studies. As a caution, it is better to make use of these sites after the student has completed a course with the case writer, not during the course itself. This is to ensure that the student does not feel that there will be special consideration given in the course simply due to providing access to a case site.

This type of case source occurred when one of the authors was teaching a segment of a course dealing with strategic management in a highly competitive environment. The student came up to the author after class, noting that he was working for a small company in an industry with a large number of roughly equivalently sized companies. He explained the situation. The author and student both agreed that the situation sounded promising from the point of view of a case study. Once the course was completed, the author contacted the student to help to set up an initial interview. The results of the interview were quite positive, because the student had already explained the purpose of a case study and had spoken positively about the background of the case writer. The case was written, with few complications, and was subsequently published in two text books (Naumes & Schellenberger, 1983).

■ **Family and Friends as Resources**

Another effective source for case sites comes from family and friends. Although the case writer may be closer to this group than to students, there are fewer of the former than the latter. Also, although this group provides situations that tend to be better known to the case writer, family and friends may be reluctant about baring their souls to one whom they know well. They may not want their relatives and acquaintances to know, directly, about the situation that occurred. This is often viewed as a bigger threat or embarrassment than telling a stranger what occurred. The individuals may want to be able to maintain distance with the case writer. This is often impossible when the case writer is a family member or friend.

A benefit, however, is that the case writer, in this circumstance, often already understands the environment surrounding the situation. This can save time and effort during the interviewing process. However, the writer, because of her or his relationship with the case subject, may be biased toward the subject's point of view, causing the case to be one-sided or to lack objectivity. A related danger is that case writer, thinking that the environment is understood, may miss some of the nuances of the situation, through a failure to ask probing questions. As it has often been said, a little bit of knowledge can be a dangerous thing.

■ Alumni as Resources

Alumni can often be an even better source of case sites than students. They have usually been exposed to a larger and wider variety of situations. Also, similar to the current students, they are already familiar with case studies through their former course work. Their own experiences may provide an interesting scenario. They may also have the authority to gain access for the case writer to the relevant individuals and information necessary to develop an effective case study. Moreover, as long as they have had an enjoyable or at least an acceptable academic experience, they are more likely to be cooperative with someone from their alma mater. This connection also gives the case writer added credibility with the individuals being interviewed.

A problem with the use of alumni as a resource is that they do not know what objectives a given case writer is trying to achieve, unless the two are in close contact. Often, the contact is through a fortuitous set of circumstances. Alumni may contact the case writer for advice concerning issues that are facing them. This then leads to the development of a case. Similarly, a colleague may have heard of a situation facing an alum. This information may then be passed on to the case writer.

■ Published Sources

Another source that both authors have used at various times comes from various print media. Although other media do provide initial ideas, print media have been more successful as leads to case ideas due to the ability to save the material concerning the individual, organization, or situation. Another advantage to this source is that the case writer is frequently provided with enough information to prepare background material for the case. The printed material also provides sufficient information to determine the appropriate contact person within the organization about which the case is to be developed. The authors keep a file of articles about individuals and organizations that seem interesting. Although only a few of these ever develop into case studies, the material is there to allow for initial contacts at appropriate times. Another advantage of these files is that they may provide material for class discussions, even when they have not been developed into full case studies.

A problem with this form of source, however, is that there is little direct information on the situation or individuals. What you know has been filtered through a third-party writer. Also, your initial contact often is made through a cold call. This may make the person being contacted wary of the case writer.

It also means that the case writer frequently has to explain his or her own qualifications as well as the process that will be used to develop the case. Additional time is required simply going through the amenities of becoming familiar with each other. Basically, a system of mutual trust has to be developed between people who had, until the initial meeting, been total strangers to each other. This also makes the process of gaining access to sensitive information more difficult and time consuming.

■ Consulting Contacts

Consulting contacts provide a rich source for case opportunities. A major benefit is that the case writer is gathering material necessary to preparing the case at the same time as developing information to meet the needs of the consulting relationship. Consultants need to have enough information concerning their clients to be able to make effective recommendations concerning decisions within the company. The situation or decision points being analyzed can frequently form the basis for the case. Lawrence and Lorsch (1967), noted behavioral researchers and consultants, used these contacts for a series of cases that they then developed for a series of case and readings books.

These types of situations can often be used as the basis for a case, even when you have not been the primary, or direct, consultant for the client. Faculty can often find such clients within their own schools. Business cases can be developed through access to sites such as those found through the Small Business Development Centers and Small Business Institutes that found at many business schools. Similarly, agriculture-oriented cases can be developed through use of extension agencies found at many schools of agriculture. Engineering and production and operations technology cases can be developed through contacts made at technology resource centers, incubator sites, and university-sponsored or affiliated technology parks.

The advantage to these sources is that the clients are already aware of the organization, if not also the case writers themselves. There is already a predisposition to provide information to someone from the case writer's institution; there is the likelihood that the client will have a positive feeling toward the institution and, therefore, the case writer. Of course, this assumes that the consulting relationship has been positive. As already noted, much of the information necessary to write the case may already be available in the form of the consultant's reports or notes.

A problem with this type of source, however, is that the original relationship was developed with the understanding that all information would be held in confidence. Because the clients typically come to the consultant to resolve a problem, the client may be unwilling to share those problems with the rest of the world. Also, even though a consulting contact exists, the issue leading to the consulting relationship may not either be appropriate or meet the objectives of the case writer.

THE FIELD RESEARCH PROCESS

■ Making Contact

Once a site has been selected, an initial contact must be made. Towl (1969) notes that this initial contact is frequently critical to the success of the overall process. The initial contact sets the tone for the subsequent interactions as well as determining the ability of the case writer to secure sufficient information to write an effective case study. It is frequently a major factor in helping to secure the final permission to publish or widely disseminate the case. It also often sets the basis for a feeling of trust toward the case writer on the part of those who will be asked to release the information provided for the case.

It is always best to have a point of access to the organization that is as close as possible to the source who can provide the ultimate release of the case information. That frequently means going directly to the individual who knows the situation best or who is responsible for the decision that you wish to describe in the case. Finding another person who knows that individual, a go-between, where there is no direct relationship with the case writer, can often resolve problems before they occur. If this isn't possible, you can approach the company or organization yourself. Find out the name of the head of the organization, and call him or her directly. She or he is the person that you will ultimately need to obtain the release to use the case. It is surprisingly easy to get through, in some cases. If not, contact the person in the organization who is in charge of public relations. One technique that the authors have used successfully in making cold calls on potential case sites was to write an initial case using published sources. Although the case had been well received, in its draft form, reviewers felt that additional information was needed to help to develop the technical side of the decision. The authors contacted the president's office, without any other relationship having been established. The president requested a copy of the case that had been written to that point. On reading the draft of the case, he referred the case writers to another source within the company who then provided the information appropriate to making the case a more effective description of the company's situation and the decision process that was the original objective for the case.

Having an intermediary who can provide an introduction, when the case writer is not directly known to anyone involved with the situation to be studied, is often the best approach to starting the process on a sound footing. As noted earlier, any number of sources may assist in this process.

One of the authors was approached by a student at the end of a class session noting that the company for which he was working had recently gone through a strategic decision process similar to the one that had just been discussed in class. There was an added twist, however, that a transition in management was occurring as well. This seemed to have potential for the development of a new case study that would be able to meet multiple objectives for at least two different courses, strategic management and entrepreneurship, because the events were taking place in a smaller company. After the end of the course, the case writer contacted the student and asked if he thought that the managers at his company would be willing to participate in the development of a case study based on their firm. The now former student approached the president of the company, with whom he worked closely, and broached the idea of a case study about the company. The president responded with some hesitation but agreed to an initial meeting with the case writer. At that meeting, the case writing and teaching process was discussed. The former student, who took part in a portion of the discussion, related his experiences with the case method as a teaching tool, which, fortunately, were quite positive. He also noted that the case writer had brought a manager from another local company to class, in connection with a just-finished case. The student commented on how effective it was to be able to speak to someone from one of the companies he was studying. The student also noted how effective it was to be able to study a local company, as opposed to always having to study some large and often distant organization. The president asked if it would be necessary for him to participate in a class discussion of his case and was reassured that, although it would add to the richness of the discussion, it was not necessary. His participation would certainly not be expected every time the case was taught, especially because it was expected that the case would be included in one of the case writer's upcoming books. The president was also concerned about sensitive information that might be forthcoming from interviews with several of the top managers at the company. The case writer assured the president that the final draft of the case would be made available to him for approval. The result of this initial introduction and further discussions led to the development of a highly effective case study that was subsequently published in books other than those written by the case writer (Naumes & Schellenberger, 1983).

This example demonstrates the effective use of an intermediary who is known to the person who would ultimately be asked to release the information for use in the case. The former student not only provided access and respectability for the case writer, he also was instrumental in describing how the case study would be used and its importance in the education process.

The process by which a case is developed and subsequently written should be discussed at this time. As noted in the example given earlier, this would often include the need for interviewing different people who might have been involved in the situation or decision to be analyzed. This, in essence, follows the reporter's rule of trying to find corroborating statements about any incident or situation. This is also the point at which you should note what kinds of additional information might be needed. For example, in case studies dealing with strategic issues, financial information is usually required to understand the environment in which a decision is to be made. For a case study in psychology, confidential or medical information might be necessary. The need for this information should be made clear at the earliest possible time. Both authors have found themselves with well-defined case studies that could not be completed or published because permission could not be secured for a key piece of information or because at a critical stage in the case-writing process, the information was simply not forthcoming.

Individuals who have not previously been exposed to case studies may need additional explanation as to how a case is used, especially for teaching purposes. People are especially interested to know who will be using the case studies, for what purpose, and who the expected audience will be. Once again, managers are often impressed when they realize that their experiences will become the basis for expanding knowledge by students. They realize that they will, in essence, become an active part of the education process, without the necessity of having to be physically in class themselves.

The authors have found that in the development of the case study, a discussion of the proposed audience and use of the case can be an especially effective technique in securing the assistance of managers at all levels of the organization. Senior-level managers, especially, like to hear that they will be studied by students at a variety of different institutions. This meets their ego needs. It is a form of flattery that appeals to their sense of importance as leaders in their fields.

■ Gaining Access

Once the initial contact has been made, there are frequently issues that arise over access to other individuals and information that might be needed to complete the case study. It is rare that all circumstances can be predicted at the initial meeting. Questions then arise as to what additional information or interviews might be both appropriate and necessary.

An issue that frequently arises is whether there is a quid pro quo involved in the case-writing process. In many instances, individuals ask for what is, essentially, free consulting or counseling in exchange for access to the material needed for completion of the case. This should be avoided at all costs. If the case writer becomes involved with the organization or individual as a consultant or counselor, at this point, then independence is frequently endangered. Although this may seem to violate the point noted earlier that a consulting engagement can lead to a case study, under these conditions, the consulting aspect of the project needs to be completed before the case study is to be commenced. It should also be noted to the individual who raises such a question that the completed case often can be as valuable as a consulting engagement. It is hoped that the individual or organization is receiving an unbiased and independent description of the incident, situation, or decision being studied. This can be an effective manner by which the individual or organization can understand what was happening and why and what the impact was. This, in itself, should provide a valuable benefit in exchange for the time and information being provided to the case writer. Also, as noted earlier, the value of the case study in the education process cannot be slighted. The individual or organization has, through the case study, assisted in the education of future analysts or decision makers in the appropriate field of study.

■ Releases and Promises

A formal release must be obtained for field-researched case studies. See Tables 3.1 and 3.2 for sample release forms. At the least, the final draft of the case should be given to the individual within the organization who has the authority to grant release of the information provided in the case. Towl (1969) mentions that Malcolm McNair had noted that he suffered serious damage to a business relationship due to his premature release of information that had been given to him by an associate outside the Harvard Business School. McNair stated that he had thought that the information could be shared with his classes. On hearing that McNair had presented the information in the form of a case study, the executive cut off all access by McNair to the company. The executive made it abundantly clear that the information had been given in confidence and that McNair should have asked the executive's permission before sharing it, in any way, with others. After that experience, McNair has always secured a formal release, even when there is a general understanding that the information is to be shared as part of a case study (Towl, 1969).

The authors found themselves in an analogous situation when developing a case study on a privately held manufacturing firm. The CEO of the firm had stated that he was pleased to be able to have his company and managers participate in a case study, especially because it would help students understand how a supplier can succeed by working closely with its customers, a major objective of the case study. As part of the discussions, the CEO explained the value of his administrative and operating staff. He noted that without certain, specified personnel policies, he would not have been able to keep so many talented managers at a medium-sized company. When he saw his comments in a draft of the case, he emphasized that under no circumstances could the statement remain in the case. He hadn't even realized that he had made it until he saw it in print. Fortunately, it was able to be deleted before the case was shared with others. Although the full statement of policies would have made the case better, the deletion did not really harm the case. Moreover, the willingness of the case writers to immediately delete the sensitive information made the executive even more comfortable with the end product as well as the case-writing process in general.

Preliminary release authorizations should be requested when the drafts of the case are shared with colleagues. This could be for the purpose of gaining outside views of the effectiveness of the case or for permission to distribute the case at a case workshop where it is to be reviewed as any research paper would be analyzed. If you are quoting someone directly, his or her permission must be secured. These authorizations may be oral, as opposed to the traditional written authorization received at the completion of the case-writing process. It is always preferable, however, to receive all authorizations in writing.

There are times when, despite your best efforts, the person whom you need to sign off on a case authorization decides not to provide the release requested. Regardless of the assurances originally given that a release would be granted once the case-writing process was completed, the relevant person may decide that the case should not be released. This may be due to simple cold feet about seeing the situation in print. It may also be due to late-breaking problems, including legal constraints. At these times, it is best to simply accept that the project is over and go on to another case study. It may be possible to revive the project in the future, but under no circumstances should you attempt to disseminate the case study without the approval of the relevant person involved in the situation being described. Even disguising the organization and the individuals would not compensate for the lack of a formal release.

One of the authors was involved in the development of a case for use as a class final project. The CEO of the company assured us, after the case-writing process was described to him, that he would provide final authorization for release of the case. After we spent half of the term researching and interviewing managers within the company and presenting a draft of the case to the company, the CEO responded that he could not authorize release of the material in the case. The legal department of the company had advised him that, because the company was preparing a new stock offering, the authorization of the case could be construed as providing limited release of inside information and, therefore, would constitute illegal insider information. There was nothing we could do but find another company around which we would develop the class project.

■ Case Disguises

Sometimes, it is necessary to offer to disguise a case study to make it acceptable for release to the public. Although a disguise is acceptable as part of the case-writing process, it is often difficult to accomplish and still maintain the integrity of the case. Robert Katz (1970) wrote a case study in the mid-1960s based on a San Francisco company but decided a disguise was necessary to be able to put more information into the case. The additional information was probably worth the disguise for most students, but it did create a potential problem. A key aspect of the case involved immigrant Italians who worked for the company and lived nearby. One option for the new owner of the company involved moving the company to a new site, with the approval of the employees. In the disguised case, the new location became South Boston. Unfortunately, as most students from Boston would understand, South Boston is a heavily ethnic Irish community. Although Boston is similar to San Francisco in many ways, Katz would have been better served stating that the company was to be moved to the North End or East Boston sections of the city. When the case was taught to students with a familiarity with the Boston area, the location became a major distraction from the key issues of the case and made it much more difficult to teach.

Other means to disguise a case frequently deal with the names of key individuals. This is usually not a problem as long as the case writer does not try to become too creative with the disguised names. Disguising the products or industry of a company can frequently be effective but only if the industry data are not a key aspect of the case. Disguising financial data provides more problems, however. Often, the financial data are key to the discussion of business decisions. Disguises of financial data usually take the form of applying a constant multiple to the data. This may make financial analysis difficult to perform. Worse yet, it may provide a false indication as to the financial health of the company. This is due to the inability to compare the disguised data with relevant industry data. The company may be viewed as either smaller or larger that it actually is, leading the reader to misread its relative strength. The use of common multiples also may well lead to maintenance of relative proportions that may not be appropriate as the firm either grows or contracts.

In summary, case writers need to take especial care when trying to disguise a case. As Sir Walter Scott noted, "What tangled webs we weave, when first we practice to deceive" (Scott, 1808).

One way to overcome some of the hesitation concerning release of actual data or information is to explain the timing of the case-writing process to the person responsible for authorizing release. It often takes at least 6 months to perform all the interviews, write drafts, present them for approval, and prepare the final draft. After that, the case writer will often seek the responses of other case writers, as well as class test the case, as will be discussed in Chapter 7. By the time the case becomes available for widespread distribution, at least 18 months will have passed. By then, much of the data and information will be general knowledge, anyway. The time lapse is lengthened when one realizes that all of the material involves a situation that has already occurred. Most individuals who are not familiar with the case-writing process assume that the case will be available for immediate distribution. Once they understand the time that will pass between the actual event and ultimate publication or dissemination of the case study, they are more likely to provide releases without needing significant changes or disguises.

GATHERING DATA

Once you have made the initial contacts and established the ground rules under which you will be allowed to study the organization, you can begin the process of collecting the actual data that will be included in your case. Although you can simply wander around and observe or sit down with an individual and start asking questions, it is helpful to plan the data-gathering process. This includes both the types of information that you want to collect and the techniques you will use to collect it.

■ Preliminary Preparation

The objectives outlined and defined in Chapter 2 should be used to help to define the questions to be asked. As with any field research, case research relies on a core set of questions relating to the objectives of the case writer. It is best to outline those questions and to follow that outline. The case writer should allow for follow-up and in-depth questioning when responses from those being interviewed show promise in developing a greater understanding of the background, definition, and reasoning behind the situation being explored.

Open-ended questions usually work the best. During this process, however, the case writer is often following a cautious path between too much and too little guidance in developing questions. Too much direction may lead to responses that are preordained and biased. This is equally true for a teaching case as well as a research case. Too little direction may cause the respondent to skip over material relevant to the full understanding of the situation. When in doubt, the case writer should always remember that collecting too much is always better than not enough. It is always much easier to cut material from the case than to have to go back and get additional information at a later date.

The use of a standard set of core questions also allows for the case writer and subsequent researchers to be able to compare the results of the material within the case studies as well as the studies themselves. For teaching cases, this means that teachers will be able to use a series of cases in the same or a similar industry to demonstrate how different firms adapt to the same environment in different ways. For research cases, this allows researchers to develop and refine concepts and theories while holding much of the research process constant.

■ The Interviewing Process

The interviews should be developed at the respondents' place of business or operation. This helps the respondents feel more comfortable because they are on their own turf. This also allows the case writers to get a better understanding of the environment under which the situation being studied occurred. We always readily and willingly accept tours of the site, whether it is a manufacturing facility, office, or service operation. This gives added insight to the environment and how it may have affected the situation. It also often causes the respondents to recollect information that might otherwise have been overlooked or forgotten without the visual cues of the workplace.

Also, always remember that the respondents are doing you a favor by letting you interview them. Interviewing them at their site means that you will be taking less of their time; this makes it more likely that they will accept the interview request than if they have to come to your site.

It is preferable to have two interviewers while collecting information. In this manner, one of the case writers can focus on the actual questioning process, including follow-up and in-depth questions, while the other case writer can focus on an accurate transcription of the responses elicited during the interview. This latter process should include as many direct quotes as possible. It is these direct quotes that often mean the difference between a rich, vibrant case and a lifeless and sometimes boring one.

If the respondents agree, it is preferable to also have the interviews recorded. A tape recorder ensures that all of the responses are accurate. It also ensures that the interviewers will not miss any important information. The ability to videotape some responses would be helpful. However, as we will see later in this book, making use of videotape successfully is difficult and costly.

Whenever possible, find out what material the respondents may have to support the case interview. This may involve company financial statements. It may also take the form of other interviews that members of the organization may have given, especially during the time being studied. Other material may include advertising by the organization, public relations material, policies and procedures statements, and a variety of data gathered by the organization concerning its customers, suppliers, competitors, and its own employees.

■ Triangulating

Field research does require that the information gathered by the case writer be verified, in some form or another. One person within the organization making a statement involving judgment or values may not reflect the true situation within the entire organization. Where at all possible, information should be gathered from multiple sources. As with a reporter preparing an article for a newspaper, at least reputable ones, all facts need to be verified before publication.

Some of this may be accomplished by interviewing others within the same organization. Other means may include interviewing individuals outside the organization. This may include customers, suppliers, and even competitors to help to validate such information and claims by individuals within the organization.

This can often provide alternate points of view to those presented by managers within the organization. Even if the original statements cannot be verified through these interviews with others, the readers are presented with these alternate points of view. The readers can then determine for themselves which individuals to believe and which points of view to accept.

There are a variety of external sources that can also be used to help in the verification process. Financial data can be found in published sources, especially for industry comparisons. You may also be able to find published interviews and articles about the individuals, organizations, or situations being studied. This material may also be used to either verify or present alternate perspectives for the reader.

Last, you may simply watch and record what is happening around you. This process has a long and rich tradition in field research to develop and validate hypotheses. Direct and nonintrusive observation can also be used to further validate information for the case. The problem with this method is that you have to directly filter and interpret the information before including it in the case. This adds to the potential for bias into the case.

AUTHORIZATION FOR RELEASE

Releases need to be received for all case studies that are developed through field research. Where an organization is concerned, the authorization to use the material in the case study should be signed by the supervisor of the highest person mentioned in the case. Otherwise, the individuals involved in the case should be the ones to sign off on use of the case.

There are times when, on reviewing the final draft of the case, the person authorizing the case does not want some material to be released in the form presented. Rather than scratching the entire case, you can offer to disguise some material in the case. This may be as simple as disguising the names of the individuals and the organizations. Other disguises, as noted earlier, may require significant changes in the case. Regardless of whether the case is disguised or not, an authorization still needs to be secured. This is to overcome the likely problem that sometime, somewhere, someone will probably see through the disguise. A colleague once told us of writing a disguised case and releasing it for use elsewhere. Another professor in a distant state used the case. One of his students immediately recognized the company from descriptions in the case. Fortunately, our colleague had secured a release from the company before allowing it to be used elsewhere.

TABLE 3.1 Sample Case Release Permission Form

Permission is granted to William Naumes and Margaret J. Naumes to include the material in the Meyers and Morrison case for publication and dissemination on a worldwide basis. This case is to be used solely as a basis for class discussion rather than as an example of effective or ineffective handling of an administrative decision.

William Naumes	Authorizing Signature
Margaret J. Naumes	Title
Date:_____	Date:_____

Two basic sample release forms may be found in Tables 3.1 and 3.2. The authors have used the first form (Table 3.1) for their own writing. The second form is a release that they have used with student case writers. Your institution, or any publication to which you may be submitting your work, may have its own form that it would like you to use.

LIBRARY CASES

Up to this point, most of the discussion in this chapter has revolved around the development of field-researched case studies. Another form of research that has been alluded to briefly deserves additional treatment. This is the case study that is developed solely through published sources or, as it sometimes described, the library case. The benefit of this form of case study is that it does not require direct access to the individual or organization. Instead, it requires access to sufficient material concerning the individual, organization, or situation so that a reasonable discussion can take place, through the case study. This is sometimes easier than one might think. Many individuals and organizations actively seek publicity and are often willing to be "on the record." As noted in Chapter 1, during the early 1970s, one of the authors saw that there were a limited number of case studies on conglomerate forms of business enterprises. He did not have the time or resources to travel to one of the several existing conglomerates, but he felt it was necessary to have a conglomerate case study in an upcoming text, to demonstrate strategic management under different corporate forms. With the help of a graduate assistant, he was able to find sufficient published information on Gulf &

TABLE 3.2 Release Form for Case Use

We release to Dr. Margaret Naumes the right to use our case,

_____,

for use in class. We also give her the release to use our case as the basis for further research and case writing. We understand that we will be given acknowledgment as the authors of this case, any time that it is used for any purpose.

Please sign and date this form, if you are authorizing this release. For me to be able to use the case, all group members must give permission. Thank you!

_____	_____
(Signature)	(Date)
_____	_____
(Signature)	(Date)
_____	_____
(Signature)	(Date)

Western Industries, a major conglomerate of that era, to be able to piece together a reasonable case study on how and why it had developed its strategic direction. A major factor in being able to develop that case study was that Charles Bludhorn, the CEO and founder of Gulf & Western, was an outgoing individual, as was his President, John H. Duncan. Both made themselves readily available to the print media and were often quoted extensively in those sources. Of equal importance was that they believed that their strategies were both consistent and exceptional. They took pride in their ability to succeed using the conglomerate organizational form. Therefore, they were happy to expound on their use of the form and the strategies that they developed to make their company a success, according to them (Naumes, 1982b).

The success of this case, which was subsequently used in several textbooks, was based on the richness of the information that was available from a large number of sources. The author did not need to rely on only one or a few published sources. That is a potential problem with library case studies. If only a limited number of sources are used, the resulting case study may suffer from the bias of the authors of the original pieces. Also, if the case writer quotes too extensively from one source, there is the potential for copyright infringement. The case writer would need to receive permission from the original source to be able to use the case study. This is often time-consuming and potentially costly.

Another disadvantage of the library case is that it often lacks the depth of treatment and presentation of the values and thoughts of the individuals involved in the incident or situation being explored. In the Gulf & Western example, the two top officers of the company were more than willing to share their personal and professional views concerning the situation discussed. There was very little information concerning other managers within the company, however. This was very different from the position the authors were in when they developed the case study on the supplier-oriented, manufacturing firm mentioned earlier in this chapter. In that situation, the authors were able to directly interview all of the top managers in the company. Those interviews indicated some disagreements among the managers as to the importance of some of the aspects of the strategy being followed by the company. One wonders whether all the managers at Gulf & Western were as committed to the conglomerate form as were its two top officers.

There are many instances, however, when the library case is the only effective method of developing a study of a particular incident. This is particularly true where there are issues of illegal activities involved on the part of the individuals or organizations being studied. This was the situation with several case studies surrounding the gas leaks at the Union Carbide plant in Bhopal, India. The company was unwilling to participate in case studies of that incident because it was being actively investigated by several agencies in both India and the United States and faced potential lawsuits. To get a case study to press in a timely manner, case writers had to rely on published sources. Fortunately, the investigations were made on a public and timely basis. As a result, there was a large amount of publicly available information on the incident itself, the situation leading up to the gas leak, and the response of Union Carbide management to the problem, both in India and the United States.

One valuable source of information can be court documents and legislative hearings. Because many library cases involve sensitive incidents, these sources can prove invaluable, because much of the information is taken under oath. There are problems with this type of information, the major one being that not all information has to be disclosed. Also, the records are often not available until after the proceedings have ended, creating a time lag. However, these sources provide a source of direct input from the individuals involved in the incidents.

Other valuable sources of information for the development of library cases are government documents. The various government agencies provide free and open access to a wide variety of studies. Examples would be industry studies that help to provide background information on competitors as well as the organization being studied. In business case studies, the Securities and Exchange Commission (SEC) requires that publicly held companies provide a variety of financial and legal data concerning the company. The SEC then publishes this data, making it part of the public domain and therefore available for use in library cases. Moreover, most major state universities are official repositories for government documents. This makes it that much easier for case writers to gain access to this information. The usual request of the government agency supplying the information is that the source be appropriately noted for the information used in the case study.

SUMMARY AND CONCLUSIONS

Field-based case studies can have several advantages compared to library case studies. The field-based cases provide a richer depth of information than library cases. They allow the case writer to follow up on potential added issues. They allow the case writer to add dimensions to the case that reliance on published sources rarely permits. They are also likely to be more lively and interesting than library cases because the case writer has a better understanding of the individuals who are the focus of the case study. Field-based cases allow the case writer to delve into the values of the individual decision makers and their reasons for participating in the actions or situations being explored.

There are a wealth of sources for field-based case studies. Most come from people with whom you, the case writer, have direct contact in one form or another, including family, friends, colleagues, students, and other associates. Using these resources in a positive manner can often lead to ease of entrance to the case site. Once entry has been established, the first dialogue with the individual around whom the case study will focus, will often determine both the effectiveness and overall success of the endeavor. The case writer must always keep in mind the objective defining the case study. Also, the case writer must always adhere to the necessity of securing permission from someone who has the authority to provide a release for the information being made available in the case. Although disguises to case studies can make the process of securing releases from the individuals or organizations somewhat simpler, there is always a danger that the disguise will create more problems than it resolves.

Library cases usually do not require release for sensitive information, because the material has all come from published sources. These cases, therefore, can be useful in developing studies of extremely sensitive material. It is rare with library cases, however, that more than one or two perspectives can be developed. It is also typical that library cases lack insight into the feelings and emotions of the key individuals that are available from a field-based case study.

The case writer needs to keep in mind the original objective of developing the study. This is the determining factor in deciding what types of material to use, how to find it, how to secure it, and ultimately, how to write the case studies.

4

Research Cases

Research cases share many of the same characteristics as teaching cases. The main difference is that research cases are designed to develop or test research hypotheses, as opposed to achieving a pedagogical objective. As such, research cases have different styles and organization than teaching cases. Because research cases are designed to both explore and present analytical results, the development and structure of this form of case study have somewhat different constraints and opportunities than those for teaching cases. The popularity and long-standing use of research cases require that we discuss this important vehicle as a separate entity. In reality, teaching and research cases can be part of an unbroken circle of professional development and preparation as a better teacher.

BACKGROUND

Case studies have been used to develop and test research hypotheses, formally, since the 1800s. They were the foundation for research in fields such as psychology and political science. Freud and Jung developed their concepts of psychoanalysis through the study of individual patient analyses. These "single n" case analyses were presented to their students as examples of various illnesses. They were also used to demonstrate methods for treating these illnesses when discovered in other patients (Feagin, Orum, & Sjoberg, 1991). The work of psychologists was extended into the behavioral sciences by Wundt, Pavlov, and Thorndike, in part, through the use of case studies.

Skinner's work on operant conditioning was accomplished, essentially, through the use of a series of case studies of individual subjects (Kazdin, 1982).

These researchers understood that field-based case studies provided an opportunity to extend hypotheses and concepts without having to rely strictly on self-reported data, such as surveys. Survey research data typically rely on the memories of individuals to state what happened and when. Case-based studies allowed the researchers to explore the full development of what happened in a given sequence of events to a much greater degree possible than with survey data. This then gave the researchers the ability to better understand some of the more subtle aspects of the situations.

All of these factors give case researchers the ability to imply causality for the observed actions. Survey-based research, which relies on statistical analysis, demonstrates correlation but cannot imply causality. Case studies allow researchers to develop and test theories and concepts through the use of direct, trained observations, as opposed to indirect methods of research.

Bock (1970) notes similar results in the field of political science. Early work in this area included research based on a combination of diaries, biographies, and direct observations. This is similar to modern case research that might combine interviews, media accounts of events, and other personal statements presented elsewhere, such as in annual reports or testimony before courts and other legal hearings.

Whyte (1984) notes that many of the most important studies in organizational behavior have come through the use of participant or observational studies. These forms of single and multiple case studies have gone a long way to extend knowledge in this field (p. 29). Much of this work is historical in nature. Its value and interest comes from its ability to study an organization or group of individuals and interactions over time. These longitudinal studies allow researchers to determine the pattern of these interactions and behavior through different environmental forces. Chandler (1962) used this method to study the relationship between organizational structure and strategy by analyzing the responses of four large firms over a long period of time. By making qualitative analyses of the similarities of these patterns of decision making and reactions, he was able to develop his theory of strategic and structural change.

Bock (1970, pp. 5-18) goes on to list seven key factors that make case research such a rich tradition in the field of political science, and by inference, in other fields as well. These include:

1. The ability to focus on issues and subjects
2. The ability to focus on the dynamic interaction of the situation

3. The ability to study a situation at a point in time
4. The ability to study a series of actions over a period of time
5. The ability to study the aspects of a situation
6. The ability to probe a situation in depth
7. The ability to corroborate theories

These same factors have led to the use of case research in other fields. These include medicine, law, and more recently, education, business, and management. All of these fields use the advantages of case research to focus on the similarities and differences in individual instances. They can then use the case studies to prescribe methods to overcome or to take advantage of the situations.

ADVANTAGES AND DISADVANTAGES OF CASE RESEARCH

The opportunity to study an actual situation in a realistic setting is the principal advantage of case research. This allows the researcher to determine not only what happened but why it happened. Case studies also allow researchers to study the impact of actions over time. Stake (1995) notes that many statements from the research case can be used to help explain the causal effects of the research, as opposed to having to infer this from traditional statistical analysis (p.18). Moreover, case studies allow researchers to place the study in the context of the environment in which it occurs. Whyte (1984) notes that case research allows researchers to go into greater depth when studying responses than would be allowed through survey research (p. 94). Last, case studies allow researchers to study complex processes in their entirety. All of these factors provide significant advantages to researchers who use case research in their studies.

There are disadvantages to using case studies as the basis for research projects, however. The major disadvantage to case research is the difficulty in generalizing from the results of these studies, in extrapolating the results of single case research into a larger context. This is especially true when environmental factors are taken into consideration. Yin (1989) argues that case research can provide analytic generalization, although not statistical generalization (p. 38). Moreover, providing data and information from multiple sources provides an added form of construct validity.

The reliability of the results is similarly difficult to demonstrate, because the circumstances surrounding the research are so difficult to replicate. The data presented in case studies are usually analyzed using qualitative methods, even though nonparametric statistical methods can be used. The case can be presented to multiple researchers and to the degree to which they arrive at the same conclusions as the original researcher, the case research can be said to be at least partly reliable (Yin, 1989, p. 45.) In any event, Stake (1995) argues that "The real business of case study is particularization, not generalization" (p. 8). Moreover, the subjectivity of case research is both an advantage and a disadvantage. It allows researchers to use their background and knowledge of the situation to follow up on issues raised during the interview process. On the other hand, subjectivity opens up the research to potential bias. Whyte (1984) also notes that it is all too easy to get lost in the mass of information and data, especially given the subjectivity of the process (p. 35).

Last, it is often noted that case research is expensive and time consuming to implement. This is especially true when considering the amount of personnel time required to effectively develop one or more case studies.

METHODOLOGY

Research cases are developed in much the same manner as teaching cases. The main difference is that the researcher starts with a specific purpose in mind, whereas some excellent teaching cases have been written primarily because information was available (the serendipity mentioned in Chapter 1). Also, the purpose of a research case is usually more directed than that of a teaching case. This purpose determines the people, organizations, or situations that are studied. The researcher seeks out situations that meet the characteristics required by the hypotheses that are being developed or tested. The researcher tries to hold extraneous factors to a minimum. Yin (1989, p. 35) notes that an effective design for research cases should include "(1) a study's questions, (2) its propositions, (3) its units of analysis . . . (4) the logic linking the data to the propositions and (5) the criteria for interpreting the findings."

The questions during the interview for the research case are also more directive than those for a teaching case. Once again, the interview, and the subsequent written presentation are driven by the purpose and objectives of the research study. Essentially, the research case study takes the form of a semistructured interview, where the interviewer has a minimum level of questions for which responses are to be elicited from the individuals familiar with the situation being studied. It is the role of the case writer to gather information from the semistructured interview without leading the individuals in their responses. The issue of interviewer bias is a critical problem with case-based research. It is all too easy for the case writer to develop questions that predetermine the responses.

Equally important is that the case writer take care that the responses are presented in a factual manner. Critical factors cannot be withheld, even if they may bring the research into question. Similarly, the case writer should not try to paraphrase the comments of the respondents. As with the teaching case, it is always best to present the comments verbatim. Then, the analysis can be made. This helps the readers to analyze the data and information for themselves. Yin (1989) notes that this is a particularly difficult process to learn, for which there is little in the way of external validation or training (p. 62). Thus, an effective case researcher needs to be a good listener who does not intrude into the data-gathering process. Moreover, the case researcher needs to make sure that both verbal and nonverbal cues are withheld during the interview process (Whyte, 1984, pp. 97-99).

Researchers also need to determine, in advance, how they will manage the trade-off between sample size and ability to generalize the results of the study. A multiple case study can heighten the ability to generalize the results. If a larger number of cases is used, the researchers need to spend more time preparing the interview process and ensuring that it is implemented in a consistent manner. When analyzing the data from the multiple case studies, the researchers need to be sure that the causal patterns are also consistent. This, typically, requires the use of independent analysts looking at the same cases and arriving at the same conclusions (Miller & Friesen, 1980, p. 595).

When implementing the interview process, it is preferable to use a team of two or more people, as noted in Chapter 3. In this manner, one person can be conducting the interview while the other(s) records the responses from the interview. Similarly, the ability to record the interviews on tape can greatly improve the validity and reliability of the data, if the persons interviewed will agree to this process. This makes it easier for the principal interviewer to follow up on appropriate responses. If the subjects will permit it, using a tape recorder in addition to the two-person team will allow for still greater precision; a tape recorder is even more important if the researcher must conduct his or her research alone. After the interview, the researchers can compare their notes and recollections of the interview. This provides a means by which interviewer bias can be reduced or countered. The final written report should be a consolidation of the material provided by all members of the research team.

USES

Cases can be used to achieve several different research ends. They can also be developed in different manners. In all of these instances, the case study has to relate to the research objectives as well as other theories relevant to those objectives. Schatzman and Strauss (1973) present a model that relates how field research using case studies can be used in anthropology and the social sciences. This model can also be adapted for use in other fields of research. The model presented by Schatzman and Strauss is based on the development of three types of field-based case research. They describe classifying field notes in these ways:

> ON: Observational notes are statements bearing upon events experienced principally through watching and listening. They contain as little interpretation as possible and are as reliable as the observer can construct them.

> TN: Theoretical notes represent self conscious, controlled attempts to derive meaning from any one or several observation notes. The observer . . . interprets, infers, hypothesizes, conjectures; he [or she] develops new concepts, links these to older ones, or relates any observation to any in this presently private effort to create social science.

> MN: A methodological note is a statement that reflects an operational act completed or planned: an instruction to oneself, a reminder, a critique of one's tactics. . . . Were he [or she] to plan on writing for later publication about his [or her] research tactics he [or she] would take detailed notes. (pp. 100-101)

Pavan (1988) analyzes these forms of notes and states that they can be effectively tied together to form an integrated case study that "can be presented to the reader, be the readers students or professional colleagues" (p. 5). According to Pavan, the format in which the case is presented determines whether the study is a teaching or research case. The fully integrated presentation becomes the research case.

Field research, as presented in this manner, according to Pavan (1988), is particularly "amenable to the study of complex, poorly defined problems, such as often confront business managers" (p. 5). In particular, such case studies can be used for both hypothesis development and hypothesis testing. In both situations, the researcher is searching for patterns in the case studies that indicate how they relate to the theories being developed or tested.

Stake (1995) follows by noting that case research allows the researcher to understand what is occurring. It also allows for a more personal involvement of the researcher into the process. Last, the researcher is better able to construct theory through case research (p. 35).

■ Hypothesis Development

Case studies have been extended to the testing and development of theories, models, concepts, and hypotheses in entrepreneurship. Yin (1989) proposed a model for the use of field-based case studies as a research method to be used either as a stand-alone method of research or to supplement more traditional forms of organizational studies. This has encouraged researchers to use this methodology in their studies. He notes that although the research design includes an understanding of the general concepts behind the development of the theory to be studied, they need not be fully established before the case data is collected.

Based on this model, recent researchers have applied field-based case studies to the development of their research proposals. This is based on the need to develop hypotheses and theories concerning, for example, behavior and decision making. It involves studying organizations or situations facing new or developing environmental factors and learning how these organizations adapt to them. From these field studies, a theory of administrative decision making can take place. The theory can then be tested through traditional, large sample studies, including questionnaire research.

Case studies provide a realistic vehicle for developing hypotheses or theories. Full-fledged case studies allow researchers to analyze a situation in its natural environment.

■ Hypothesis Testing

An alternative model is to test a previously developed theory or set of hypotheses by intensively studying a small set of situations or companies facing the factors outlined by the theory. This type of theory testing is exemplified by the work prepared by Porter (1990) in his study of the development of competitive advantage among nations. A variation on this form of case research is to use case studies that have already been written by other authors in theory development and testing. Although this method takes considerably less time than developing the cases personally, it also contains problems that lead to previously noted potential difficulties in reliability and validity in the research process (Hofer, 1973).

Of particular benefit is that case research can elicit the reasons why people act in the ways they do. This helps researchers to attribute actions to specific stimuli and values.

The case method can be especially valuable as exploratory research. It allows the researcher to investigate interactions of behavior and decision making. It also allows the researcher to study the impact of personal values and the background of those being studied on their actions and decisions.

This process can also be used to validate and extend other forms of research. For example, various researchers have hypothesized that entrepreneurs either are or are not responsible for the advancement of innovation and extensions of competitive advantage in developing industries. Case studies can help to explore these conflicting theories in a dynamic setting.

PREPARATION

The case writer needs to prepare carefully before initiating a case research project. Similar to the teaching case, a site needs to be selected that is likely to achieve the research objectives. The individual, organization, or situation to be studied should meet the constraints and characteristics required by the hypotheses being proposed. Porter (1990), in his study of competitive advantage, looked for industries where the companies were clustered in a particular geographic area within a country. He then developed a structured approach to evaluating the history and environment surrounding these companies. Porter developed a team of case researchers to seek out information on these industries and companies. They then went in and studied the individual companies to determine whether and how they had developed distinctive competencies and advantage over their competitors in other geographic areas.

The researcher needs to determine just what the focus of the research is to be. That determines what types of situations are to be studied. The focus of the research typically is grounded in the literature of the field to be studied. The literature helps to define the hypotheses. It provides the basis for proposing those hypotheses. The literature also helps to determine what type of individual, organization, or situation should be selected for the case research. Porter (1990), in the previously mentioned studies, did not arrive at his hypotheses on a whim or out of the blue. If we were to study his previous work, we could see the genesis of his concept and hypothesis of competitive advantage.

Porter and his research team then studied economic and demographic data to determine which industries to study. This then led them to approach particular companies for further in-depth studies. As can be seen, there are ways that the search for an appropriate research site can be made more efficient. A random search for a site should not be the norm. The characteristics of the type of site and situation should be clearly defined. These characteristics come from the definition of the hypotheses as well as the literature around which they have been developed. Moreover, Porter and his research group determined to test their theories through the use of multiple cases using the same questions and design. By doing so, the group was able to provide both validity and reliability to their research findings.

In a study, which will be presented later, on competitive advantage of New-Hampshire-based suppliers, the New Hampshire Industry Group (NHIG) developed a model of how suppliers can develop competitive advantage. Based on an analysis of the results of survey instruments, as well as demographic data, the NHIG chose several industries from which to select firms for further study. This led to the selection of a series of firms in leading economic industries. A number of firms were contacted by members of the research group. Several of the firms declined to be interviewed for the in-depth case studies. Others indicated a willingness to participate. Members of the group then interviewed managers within these companies, using a structured series of questions that were designed to test the reactions and strategies of the companies in their relationships with their customers as well as their technological environments. The companies fit the profiles established by the prior research studies. The companies were approached through several different sources. One was approached through a contact developed through previous consulting contacts with one of the members of the research group. Another was contacted through the school, because the head of the company was an alumnus of the school. A third was contacted because the CEO was a member of the advisory board of the school. A fourth was contacted through a personal contact of one of the members of the research group.

As can be seen from this example, a combination of sources is used to select appropriate case sites for research purposes. The first factor is, as noted earlier, a combination of the hypothesis and the relevant literature. A variety of demographic data as well as the results of previous research should also provide the basis for selection. Last, appropriate sites should be approached based on the likelihood that they will participate in the research. The criteria for securing access and release of information for a research case, discussed in Chapter 3, apply to a research case equally as much as to a teaching case. Yin (1989) further notes that there are a variety of other sources for such data. These include internal documents, reports, other studies, and material from published sources other than those already noted (p. 85).

PRESENTATION STYLE

The research case also starts with its own version of the "hook." In this situation, the hook is a statement of the purpose of the research. Often, this is found in an abstract. In other situations, it may be in an introduction. And still other research may start with a statement of the hypotheses to be developed. The presentation of the case then becomes a combination of the statement of the case facts and the research project. In many respects, the research case is a combination of a focused teaching case and its attendant instructor's note.

The written presentation of the case study is more focused than that of the teaching case. Typically, only those aspects of the situation that relate to the research objectives are presented. These statements are not presented in a contiguous manner, however. Unlike the teaching case, the research case is interspersed with the material relating to the research objectives and definition.

The opening statement, as noted, would be a statement of the research purpose. This might take the form of an abstract of the paper, as well as the statement of the research hypothesis. The basic situation would then be described. The segments of a traditional research paper would be presented with relevant segments of the case.

An example would start as just noted. It would be followed by a general description of the situation presented in the case. The literature review would then be presented, followed by more description of the case, specifically, those aspects of the case that relate to the relevant literature. The literature review would then be followed by a statement of the research hypotheses or of the conceptual model to be tested.

At this point, a further description of the situation would be presented, with examples chosen to help depict how the case applies to the model or hypotheses. This would include those environmental or extraneous factors that help to define the background, not just the direct aspects of the situation presented in the case. At this point, the case is enriched to include the data and information that would be needed to enhance an understanding of how the case relates to the hypotheses or model. In particular, appropriate quotes and information from other sources, both inside and outside the organization, would be presented. This is where the case writer would provide the data that support, or fail to support, the hypotheses of the research. This is where the validity and reliability of the research are developed. Whyte (1984) notes that not all participants' information is of equal value, however. The case writer has the responsibility to ask questions that will indicate the level of importance and responsibility of each of the respondents (p. 105).

This is then followed by a simple statement of the methodology. Because the whole focus of this type of presentation is for a research case study, a brief description of the role of case research would be presented here. This would be followed by a description of the rest of the case study, including information on how, when, and where the information was collected. Also included would be information about the individuals interviewed, including the method by which the questions were both developed and presented. The method by which the collected data is analyzed is also described; basically, the analytical methodology is presented at this point. The presentation of this additional material is analogous to the presentation of research data in a more traditional research paper.

As with any research paper, this would be followed by an analysis of the research case. At this point, the case writer demonstrates how the research objectives have been proven through analysis of the case. This would include a restatement of the hypotheses and their proof, if the case was designed to be explanatory in nature. However, if the case were to be used in an exploratory way, then the results would describe the further development of the theories, concepts, or hypotheses that had been illustrated through the case.

The summary and conclusions would repeat those aspects of the case that were critical to the research objectives of the study. The results of the analysis would also be summarized, with the addition of references to the case to provide added emphasis. During this recapitulation of the results, the fact that the study relies on an actual situation is stressed. Although the limitations of the study are noted, the fact that this analysis was based on field research should also be noted at this point. The study, therefore, does not possess the limitations of other forms of research. The positive as well as negative aspects of the case study are presented in this manner (Stake, 1995, pp. 123, 131).

It should be noted that many of our colleagues do not place as much credence in case-based research as in more traditional, parametric statistical types of research. Although there is a long tradition of this type of research, there are universities where it is simply not as well accepted as the more traditional forms of large-N-based research.

The case should be presented in as complete a manner as possible. Moreover, the case should be clear and adequately defined, while meeting the needs for brevity and efficiency. Moreover, the material in the case should be significant to the objectives of the case.

■ An Example

NHIG, at the University of New Hampshire, has used case research to both develop and test theories and hypotheses, as noted earlier. The initial hypotheses developed by the NHIG involved a test of Porter's (1990) concept of competitive advantage, especially as it relates to a regional industrial base.

Secondary data were initially used to allow the researchers to focus on a group of New-Hampshire-based industries that appeared to have developed an advantage over their competitors elsewhere. Two companies were initially interviewed to develop a mail survey questionnaire. The results of the questionnaire were then used to develop a hypothesis that defined successful customer or supplier relationships. This hypothesis was then tested with a series of individual case studies. Firms were selected that were in the industries included in the initial survey study. Several of these firms were assigned as focuses for research projects in a graduate seminar dealing with the concept of the development of competitive corporate strategy in a dynamic environment. The students were asked to develop background information on the industries within which these firms operated.

Members of the NHIG then started interviewing the companies, using a consistent format. This format consisted of a series of semistructured interviews with various members of each company. The interviews were designed to determine the responses of the company to a series of environmental inputs, based on the perspectives of different managers within the company. The questions all revolved around the manner in which the firms developed, or failed to develop, relations with their customers and suppliers. Factors such as technology used, management strategy, organization structure, training, research and development methods, and a variety of other internal and external factors dealing with collaboration and technology were discussed during the interviews.

The interviews followed a question-and-answer approach. The questions were neutral in tone, so as to eliminate biased responses. The interviewers were the trained case writers within the group. They allowed the various managers to follow their own paths in responding to the questions. As such, the interviews were open-ended in nature. The interviewers were also trained to develop follow-up questions when the initial responses indicated that there may be more information available through such well-placed questions. These interviews resulted in a series of case studies that have been used to further test and refine the hypotheses.

The first of the case studies published, based on HADCO, Inc., helped to define in a practical manner the concept of a collaborative technology specialist. The research case helped define the strategic stages that such a company might follow to achieve its goals for growth through customer collaboration, in a technologically advanced environment (Wood, Kaufman, & Merenda, 1996).

Other case studies have explored the manner in which these companies have developed their strategies when faced with similar environments. These succeeding cases have helped to refine the basic concept that was originally developed through the original and succeeding survey instruments. These succeeding conceptual developments and new survey instruments were refined with the information and analysis from these case studies.

As can be seen from this example, research case studies can be used for a variety of purposes. Initially, the main purpose of the research case studies was confirmatory in nature. The research group had developed a conceptual framework based on the results of a series of survey instruments. There was a question in the minds of the researchers as to the causality of their research results. They wanted to be able to test whether the model actually worked the way that they had predicted it would in their model, as a result of the previous studies. Later research cases helped to develop the explanatory nature of the previous results. This then helped the group to further refine their research goals and to develop a more elaborate definition of their model. It also helped the group to develop an enhanced survey instrument for successive tests and hypotheses.

CASE RESEARCH TO CASE TEACHING:
THE UNBROKEN CIRCLE

Case research has an additional advantage for case writers. Both research and teaching cases provide case writers with direct experience with actions from actual situations. The ability to analyze these situations in the context of a set of theories and hypotheses allows case writers to broaden their pedagogical repertoire. It is one thing to be able to present hypothetical concepts and situations from a theoretical perspective, especially those that have been developed by others. It is another thing to be able to discuss those theories and concepts when they are your own. This is made more realistic when the teacher can refer to situations where the theories and concepts have actually been tested and applied. When these situations can be associated with real, identifiable individuals, the concepts and theories provide an even more believable teaching tool. The addition of the research case to the teaching process adds to the credibility of the teacher as well as the concepts being presented.

The case research developed by the NHIG, as just described, has been used by the members of the research group in their teaching. They have been able to adapt their studies for classroom use. Moreover, not only has the research been effective for describing entrepreneurial actions in a lecture or discussion setting, but the studies have also been adapted into teaching cases. The aforementioned HADCO, Inc., study has since been developed into a teaching case, as well as a research case. Similar studies to this have occurred at Harvard and other business schools, where the research studies have been turned into effective teaching instruments as well. Research cases have also been prepared and developed into teaching cases in other fields. Cases in the fields of agriculture, education, and health care have recently been presented at the annual meetings of the North American Case Research Association. Researchers in these and other fields have returned to the use of case research and have incorporated this type of research into their pedagogical repertoire.

What we had to do to successfully turn a research case into a teaching case was to disaggregate the factual information from the research results. In essence, we split the material into the case and the Instructor's Note. The way to do this is to go back through the source material and the interviews and develop a teaching case, as will be described in Chapter 6. The results of the research are placed in the Instructor's Note, with added material to note the pedagogical purpose of the case, as well as teaching hints, a summary, suggested questions and responses, and any additional analysis that is necessary to complete the Note. More on the structure of the Note will be described in Chapters 5 and 8. The result is a teaching case that has been developed from the same interviews that were used to develop and test research hypotheses.

The differences in style between the two types of cases involve the placement of the research results. In the research case, the focus is on the results. In this manner, the research case includes your, the researcher's, opinions and judgments. In the teaching case, as will be noted, you as researcher are acting as reporter, withholding your opinions for the Instructor's Manual. In the research case, there is no separate Instructor's Manual.

What we see here is the closing of the teaching-theory-research circle for case writers. It has been noted that teachers can become more effective if they are able to incorporate their research into their teaching. If that research has direct application to actual situations in the fields and areas in which they teach, the effectiveness of the presentations is intensified.

SUMMARY AND CONCLUSIONS

Case research has a valid and valuable place as a research tool in the study of administrative disciplines, a place it has long held in many of the social sciences. It has developed as a means to develop, test, and extend theory. This method can be especially valuable for administrative research, due to the dynamic nature of the research. It is also valuable due to its ability to demonstrate the interaction over time of actions and decisions with values and environment factors. Case research presents the added advantage of allowing the researcher to follow up on questions and issues that are developed during the interview process. Moreover, case studies allow researchers to study a variety of aspects of the situation being analyzed as well as the theories and concepts under review.

Case research has the advantage of allowing the researcher to study the concepts in a realistic setting. It allows the researcher to place the research in the context of the environment in which it naturally occurs. The disadvantage of case research is that it is difficult to replicate, due to the variety of extrinsic factors that are present in any real setting. Also, it is difficult, time consuming, and expensive to implement. Its validity can also be called into question, because it relies on the observations of a potentially biased observer.

Research cases are developed much in the same manner that teaching cases are developed. The focus and objectives of the research, usually defined by the hypotheses or theories being studied, define the setting and constraints of potential case sites. An appropriate literature search helps to determine where and how a case site and subsequent observation should be developed. A main difference between the teaching and research case is that case writers use more structured interview techniques when implementing the research design at the case site. Another difference lies in the writing style, because the intended audience is professional colleagues, rather than students. The tone of the research case is often more formal and structured, as well.

The written research paper itself is a combination of the material that is found in a well-balanced and thoroughly developed teaching case and its attendant instructors' note. The research case starts with an introduction or abstract of the concepts to be presented. A brief explanation of the case itself, is presented, similar to the teaching case's summary. This is followed by the literature review used to develop the hypotheses, which are also presented. These are analogous to the Key Issues and Theoretical Linkages sections of the teaching case's Instructor's Manual, as will be discussed in the next chapter. The case description and data follow this presentation. Next follow the analysis, summary, and conclusions, including how the research relates to the situation being described in the case.

Case studies can be used to both validate and extend current theories and hypotheses, as well as to develop new concepts and theories. There are numerous examples of each type of use in the research literature of many fields, including psychology, political science, organizational behavior, anthropology, and the administrative disciplines.

The fact that case research can be extended into an effective teaching tool only serves to demonstrate the overall value of case research. Faculty in a variety of disciplines need to present and instruct on theories and concepts in their courses. The presentation of this material is made more realistic through the use of case research and studies. Pedagogically, it is more sound for the faculty member to have experienced the concepts directly through case research. It is also stronger pedagogically for the students to take an active part in the development of the concepts through their involvement in the analysis of issues and decision making in an organizational setting. In this manner, the use of case studies for research writing and teaching closes the unbroken circle of literature review, teaching, and research.

5
■

The Instructor's Manual
(Part 1)

■

Written guides to teaching cases, including the Instructor's Manual (IM) or "Teaching Note," serve a variety of uses and users. They are more than the last resort of an overworked instructor. They are memory joggers, class- and course-preparation guides, guides to linkages with theory, and sources of teaching techniques, and they may even provide additional information about the case. Unlike the research cases discussed in the previous chapter, a teaching case contains only the facts, the data; thus, the IM must also serve as the Analysis or Research section of case writing and research. In this chapter, we deal with the basics of the case note, in particular, those aspects of the note that can—and should—be written along with the case. In Chapter 8, we will cover those aspects of an IM that can best be completed after the case has been tested in class.

THE IMPORTANCE OF THE INSTRUCTOR'S MANUAL

The IM or case guide for a teaching case serves many different functions. There are at least four primary users of instructor's manuals: teachers, the writer himself or herself, researchers, and readers who wish to evaluate the quality of the author's case research process (this category includes tenure committees and deans, in addition to editors and others concerned with the validity of both research and analysis). Our focus will be on writing a case note suitable for the first three users. If done thoroughly, the result should also satisfy the fourth, evaluative, reader.

The process of writing a case note should be an integral part of the case development process. Its primary role is to help the case writer organize material by forcing her or him to think in terms of the function of the case that is being developed. The initial question concerns the purpose of the case: How could the case be used? For what academic courses would it be appropriate? Are the issues relatively straight forward; symptoms of underlying problems that must be diagnosed; or complex and interrelated, requiring mastery of most of the course's content? The body of information collected by the case writer may determine the answer (it's hard to write a complex case from data that describes a single problem area). Often, however, there is sufficient information to write a small book! The problem then becomes one of selecting the details and areas that will be most useful to the readers. This requires a decision concerning who those readers will be and what learning objectives you have chosen, following the guidelines in Chapter 2. The case note informs the teacher or user of the case's intended uses.

In addition to its initial role in determining the focus of a case, the case note can also contribute to the writing process. Barra Ó Cinnéide (1997) argues that the teaching note should in fact be written in detail before the case itself. This allows it to serve as a template for the composition of the case. Not only does he feel that this process of "front loading" makes writing the actual case more efficient, but he also feels that it makes training easier for new case authors. "This should mean more substantial and higher quality teaching and learning material and, consequently, better learning experiences, hopefully" (p. 6).

The case note also provides an outlet for the case writer. It is human nature to evaluate, yet students will learn more if presented with the bare facts so that they have to perform that evaluation. The Visiting Professors Case Method Program at Harvard suggested that the case writer

> carefully record what he saw and heard, then develop worksheets to help him discover the meaning of what people did, with whom they did it, and the value to them of this experience. . . . Comments [should] be separately recorded in an analysis of the case and as a guide to teaching the case. (Towl, 1969, p. 112)

If the writer has personal reactions or impressions, the teaching note is the appropriate place to express them. The case writer must be careful to leave evaluation to the student, not to include personal evaluations of the appropriateness of the actions or beliefs described. But the case writer does have opinions and access to extra information and understanding that even the experienced case teacher and case reader cannot match. One of the many functions of the case note is to provide a means of passing on that expertise to subsequent readers and users.

The author's biases, if he or she is aware of them, should be stated. More subtly, a case may have been written with a particular point of view or use in mind. For example, a case that appears to have sufficient information to be useful in an integrative strategic management course may, in fact, have been developed to illustrate the importance of market research and may therefore not have the necessary depth to evaluate production or human resource ideas. Knowing the author's vision of the case is not intended to limit the case's usefulness but rather, "to help the professor who is building a course of his own know the possibilities of the new case" (Towl, 1969, p. 85).

The case note offers the author the chance to record more information. Background on the industry is one topic that might lengthen a case unduly yet might be useful to some readers. Additional material of this type can be incorporated into the IM in a format that allows the teacher the option to hand it out to students—for example, as an appendix to the IM. Similarly, the writer might give references that would provide supplemental information or suggestions for related readings, as well as ties to theoretical material or even ideas for projects or further research.

Most educators and case authors agree that the purpose of a case note is not to replace individual preparation by the instructor.

> Teaching notes are written to increase the value of the case for classroom use. They are not a replacement for in-depth study required of the case instructor. A teaching note can increase the breadth and depth of thinking of the instructor by adding the case writer's ideas and analysis. (Scott, 1980, p. 39)

Case notes are not intended to make life easy for the lazy or to give correct answers, as a mathematics text guide might do. They are intended to help the instructor provide students with the opportunity to experience a small slice of the real world. A case doesn't tell the student what's relevant; instead, it describes a situation and allows the students to figure out for themselves what the problems are and how to solve them. Each student's approach may be different. The case note is a means to broaden the instructor's horizons and better prepare him or her to lead students in this kind of learning, and to get the most learning out of this particular case. As the computer literate might say, it makes the case more user-friendly.

■ Who Should Write the Case Note?

As is evident from the previous discussion, a strong argument can be made that the case note should be written by the case's own author. She or he has the strongest understanding of the material, having determined the objectives of the case and collected and organized the data. In the absence of an author's note, notes for teaching cases are often produced by textbook authors (or their assistants) in need of explanatory material to accompany the cases they have selected or using the text authors' own models of analysis. Many of us have also made informal notes of our own concerning cases we have used in class: what questions worked best, points that are likely to come up or that should be tied to theory, further information that students are likely to need, and so forth. All three types of notes may exist for the same case. They are each useful because each serves a different need, even though all are ultimately focused on the classroom. A richly detailed case could be used to provide data for subsequent analyses by researchers, who would then need to provide their own notes, tailored to their methodology and research questions.

A QUICK OUTLINE OF A TYPICAL INSTRUCTOR'S MANUAL

A typical IM performs a variety of functions and is intended for at least three users: teachers who will be considering the case for their courses teachers who are preparing the case for class discussion, and the case author himself. An outline for a typical business case's IM is given in Table 5.1. Although different authors may prefer other arrangements, this basic list of headings is quite comprehensive and includes those topics that case users and journal reviewers will expect to find. (The "Checklist for a Well-Written Instructor's Manual," Table 8.1, is based on one created for reviewers for the *Case Research Journal*.) In this chapter, we will discuss only those parts of this outline that can and should be written before the case itself is completed and tested. The remaining sections of the IM are primarily concerned with preparing the case for classroom use. They will be discussed in detail in the second chapter on the IM, Chapter 8.

Although all of the sections shown in Table 5.1 have relevance to the classroom, the sections on objectives and key issues of the case, linkages to theory, and basic pedagogy are also very useful for the case writer. Your reasons for wanting to write a teaching case, discussed in Chapter 1, are the beginnings of your discussion of pedagogy: What gap or need in your course

TABLE 5.1 Outline of a Typical Instructor's Manual

[a]Objectives of the case

[a]Basic pedagogy
    Course
    Level (e.g., undergraduate, graduate, doctoral, executive program)
    Position in the course
    Prerequisite knowledge needed (including other readings to be assigned)

[a]Case summary

[a]Key issues—List

[a]Theoretical linkages (if not fully covered under Key Issues and in the discussion questions)

[a]Discussion questions

Suggested responses

Teaching tips
    Time or class length best suited for teaching the case
    Board layout
    Other techniques

Bibliography or "For Further Reading"

Epilogue

Tables for the instructor's use (at the end, for ease in removal for reproduction, etc.)

Transparency masters and handouts

Data workouts

a. Topics discussed in Chapter 5. All other topics discussed in Chapter 8.

are you trying to fill? What issues or topics are not covered or could be better understood via class discussion? Often, one of the reasons for writing this case will be to illustrate how theories can be applied in the real world. Knowing how you want to use this case also gives you the first draft of your key issues. In deciding what type of case is most appropriate, discussed in Chapter 2, you have established both educational objectives and the amount and types of data that you will need. All of these issues—your objectives, the teaching objectives, key issues or topics, and linkages to theory—are factors that you have already considered in beginning the case-writing process.

OBJECTIVES OF THE CASE

From the viewpoint of the case writer, this is your reason or reasons for writing this particular case. The "Objectives" section of the IM, however, serves multiple purposes. Your objectives help you focus your research on the types of information that will be needed. Once you have that information, your objectives help you to organize it by providing the framework of what you want, or want your students, to learn from this situation. The amount and types of information and the degree of structure will have been determined by your choice of educational objectives, as was discussed at length in Chapter 2 and shown in Table 2.1.

The "Objectives" section is designed to give the prospective user a quick look at whether, and how, your case would fit into his or her course. If the degree of difficulty is too great or too small, or if he or she already has sufficient teaching materials relating to your key issues, then he or she doesn't need to read any further in the IM, much less the case itself. Generally, one paragraph is sufficient to provide this information.

The "Objectives" section of the IM should also make your objectives clear and give a little bit of information about the case. Tell the reader, in one sentence, what type of case it is. Is it intended as an illustration of a theory or model? Is it evaluative, designed for students to analyze what actually happened or critique the decisions that were made? Or is it structured so that students will be able to make their own recommendations? Where does it fit in Chapter 2's Table of Educational Objectives (Table 2.1)?

Briefly, give your objectives in writing this case. It will be more interesting if you start with one or two sentences about the situation that the case describes, but keep this as short as possible. (You will have the chance to write a more detailed description for the IM once you have completed the case.) Then, tell the reader why you wrote about this particular situation—because of its uniqueness or its typicalness? Many business cases focus on well-known products or companies; for a different perspective, you might have chosen to write about a small manufacturing company. An example would be of the Post Manufacturing company, where one of the authors was trying to demonstrate the problems facing an entrepreneur who had led a management buyout and then had to develop a strategy for expansion while faced with the constraints of heavy debt (Merenda & Naumes, 1993).

A case can be used to illustrate a particular theory or to apply a specific model. It can also give students an opportunity to sort through a complex situation and define for themselves the important issues. The authors wrote a case on the merger of Merck and Medco Containment Services. The issue of reduced costs in the medical services and pharmaceutical industries had to be offset by the potential for unfair competition due to the combination of these two very powerful firms. Public policy considerations, as well as strategic advantages, strongly enter the discussion of this decision (Naumes

& Naumes, 1995). The need to include objectives in the IM not only helps you to define your own purpose more clearly, but it also will help prospective instructors decide whether this case fits the objectives of their course without having to thoroughly read and analyze the case.

CASE SUMMARY

Early in the IM—some say, as its first element—there should be a summary of the case itself. This should be more detailed than the one or two sentences that you wrote to start the section on objectives. It can range from a paragraph to a page in length, depending on the teaching objectives and complexity of the case. Because the case is not yet completed (and perhaps you have barely begun to write!), it may feel awkward to write a summary now. However, as with several of the other topics presented in this chapter, the intent is to help you organize the volumes of data that you have collected, by asking you to state briefly what you think will be included in the ultimate case. If needed, you can rewrite this section later, to conform with the case's actual organization and contents.

Why include a summary in the IM? It has several purposes. One is to offer more information to the potential instructor who is trying to decide which cases to include in his or her syllabus. For a business case, it would typically identify the setting—company or organization, industry, and geographic location (if important). It should identify the time frame: When does the case take place? Does it follow the situation over a long period of time or does it describe a specific moment? It should also identify the decisions to be made (if any) and the aspects of the organization that will be the focus of the teaching objectives.

The other major use for the case summary is to serve as a reminder for the instructor before going into class. Teaching schedules frequently call for the instructor to shift from one class or subject to another, with very little time in-between for detailed preparation. She or he will have studied the case carefully but frequently will have had to prepare it a day or more before the class itself. For this reason, the summary should include the names of all important people who are featured in the case. It should also remind the instructor about the key details that will be needed to match the case with its theoretical linkages or to discuss the key issues. There is nothing more embarrassing, or that makes the instructor look less knowledgeable, than to have a student correct her or him on facts during class!

BASIC PEDAGOGY

Case writers often forget to include this very basic information in their IMs—it is implicit in their reasons for writing the case. However, any teacher who is considering assigning the case could use a sentence or two identifying the course or courses for which this case is appropriate and when it could be most profitably used during the course (early as an introduction; at the end because of its complexity, etc.).

If you are writing the case to fill a personal need in a course, you will already know how this case is intended to be used and where it would come on your syllabus. Because of this, you have determined what other topics will have already been studied, both in your class and in other courses that the students will have taken. However, even after reading your brief description, someone else might still not know whether this case was appropriate for her or his course and students. Do they need to have completed several previous courses to have enough background to understand this situation? Or is it relatively simple to understand, suitable to introduce new topics to the reader? For what level of students is it most appropriate, for example, for college undergraduates, for older students who have more real-life experience, or for students in a graduate degree program who have completed more advanced course work? If your case is developing from a serendipitous situation, you will have to make a conscious decision about the type of course and level of students for which you are writing.

In either situation, it is important to consider the models and theories that students will already have studied at that point in the course. Having designed the course, you have an intuitive feel for the students' academic preparation and are writing the case based on assumptions about what students do and do not already know. Another instructor, however, would not have this knowledge unless you provide it. It will also be helpful to you, once you start to write, if you can be specific about the background that students need in order to use the case "correctly," according to your objectives. Some previous topics or models in the course may not be needed; if so, you do not need to include information that would be used primarily to do this analysis. By identifying the prerequisite concepts that are necessary or useful, you are helping any other instructor, and you are also clarifying for yourself how the case will be used. This will help you to decide what information must be included.

As you write the case, and particularly as you begin to teach it, you may find that your initial ideas change. Students may need more information to accomplish your initial objectives than you have provided. Or the case may be less complex than you had anticipated and consequently could be used earlier in the course or with less background. Sometimes, students will find relationships in your case data that you had not thought about or had not expected them to identify, given their background. Don't be concerned if this happens. It is always possible to redefine your objectives and rewrite these sections of the IM, if necessary.

KEY ISSUES OF THE CASE: "STUDENT TAKE-AWAYS"

We have already stressed the importance of knowing your objectives for the case, in terms of the type of learning that you want students to experience. In the previous section, we have also begun to talk about the specifics of students' learning, by identifying the subjects that they already need to know before tackling the case. The IM should also contain a brief description of the important issues or concepts raised by the case, often in the form of a list, and also of theories or models that students could be expected to apply. This list of key issues serves as a checklist for the potential instructor to match the case with concepts in her or his course.

On the Key Issues list, there should be two or more short phrases or words, each referring to a topic that could be discussed, using your case. If you can only think of one phrase, either your case is very simple, hardly more than an example, or you are thinking too broadly. Because these are intended to be guides to important points for class discussion, they should be specific enough to identify when or how the case will best fit the instructor's syllabus. They should include any theories or models that could be applied to the case's information. Some examples could include "management succession in a family business," "cost-benefit analysis of alternative pesticides," "Maslow's (1943) hierarchy of needs," or "identifying a market niche," for example.

Using the Key Issues list, the instructor can learn more about your case than your brief description has provided. In a few situations, it may be enough to have told the reader that this case is about leadership styles at Microsoft. Any business student or instructor, and many other people, will recognize the name of the leading computer software company and most will already know that it was founded, and is still run, by Bill Gates. However, the reader may not have much prior information about the leadership of the company in your case. He or she will want to know what kinds of problems or issues these leaders might have experienced. Is it a question of how to turn the organization over to a new generation in the same family? Or of a new manager trying to establish control over an unruly work force? These topics would come at very different points in the course. So, for the instructor, it would be very helpful to find "Management succession in a family business" or "Dealing with a 'Theory X' workforce" in the key issues.

The same principle applies also to other fields, such as law, medicine, or political science. If the course case is relatively recent or the example is not the one that is commonly used, it might be helpful to list the specific legal points or questions that distinguish this situation. This gives the instructor an idea of the complexity of the issues or whether in fact they are quite straightforward. A brief listing of the key symptoms and background factors that would be most important for diagnosis could be helpful, particularly to an instructor who is looking for relatively unusual situations or symptoms for his or her class. The factual description of a particular event could lend itself to discussion of different issues depending on the focus and the specific details that you, the case writer, have included. Your list of key issues will enable a potential instructor to determine quickly whether the case has the focus on behind-the-scenes politics that he wants, for example.

The instructor, of course, may not be interested in all of the topics you list. He or she may prefer to focus on only one or two of them. If there is not enough information in the case to serve as the basis for a useful discussion, that topic should possibly not be included as a "key" issue. The items on your list should each be identifiable in the case or easily raised in discussion. However, sometimes, the interrelationships between the issues are also important. An instructor who chooses to focus more narrowly on only one issue may not be aware that there are other aspects to the case, and she or he should be prepared for the possibility that students may also be interested in these other aspects.

THEORETICAL LINKS

In addition to a brief mention under Key Issues, important theoretical applications also deserve a section of their own. What theories or concepts or models do you want students to apply? If the case was written to meet a specific need—a gap in your course—that gap is often the need for a case to illustrate a particular theory or concept. Many, if not most, other cases also describe situations that could be used as the basis for class discussion of theories or models. This section of the IM outlines the links between the theory or model and the facts in the case.

An important reason for writing a draft of the Theoretical Links section before you complete the case is to help yourself identify what information to include. If one of your reasons for writing the case is to discuss the personal characteristics of an entrepreneur such as Steve Jobs, founder of

Apple Computer, then it will be necessary to include details of his actions and if possible, his beliefs. In the case, you will have to describe how he turned over the management of his company and its very successful product, the Apple II personal computer, so that he would have time to devote to developing an entirely new type of computer, later named the Macintosh. Then, after reading the case, students will have enough information to discuss whether Mr. Jobs was motivated by the need for achievement as opposed to a need for power, using McClelland's model, or what stage of Maslow's Hierarchy of Needs best applies.

The Theoretical Links section is also an important part of the IM because no one knows your case as well as you do. It would take several careful readings before an instructor would understand all of the details of the situation or company, whereas they are readily apparent to you. In this section, you are showing how one or more theories can be applied to this situation. This is not just to make the instructor's life easier. It also ensures that he or she is prepared to help the class make these links between the real world and the models from their text or lectures. As you write this section and identify how a theory can be applied to your case situation, you are developing an idea of the class discussion that the instructor would like to have. You should be beginning to think of questions that you would ask to lead students in that direction, as will be discussed later.

At this point, it is also helpful to develop a brief bibliography with specific references to the literature on which your theoretical linkages are based. This is particularly useful if the theory or concept is not well known. A case coauthored by one of the authors involved the question of whether it was ethical to blow the whistle to the federal government on a competitor's activities. Whistle blowing is not a subject that is found in most texts. We had to research the literature to be able to analyze the options in this situation, even though we had collected the case data ourselves. It was then necessary to provide potential users of the case with references to the more useful articles, to supplement their understanding of the issue (Naumes & Oyaas, 1995). Even with better-known theories or issues, some instructors prefer to assign the original article rather than have students rely on a textbook's summary. Footnoting one or more sources for the theoretical links will make it possible for the instructor to identify and use them. The theoretical references may also be listed separately in a Suggested Readings section in the IM along with other references, as will be discussed in Chapter 8.

Just as research cases are developed in conjunction with theory, a teaching case may apply and test theoretical models. Cases, both research and teaching, have become more accepted as a form of research precisely because they are based on theory and are testing theory. For teaching cases, however, this relationship is not obvious in the case itself. It must be made explicit in the Theoretical Linkages of the IM for the teaching case to be considered as evidence of valid research, rather than simply storytelling.

QUESTIONS FOR STUDENT PREPARATION AND DISCUSSION

You have already thought about your case's key issues and how the situation might be tied to one or more theoretical concepts. A set of discussion questions is the means to translate the case's educational objectives and key issues into student learning. It may seem early in the case-writing process to be developing specific questions. However, they can, and probably will, be changed once you have written and tested the case. Writing them now will help you determine the specific information that students will need to perform the type of analysis or make the type of connections with theory for which the case is intended.

You will probably find it easiest to start with the most advanced questions. These would be the ones that challenge students to apply theory or to develop their own recommendations or any other educational objectives that you have just identified. From these complex questions, you will need to work backwards. How should the discussion develop to get them to carry out your objectives and analyze the key issues you, as the case writer, have included? How should the discussion start—what will get the students involved with the case and willing to talk? Students at more advanced levels may be able and willing to jump right in to a discussion of the most important issues. A question such as "So, what do you think of Mr. Jones's actions?" may be all that is necessary to start the class talking. This type of introductory question works best with students who are experienced in learning via the case method. It also is more effective for cases that have some kind of conflict or controversial issue than for a case whose objective is primarily application of theory.

Many students need more guidance, however. It may be that they are simply shy, less willing to commit to an idea in front of others. Or they may not have prepared the case thoroughly or identified and thought through all of its implications. In either situation, it will be helpful to structure the questions in such a way that the analysis is built up from simpler concepts to more detailed and complex ones. We often start case discussions in the Strategic Management course with the question, "What business is this company in?" This, in most situations, is quite obvious. For some cases, however, it can be a critical issue; for example, the 1997 decision of the U.S.

government that office supply superstores were in an industry of their own, competing primarily with each other, rather than more generally with all places where office products could be purchased. The question of "what business" leads directly into a discussion of Michael Porter's (1979) Model of Competitive Advantage, which describes the impact of forces inside and outside an industry on the individual firms in that industry. A simple, almost obvious question leads to a more complex, theoretically oriented discussion. One additional benefit to starting with a basic question is that it will allow the less aggressive student to prepare a response ahead of time and feel more confident about entering the discussion.

The types of questions should be varied. They should not all begin with the same wording, for instance, "Evaluate . . . " or "What is . . . " or "Solve . . . " Identical beginnings mean that the students are being asked to perform the same type of analysis for each question. They are not being asked to demonstrate other levels of learning. Not all questions need to be at the highest level of learning objectives. Professor George Lombard, speaking to participants in the Visiting Professors Case Method Program at Harvard University, gave guidance to note writers and case users:

> I have come then to realize that there are five or six different action questions. First, what did X do? Second, what might he have done? Third, what will he do now? Fourth, what would you do? Fifth, what should be done? . . . The first, it seems to me, is *descriptive*, the second deals with *possibilities*, the third is *predictive*, the fourth *personal*, and the fifth *normative*." (Towl, 1969, p. 186)

Each of these questions represents a different type of thought, a different approach to learning, as was discussed in Chapter 2.

It can be helpful to build the analysis from simple questions to more complex, as already noted. It is often necessary to use lower level skills, such as analysis (Level V in the Educational Objectives Chart in Chapter 2), before being able to "solve" a problem or recommend a solution. The Gustafson Farm case (Noetzel & Stanford, 1992) concerns a farmer whose fields were being threatened by grasshoppers, who will devour everything green. He had several alternative courses of treatment, at different costs and effectiveness, that he could use. But the grasshoppers were coming from vacant fields owned by someone else, and any treatment would be effective only if they can be prevented from crossing into the farmer's land. Before students can make a recommendation, they must consider both the cost-effectiveness data and the ethical issue of whether the farmer has the right, or the obligation, to treat the neighbor's fields also. The question about cost effectiveness represents a Level IV or V educational objective, a somewhat complex problem with the method of solution fairly evident. The ethical issue requires thinking at Levels VII or VIII, where opinions and even value systems will vary among class members. Both types of reasoning are needed before the students can make an informed recommendation.

The number of questions will vary according to the complexity of the case itself and the needs of the students. Because the case writer cannot possibly anticipate the preparedness of every instructor's class, he or she should provide questions appropriate to the courses and position in course identified in the Basic Pedagogy section of the IM. There should be at least three or four questions. If there are fewer than three, it is probably because they are each quite broad. Consider whether you are asking the student to perform several types of analysis or accomplish several objectives in the same question. Generally, each key issue will have its own specific question, unless the issues are highly interconnected. Vary the wording of the questions so they appear to be different, even if the skills involved are quite similar. For example, "Solve for the best . . . " could also be written as, "What do you recommend and why?" This also gives the instructor a way to reword what she or he is asking the class, if the first question did not generate sufficient discussion. If the questions build logically on one another, carrying students deeper and deeper into the implications of the case, the final question or questions should call for the highest level of skills that students are being asked to develop.

The questions should be listed together in a separate section of the IM. This list should not be included with the case itself, once it is written. If it is included with the case, as often happens in textbooks, students will tend to focus only on the issues specifically raised by the questions on the list. Having the list of questions only in the IM gives the case's instructor more flexibility in how the case is used. She or he may assign all of the questions to the students in advance or may proceed through them systematically in class. The instructor may, however, prefer to start the discussion with a more difficult, higher-level question and proceed back to the analysis to support or develop students' ideas. The instructor may also prefer not to follow a fixed format but rather, ask one question and let the discussion evolve. The instructor may even be using the case in a different course context than the one for which the questions were developed. In all of these situations, a list of questions packaged with the case would make it more difficult for the instructor to manage the discussion in the way she or he preferred.

These draft questions will be tested along with the case, as described in Chapter 7. For now, they will serve you as a guide and a reference as you sort through and structure your information and begin to write your case.

METHODOLOGY

A good case, as already noted, is based on research. Whether by personal observation, by interviews, or from already published information, the case writer's task is to collect data from the real world. It is important to let the reader know what types of research you used. In a teaching case, this is usually just a sentence to let the reader know whether the case was researched in the field. This includes information about your sample size: specifically, whether information came from one or more sources, such as interviews with multiple people. If material from published sources was also included, this should be noted. As discussed in Chapter 3, "Finding a Case Site and Gathering Data," information from published sources has already been filtered by previous data collectors and writers, whereas field research is based on personal contact. This section also gives you the opportunity to thank those people who helped you with the research, particularly if they provided the opportunity for on-site or personal research.

PRACTICE SESSION

In this section, we will concentrate on Appendix 2, the draft of the IM, and compare it with the final version found in Appendix 4. We have already read Appendix 2, hoping for guidance on the case's objectives, as discussed at the end of Chapter 2. This time, when you read the draft IM, look for the features discussed in this chapter: an explicit section on objectives, the case summary, basic pedagogy, theoretical linkages, and methodology. (You may also want to skim the case draft in Appendix 1 to refresh yourself on its details.)

Even a careful reader of Appendix 2 will not find much useful information on these topics. There is only one short paragraph before the author plunges into specific questions to ask. The only statement of purpose is that the case may be used for "studying the interactions" among a series of topics. This gives the impression that the case is useful for evaluation only, though the questions clearly ask for students to make a decision. It gives the instructor no guidance, however, as to the basis, theoretical or otherwise, that should be used in that analysis.

The ideal instructor's note would include a brief summary of the case, including the decisions to be made by any key characters. This IM doesn't contain any summary, although the case itself is so brief and with so little detail that it itself is little more than a summary of events.

There is only a brief summary of basic pedagogy. Four different courses are listed, which is too many. It is unlikely that any case can be used effectively in this many different settings. The level of students is not given. Not all cases are equally appropriate for undergraduates and executive MBAs. As written, the best audience is probably upper-level accounting students, who should understand the professional standards involved, or graduate students, who are more likely to have experience with the interpersonal dynamics of a small work organization. Position of the case within that course or courses? Prerequisites, if any? There is no guidance for the instructor as to when in a course to use the case or what background the students will need.

What should students learn from discussing this case? The draft IM summarizes the key issues in the first paragraph: the hiring process, professional ethics and standards, personnel review procedures, and customer relations. All of these are potentially important issues, but as written, the case will not support an extended discussion on any of them.

There are no links given to any theoretical framework and no potential ancillary readings. However, it will be easier to develop these linkages once the focus of the case is clearer. Alternatively, the author could decide on one or two theories and rewrite the case to provide enough information to explore them. Question 2 assumes that students understand the concept of *stakeholders* (anyone with a stake in the events of the case), which is a model generally introduced in advanced management courses.

The questions themselves follow a relatively logical progression, with Questions 3 through 5 asking for more complex thinking than the first two questions. Question 2, on stakeholders, is a simple list, whereas Question 1 asks students to determine cause and effect, a more complex concept. Perhaps these two questions should be reversed.

Last, there is no description of the research methods employed. Because this is a small, local company, it is most likely that the case is based on field research, but this should be stated.

Now, look at the published version of the IM, Appendix 4. It begins with an extensive summary (Case Overview), which also includes a paragraph describing the research methodology. This is followed by a section labeled "Purpose." The first paragraph of the Purpose section identifies the basic subject of the case, professional ethics, and the degree to which the discussion can be generalized beyond its setting in an accounting firm. The next paragraph deals with the types of learning that students will use. The ethical issues are described as "somewhat muddy," which would imply a high-level educational objective, according to Table 2.1. Two other issues are summarized in terms of the types of knowledge that students will develop. The next section, Key Issues, contains most of the same points that were mentioned in the draft IM but presented in an easy-to-read format and with the inclusion of the stakeholder model. There is no explicit discussion of theoretical linkages; the focus of the case, as implied in the IM, is on allowing students to develop their own judgments.

The section on Teaching Methods identifies the course for which the case is intended, as well as several others in which it could be used in a discussion of ethical issues. This section identifies the target audiences: MBA students and undergraduates. It describes the background material with which students should be familiar and the resultant position in the course. The remainder of this section is concerned with specific ideas for teaching the case. This aspect of pedagogy will be discussed in the next chapter on the IM, Chapter 8.

Last, the questions included in the revised IM are substantially the same, and in the same order, as those in the draft IM. The only difference is that the wording of Question 2 has been changed from "Who are the stakeholders?" to "Develop a stakeholder analysis." Instead of asking students for a simple list, they are now being challenged to relate that list to the issues they identified in Question 1.

SUMMARY AND CONCLUSIONS

All of these sections of the IM are concerned with subjects that the case writer is, or should be, thinking about when beginning the case-writing process. You have already established the methodology for your research when you chose what types of sources would be used. Establishing your educational objectives and the key issues for the case helps to clarify its focus, as does a consideration of basic pedagogical information on the type of course and the level for which the case is intended. The key issues, theoretical linkages, and discussion questions also aid in determining what information is necessary if students are going to achieve the objectives that you have set for them. Theoretical linkages, in combination with the brief section on methodology, also demonstrate that your case is truly a form of research, comparable to other professional papers.

These sections are not necessarily in their final form, however. This is a first draft, subject to change as you actually organize and write the case and especially as you begin to use it in class. You may find new issues, and new linkages, as you work with the information that you have gathered. Other readers, particularly students, may give you new insights or cause you to rethink your objectives or pedagogy. However, the benefits of writing these sections early in the writing process, as outlined in this chapter, make it worthwhile to proceed, even though they may turn out to be only the first draft.

6
■

Organizing the Case

■

Writing the case becomes the most difficult aspect of the case-writing process. Although this may seem like an obvious statement, many case writers forget this maxim. You, the case writer, need to remember that simply securing information, facts, and pieces of data does not mean that the process has been completed. Although information gathering is frequently the most fun and enjoyable aspect of case writing, it is the finished product that makes the process a total success. Case writers should follow some reasonable guidelines in actually writing the case study. Although these will not necessarily ensure success of the endeavor, approaching the writing process in a systematic manner should help to ease this difficult aspect of case research. Issues such as the appropriate style, length, focus, and actual material to present in the case all must be carefully considered. You will always need to consider the audience for which the case is intended.

LENGTH AND STRAIGHTFORWARDNESS

■ Selection of Facts

Case writers are often confronted with a mass of data, information, and facts when they finally get ready to write the case study. They have gathered material from a variety of sources. Some of it may even be contradictory. A question soon develops as to exactly what of this material to actually put into the case. Typically, the selection of material to be included will be determined by the objectives and focus that drove you, the case writer, to start the entire process.

The objectives of the case, as described in Table 2.1 and discussed in Chapter 2, help to determine just what material is to go into the case. A case that is designed to develop technical skills in the use of specific techniques, such as quantitative algorithms, may require little more than a basic description of the data that is to be manipulated, as well as a simple description of the use for which the data is intended. There need not be much in the way of descriptive information concerning the overall context, for example, the organization or its decision-making process. Although quotes from the decision maker provide added interest for the reader, they need not be extensive in this kind of case.

As the purpose of the case becomes more complex, however, additional information is needed to provide the reader with a better understanding of the context of the situation or decision. At this point, quotes from the key players in the situation become more important to the reader. Quotes help to provide a feeling of reality to the case. They also help the reader to feel he or she is observing a living person. Of equal importance, the addition of quotes provides a description of the environment in the words of the people who are directly involved. In this manner, you, the case writer, are not filtering the information that is provided to the reader. There is less likelihood that your values will be introduced directly into the case. The use of quotes allows the reader to analyze the situation directly, as opposed to having the case writer perform the analysis through the distillation of the material that is presented in the case.

One of the authors wrote a case study concerning the interaction between the two owners of a firm and a recently hired subordinate. The original version of the case was reviewed for publication, and the reviewers all stated that the case had much merit but was considered "dry" and "lifeless." They were also concerned that the case writer had introduced his own interpretation of the events when paraphrasing the statements and thoughts of the owners. The case writer agreed with the reviewers' comments and rewrote much of the case by simply putting the owners' own words back into the case. Because the case had been initially developed from these interviews, the solution to the reviewers' concerns was relatively simple. The revised case, with all the owners' direct quotes substituted for the case writer's summaries of their comments, was accepted for publication and was subsequently reproduced in a textbook as well (Naumes, Wilson, & Walters, 1995). The reviewers commented that, now, not only did the quotes give the case "life," but they also allowed the readers to draw their own conclusions concerning the appropriateness of the actions and responses of the principals to the situation they were facing.

For complex decision processes, sufficient material also needs to be added to the case to help the reader understand the total environment facing the decision maker. Frequently, for cases that are designed to help students develop skills in unstructured and complex decision making, material from outside the organization must be added. Examples would include information on competitors and the legal environment for cases dealing with strategic management or environmental issues. In case studies dealing with agriculture, as an example, the reader may need to know the composition of the soil, government regulations, and the personal values of the farmer concerning the use of pesticides and other materials. Education case studies may include the form of organization structure and the amount and type of governmental interaction surrounding the decision that is being analyzed. The case writer, as has been noted earlier, needs to keep in mind the purpose, as well as the intended audience, of the case.

■ Appropriate Length

There is no simple answer as to how long the case should be. The only answer is that it should be as long, and only as long, as is necessary to meet the concerns noted earlier. Some case studies that are designed to focus on the practice of a technique, such as problems dealing with straightforward quantitative methods, can be relatively short, possibly only one or two pages. Others, dealing with the development of unstructured problem-solving capabilities, can often extend to 20 or more pages.

Even this relatively simple prescription can be misleading, however. There are situations where a case study can be developed in a relatively short space and still meet the objectives of the case writer. Ken Hatten wrote a case study of less than one page in length that was designed to describe discrepancies in managerial style (Hatten, 1987). The case describes a conversation between the case writer and a manager who had stated that his style was to know and understand the needs of all his employees. While walking through his plant, he stopped often to talk with employees. He came to one of his employees, calling him by his first name, as he had done with other workers. He asked how his wife was doing. The case ends, approximately two thirds of the way down the first page, with the man's response, "Still dead, sir." Ken has clearly and concisely presented a case study that met his objectives of noting that there are often differences between the stated and actual styles of a manager. Other cases dealing with this same issue may cover several or more pages to be able to provide the student with similar information. In Hatten's situation, the conflict between belief and reality were able to be presented succinctly in one incident. In other situations, the case writer may need to present the same issue by developing a series of such incidents. A case study was developed by Thompson (1993) to achieve a similar objective concerning the management and decision-making style of Ted Turner, the media mogul, that was in excess of 20 pages.

■ "Red Herrings" and Extra Information

There are times when the case writer may decide to add information that is not absolutely necessary to the development of the case. The most common situation where this occurs is when the writer is trying to make the case as realistic as possible. In any real situation, there are many influences at work simultaneously. It is often an art to be able to sift through the overabundance of material and use only that information or data that is truly useful. Included in the information that is needed to make an effective decision or carry out the necessary analysis is what is commonly called *noise*. This is information that is more of a distraction than a help. It is, however, the kind of material that is frequently found in real life. To help students become more adept at performing this process, adding extraneous material to the case can be a worthwhile exercise.

Another reason to add information is to make it more difficult for the reader to determine the underlying reason, or purpose, of the case. This is done so the instructor can use the case to determine levels of mastery of different students. Our colleague John Seeger often places a hint to what appears to be an easy or obvious solution to the situation or decision in his cases. His intent, as he states, is to be able to distinguish between the "A" and "C" students. The C students will see the obvious solution and stop there. They will accept the red herring and go no further with their analysis. The A students, on the other hand, always ask more questions during their analysis. They ask the "why" and "how" types of questions to determine if the apparent answer is the best one, or even an appropriate one, for the case. This process is similar to the mystery writer who adds potential suspects to a crime at the early or even middle parts of the story, only to provide information that clears the innocent suspects as the story progresses.

Although these kinds of procedures may add to the length of the case, they are also valuable teaching tools. They help the instructor to further develop the skills of the students using the case, as well as providing a sounder basis for evaluating those skills. You, as case writer, should always keep in mind that merely adding information for the sake of a longer case is never a good idea. There should be a sound basis for the additional information. As with the example of the mystery writer, you should always provide sufficient information for the reader to be able to work out an acceptable solution for the problem presented in the case. If there is one, and only one, correct answer for the case, as in an algorithmic problem, then the student should be able to sift through the extraneous material and arrive at that solution. Where the problem is heuristic in nature or one where there may be a wrong answer but several or more acceptable answers, then the reader should have sufficient information to be able to arrive at one of them.

■ Missing Information

There are situations where the case writer may deliberately leave out information that is critical to the analysis or solution of the case. This is done when the objective is to help the student develop external research skills. Although there may be a significant amount of noise in the decision-making environment, there is rarely sufficient information to be able to make a perfect decision. This is especially true for complex decisions. Students, especially undergraduates, often come into advanced courses assuming that all case studies are self-sufficient and that there is no need for any external analysis. Requiring students to seek additional information from sources outside the case can be a valuable teaching tool.

This kind of exercise can be as simple as requiring students to determine what the external environment was like at the time of the case. Because all case studies took place in a time frame earlier than that in which the class discussion takes place, they may need to have an understanding of that prior time frame. This may take the form of understanding the economy, laws, or even societal norms existing at the time of the case. These help the reader to fully understand the context in which the action took place or in which the decision was to be made. This helps the student to understand that different environments produce different actions and decisions. In essence, this helps them to develop a contingency form of analysis and decision making.

A more aggressive form of objective where information is deliberately left out of the case involves a situation where it is the purpose of the case writer to have the reader develop information search and research skills. As noted, there is rarely sufficient information readily available to a decision maker to come to the optimum solution without assessing external data or information. A case study may be developed where the reader has to perform this type of research to fully analyze the case. This outside research frequently requires the use of the library, or now, the Internet and World Wide Web skills. Such a case study forces students to develop these skills to complete the case analysis. Once again, the extent to which they fully use those skills can be a part of the process used to evaluate students through these types of cases.

The caveat regarding the use of these types of cases is that all potential readers of the case must have access to the information necessary to complete the analysis. The appropriate information cannot be accessible only to those readers who happen to be close to the original location of the case study. Also, all libraries are not created equal. Not all libraries are depositories for government documents, for example. This may make it difficult for some students to be able to access critical information or data necessary to complete the analysis of the case.

These issues do not mean that this type of case is inappropriate. They simply mean that you need to take extra care, if you are writing this type of case, to ensure that information is available to the average student. You should also state in the Instructor's Manual what types of information need to be secured from outside sources by the students. The specific references should be noted, at the very least. It would also be kind of you to provide samples of the appropriate material in the Instructor's Note. This is not to imply that the teachers are incapable of securing the information themselves but simply that time is a precious commodity for most teachers, and providing the information in the IM saves time and labor. It is also usually appreciated.

THE "HOOK"

■ To Direct the Student or Not?

The "hook" is a statement at the beginning of the case intended to get the reader interested in the case. Many management case studies start with a description of a manager facing a perplexing or difficult situation. Often, the hook is presented like this:

> John Smith, CEO of Pocahontas Industries, stared out the window of his office at the gently falling snow. He was concerned about the fallout from the allegations that his company had polluted the environment near its largest

manufacturing plant. He knew that he had to develop a response to the allegation but was unsure as to what his next actions should be.

This introduction presents a focus for the case. The statement provides enough interest to motivate the reader to continue with the case. There is a problem statement that should be consistent with the issues or concepts to be developed in a course.

This kind of introduction also provides a person with whom the reader can identify. There is a decision maker who has become an integral part of the process. In addition to all of this, the basis for the case has been developed. We now know that there is a problem dealing with pollution control, involving a specific company and a manager who has to confront the various parts of the internal and external environment. The reader has an individual, an organization, and an issue to act as a guide during the rest of the case. This helps the reader fully develop and analyze the case as it is presented. In a situation that is likely to be complex and even contradictory, the hook helps the reader to focus attention on those factors that are critical to the objectives of the case.

There is an argument that a hook can provide too much focus for the reader, however. The case writer needs to walk a careful line between providing enough information to interest the reader and providing so much information that there is little left for the reader to analyze. The hook should be sufficiently vague that the case allows for an interesting as well as informative discussion. The classroom interaction should allow the students to be able to learn from their discussion, not to just follow the logical sequence of events as signaled by the hook.

There are alternatives to this approach, however. One is to simply introduce the principal players and the organization or situation to the readers. The issues are developed through the telling of the case. There is no attempt to present the readers with any focus other than the facts of the case. The readers are left to their own devices to determine the focus of the case. This certainly allows students the maximum amount of learning potential from the discussion of the case. The major difficulty with this form of introduction is that it can often be quite dry. It also can be difficult to draw in the attention of the readers to the case. This can be a problem with some students who have not developed reading skills. The authors have noted this as more of a problem as we see the members of the MTV generation enter into the academic process. They are used to quick action and limited time frame sound bites. They are also more accustomed to visual cues as opposed to written cues. The lack of a hook that draws attention to the issues may cause a problem with their development of the analysis and discussion.

Another type of introduction is a more direct form of the red herring discussed earlier. In this situation, the introduction describes the individual and the organization but presents a decision that is not the primary focus of the case. One of the authors used this format in a case that involved issues of family transition, growth strategy, and reaction to larger competitors. The introduction, however, described the executive vice president of the company—not a member of the owning family—who was concerned about the impact of the closing of its original store on the image of the company, as well as the surrounding community. Although this was indeed the VP's concern, it was not the true focus of the case as envisioned by the author. It did, however, allow the development of the true issues through the discussion of the store closing. The better students were able to determine the actual problems, whereas the average students focused only on the red herring of the store closing, a good example of the A-student/C-student split. This proved to be a worthwhile approach for the case. The case was subsequently widely adopted by teachers (Naumes, 1982a).

This is, once again, a fine line to follow. Too much of a red herring and the reader may not be able to recover and follow the development of the desired objectives from the case. If this happens, the case may not provide the educational objectives proposed by the case writer and desired by the instructor. The author should warn the instructor of this potential problem, this A-student/C-student split, in the IM. The recommended questions should provide the route for the instructor to guide discussion back to the case's actual learning objectives. In the worst scenario, the red herring in the introduction may be so distracting that the reader loses interest in the case and does not develop even a minimal understanding of any issues through the discussion of the case.

Overall, a well-constructed introduction with an interesting hook is probably the best way to start the case. A hook that provides some, but not full, direction for the reader is most effective. The hook should include enough information about the individuals, organization, situation, and issues that the reader is motivated to continue reading the case and to fully develop the analysis and discussion of the case.

CASE ORGANIZATION

An effective case is an interesting story. The case should be written in a manner that grabs and holds the interest of the reader. This calls for a presentation style that is interesting, informative, and meets the objectives of the case.

■ Appropriate Style

In a relatively short, focused case study, it is best to present the situation in the time sequence in which it developed. The length of the case does not permit you to develop much in the way of digressions from the focus of the case. You need to get to the point of the case as quickly as possible, to establish the information or data needed to meet the case's educational objectives. This is true for cases that are designed to develop specific, technical skills, such as a statistical technique or even an analytical skill, such as analyzing a behavioral concept. The main point of the case is to provide a context within which you provide the basic data, information, or description of the situation in a way that both appeals to the reader as well as meets the objectives of the case.

A case where the objectives are more complex can take different forms, however. There is more information that has to be presented. This can often mean that a combination of styles is appropriate.

The use of a time frame context is the easiest for the reader to follow. Most people comprehend situations in a sequential manner. However, as the situation and objectives become more complex and as you develop a case further on down the learning curve, information may need to be presented out of order so that it makes sense to the reader.

In these more complex cases, such as those used in courses dealing with strategic management, political science, or other areas of decision making, telling the story in other ways may be more appropriate. Management cases dealing with multiple functional disciplines can often be told better by describing each of the functions separately. In strategic management or international business cases, the description could start with an overview of the situation, including the hook. The case could then go on to describe different functions, such as finance, research and development, manufacturing, personnel, and other areas, in a sequential manner. Within any given area, however, the description may take the form of a time sequence discussion of the events that take place within that function.

An example would be the process by which Intel has developed its policies of continuously improving its computer chips. This process was developed early in the history of the company. Early on, Intel CEO Andy Grove encouraged and expected the research arm of the company to double the capacity of their chips approximately every 18 months, while holding prices stable. This policy required a highly focused research strategy that constantly looked generations ahead in the product life cycle. This could best be described by having the CEO and then the head of Research and Development each describe how the company arrived at its dominance of the personal computer chip market through the development and continuation of this policy. This would require following the product development process from the perspectives of both people over time. This might require a case study that goes back and forth between the two individuals as well as over time in their respective discussions. In essence, a point-and-counterpoint discussion might ensue, although in this example, there would probably be more consistency than counterpoint between the telling of the story by the two principals.

In a similar type of case study involving a societal issue, protagonists might well provide alternative views of the same situation. An example might involve a situation where two or more organizations dispute an action, and the discussion takes place through testimony before a federal agency or Congressional committee hearings. In this type of case, you might follow each of the points presented by the government with presentations from the people or organizations disputing one or more sides of the issues. In this manner, each of the issues briefly becomes the focal point of the case. The reader is able to analyze each issue separately and does not have to constantly shift back and forth between the presentations of different individuals or organizations to determine the different points of view on each issue. It is still left to the reader, however, to determine how all the presentations and issues affect each other from the perspectives of the various protagonists. In this type of case, the reader may be asked to analyze each of the perspectives and develop a plan of attack for one of them to follow after the testimony has been given.

In most cases, the point of view is that of a neutral observer or a reporter who is describing the situation. Sometimes, however, you may want to write a case with a particular point of view. Organizational behavior is one field in which cases of this type are useful. The case is intended to tell its story from the point of view of one person, revealing that person's version of events, preferably in his or her own words.

The case would most likely not contain multiple points of view or data sources to remain true to its view of the situation as seen by a particular individual. You, as the author, should still take care to be objective in your descriptions.

TONE AND TENSE

■ Objectivity

A major concern that has been alluded to earlier involves the issue of the objectivity of the case writer and, therefore, the case itself. This is a twofold problem. The first concern involves the way material is included in the case. Many readers, especially undergraduates, tend to believe what they see in print. Case writers, therefore, need to be careful how they present material. It is inappropriate for case writers to lead the readers in the interpretation of data, information, and facts. Adjectives are particularly problematical. A reader may form an impression even from a single word, such as *successful* or *friendly.* Instead, the situation should be described as it occurred. Value-laden statements, such as "the manager made an excellent choice given the situation" should be avoided. Readers should be allowed to analyze the situation as presented and determine for themselves the effectiveness of the decision in the example. After all, the purpose of the case is to involve the readers in the learning process. By presenting them with the prejudged statement that the choice was excellent, you would have made it much more difficult for the instructor to develop a balanced class discussion. Allowing the people in your case to describe the situation in their own words provides an even better approach to developing an effective case. Having the principals present the situation in their own words also adds life to the case. The combination of direct quotes and objective observations has been shown to be the best way of presenting a case study.

The issue of objectivity becomes even more of a problem with the development of a library case. The material has already been filtered at least once by the authors of the original source material. The case writer then has to paraphrase, reduce, and combine material from these original sources. This leads to a greater potential for subjective statements in the case study. Because published sources will typically contain fewer direct quotes from the principals in the situation, it is more difficult to present the case in the words and direct actions of those principals, thereby removing a primary means of overcoming the objectivity problem.

A second problem that may be more difficult to observe as well as to overcome is that of affecting the case's objectivity through the selection of what material to include. As has already been noted, there is frequently far more information available than can be readily accommodated in a reasonable case study. It is up to you to determine just what will be included in the final version of the case. But this choice can bias or reduce the objectivity of the case study by selecting details that favor or omit one interpretation or point of view, errors of both commission and omission. This, however, is a problem shared by anyone taking on a reporting role.

Problems of objectivity can be difficult to spot. You, as the author, do have a definite purpose in mind and have to select the information that is appropriate to that purpose. You also have probably formed a personal opinion about the situation, as is only human. Sometimes, it may be evident in your use of a single word, particularly an adjective ("an excellent manager") or adverb ("undoubtedly"). If, for example, either of these comments were the opinions of people in the case, then it is again better to quote them than to paraphrase their remarks, thus making clear whose opinion it is. If you have no direct evidence among your data, these simple words most likely reflect your own reaction to the situation and compromise the case's objectivity. This is one reason why it is very helpful to have other people look at your case. They read with a fresh eye and their own opinions. Trying out the case with students in class is one way to receive valuable input, particularly concerning whether there is enough, or the right, information. Other outside reviewers, particularly those who are also case writers, also read with a critical eye and will give you feedback, including identifying those spots in the case where your editorial opinion is in evidence. Both class testing and outside reviewers will be discussed in more detail in Chapter 7, "Testing and Refining the Teaching Case."

■ Past Tense

Your case should be written in the past tense, except for direct quotes. All of the events presented in the case have already occurred. Using the present tense, therefore, is potentially confusing to the reader. Students often have difficulty understanding the time frame of the case when it is all couched in the present tense. For example, this description of a situation, "the managers now want to make changes to the compensation policies," brings into question the time frame being used. The reader has to decide just when "now" is. Your intent is that the situation be analyzed in the context of the time frame in which it occurred. Students may, however, interpret in terms of the time when they are actually reading the case, thereby shifting the action to a future period and potentially completely changing the analysis.

Changes are likely to have occurred in external factors involving the case between the time that the situation actually occurred and the time frame when the case is analyzed in class. These would include factors such as the economy, legislation and regulations, societal norms, and competitive factors. The degree of interaction with these and other external forces may also have changed. Also, the principals may have changed over time as well. This would lead to added confusion on the part of the reader. At the very least, the discussion would diverge from the original intent of the case. The issue of corporate downsizing or outsourcing would seem quite different if the case were set during a recession than if the case described layoffs during a time when the economy was booming. In the field of political science, a few years' difference in perceived time may also mean a more liberal (or more conservative) power structure. In education, there could be a substantial difference in the type of home background that a typical child would have, depending on the date of the case. Placing the case in a specified time frame makes it clear what the environment was like and helps to anchor the subsequent analysis and discussion.

Direct quotations that are included in the case and displayed in quotations should be presented in the form in which they were spoken by the individual, however. This simply follows traditional rules of writing.

PRACTICE SESSION

An observant reader may have recognized that the discussion of using quotes, at the beginning of the chapter, used an example that sounded familiar. The case situation presented is actually the story of our case draft (in Appendix 1). The revised and published version of the case may be found in Appendix 3. This practice session will compare these two versions according to the concepts discussed in this chapter.

The very brief case draft in Appendix 1 has potential. There is at least one character with whom students can identify, and there is a very graphic image that should help students to visualize his behavior. Unfortunately, we are asked to take the role of his employers, to determine what they should do next.

The case draft is a very short, chronological presentation of a situation that developed over a 2-year period. The case is probably too short. In the practice session in Chapter 2, we have already concluded that the author's objectives are not clear and appear to change as the case progresses. This has important implications for the amount and types of information that are needed. If the original issue, recruiting and hiring at M & M, is to be analyzed, students will need more background on Mr. Adams's qualifications, as well as on the position. To discuss behavioral or motivation issues, they would also have to know more about his personal life, or at least his job responsibilities, and the partners' expectations. Information on his performance reviews would be helpful. Even more helpful would be an interview with Mr. Adams so that readers could understand his frame of mind. The final question and its ethical implications require that readers understand how an accounting firm operates. Is it illegal for Mr. Adams to be soliciting his former employers' clients? How loyal are M & M's clients likely to be? We are not recommending that the case include information on the human resource issues, motivation, ethics, and decision making. Rather, once the objective of the case has been decided, it will be possible to determine what additional information should be added. As written, the draft is a series of red herrings, without the data for students to be able to follow through with any of them.

Mr. Adams is a vivid character, primarily due to the image of him biting his fingers until they bleed. We also know that his wife is unhappy. All we know about the partners is their approximate ages and that they are accountants. The case is told primarily from their point of view. To be able to recommend a course of action for the partners, however, readers will need to put themselves in the partners' position. This means that the reader must understand the partners' expectations, both for the firm and for Mr. Adams. Allowing the characters to speak in their own words would be very helpful and would give them personality. Quotes may well be available. The author says that "[Mr. Adams] stated to the partners that his wife was unhappy" and that the office staff stated they were uncomfortable. He is paraphrasing their comments, instead of letting them speak in their own words.

The case does not begin with a so-called hook. In fact, it tells us that it is going to be about recruiting and hiring, and the first paragraph is a brief history of the relationship between the partners and Mr. Adams. This does not grab the students' interest, and it is also misleading as to the real issue of the case.

The draft is organized chronologically. This does not mean that the timing of events is clear, however. In particular, the reader doesn't know when the meeting with the partners took place—whether it was during the tax season mentioned in the third paragraph or some time later. The reader also doesn't really know why the meeting was called or even who called it. The partners asked for time to consider their options, but "shortly after," they heard about the letter. Was this a matter of days or weeks? The timing surely affects the interpretation of the partners' willingness to consider Mr. Adams for partner. The case would be clearer if the exact timing could be established.

The tone of the case is objective. There are no obvious value judgments by the author. All opinions are credited to someone in the case: the partners, the office staff, or Mr. Adams himself. For the most part, the case is in past tense, except for the last sentence. This may have been intended to give the students a feeling of urgency and importance. However, the decision will have certainly been made by the time students are reading the case, so the last sentence should also be in the past tense.

Overall, the case is actually rather dull. It has one vivid image, but even that does not give the reader a lot of insight into the characters involved. More details—whether about the job requirements, Mr. Adams's personal motivation and situation, or the clients' and the partners' expectations—would help readers put themselves into this situation.

In contrast, the revised case (Appendix 3) is still quite short but much more lively. The hook puts the focus on the decision makers, Mr. Morrison and Mr. Meyers. They have just received a phone call from a client, a situation that gives insight into the (now clearly defined) central issue. Quotes from their conversation also give insight into their expectations, as well as introducing the controversy and the other main character, Mr. Adams.

The case writer has maintained his status as an objective reporter, but the case is now told from a definite point of view, that of the partners. Mr. Meyers and Mr. Morrison are quoted extensively. Mr. Adams's views are summarized by the partners, who also contribute their observations concerning his behavior. Except for the quotes, the case is entirely in the past tense. It also now contains background information on the company and on industry norms, interspersed with the chronological sequence of events. It concludes where it began, with the client's phone call to Mr. Morrison, refocusing the reader on the central issue of the case. The actual letter from Mr. Adams, which was the pivotal event in both the finished case and the draft, is now included as an appendix. Also included is an appendix with excerpts from the accountants' professional code of conduct. This is potentially an important input into a discussion of the ethics of Mr. Adams's behavior.

SUMMARY AND CONCLUSIONS

Case studies should be written with the reader in mind. The objective of the case should also drive the presentation of the material. These factors help to determine the length as well as the material that is included in the case. A relatively focused, unidimensional case study would probably be short. The material would be limited to that which is necessary to describe the situation. Extraneous material would not be included. The purpose of this type of case is to help students understand and practice specific techniques and tools, such as mathematical models and quantitative methods. As the case objective becomes more complex, the length increases. Also, the case might include material not directly relevant to the analysis and class discussion. The case writer might want to deliberately include irrelevant or even misleading information or data, to make the case as lifelike as possible. It is rare in real life that issues are clear-cut and obvious. Putting such information into the case provides realism. It requires the reader to go through analysis similar to that which would be required in the actual setting. This format can also be used as a tool for developing research skills for complex decision making on the part of the students.

The reader needs to be drawn into the situation at the outset of the case study. Providing an introduction that presents a hook to secure the interest of the reader is an effective way to start a case study, especially one where the issues are complex and the case is likely to extend into many pages. Most students do not want to wait until they are halfway through a lengthy case study before they have a clue as to why they are reading it. The case writer needs to consider just how much direction the hook provides to the student. Too much direction, and the subsequent analysis becomes limited and possibly even eliminated. Too little direction, and the reader becomes frustrated, leading the student to lose both interest and involvement in the issues and the case itself.

There are, however, a few general rules for case writers. The case study should be written in the past tense, because all of the events that are presented in the case have already occurred. Presenting the case in any other form can be misleading and lead to discussions that fail to meet the objectives of the case.

The length and presentation style should match the objectives of the case. Highly focused and limited, objective case studies are likely to be shorter and limited in style. More complex case studies are likely to be longer, with more extraneous information provided to the reader to make them more realistic and lifelike.

Last, the case needs to be written from the perspective of a reporter, rather than that of an editorial writer. The case writer should be objective in style. Value-laden statements have to be avoided so as not to lead the reader during the analysis. The material should be factual in content. The reporter's guidelines of "who, what, when, where, why, and how" often provide a useful framework. Direct quotes lend both interest and factualness to the case.

The case study is designed to be used as a teaching tool to develop decision-making skills at various levels. An effective case study is one that is both interesting and leads to a discussion that meets the objectives of the case. The appropriate style for writing the case is the one that meets the writer's objective for the case.

7

■

Testing and Refining
the Teaching Case

■

Once the facts are collected and organized and committed to paper or computer disk, there is a tremendous feeling of satisfaction: You have written a case. The case is not yet complete, however. You do not yet know whether it is effective. How will it work in a classroom? The next step is to evaluate your case, to see whether it can accomplish the educational objectives that you have set. Based on this critical look, you may need to refine your case. This may take the form of adding or reorganizing information. It may also mean that you reconsider the case's possibilities and find that it can be used in ways that you didn't expect—and as a result, you modify your educational objectives and key issues.

There are a number of different ways to learn about your case's effectiveness and potential. However, at this stage, you will need to allow your case to find other readers. No one knows it better than you, but that is now potentially a problem. You know what each paragraph, each sentence is intended to convey. You selected the details that you felt would guide students to your key issues and help them develop the skills that you envisioned. Now, the case needs someone else to read it, discover its depths, perform its analyses. These new readers will give you the feedback you need to improve it and make it more effective.

The ideal test for a teaching case is for it to be taught. Because students' learning is the reason for writing the case, it is highly appropriate to learn from them. Other readers, including other case writers, are also a valuable resource. Some case writers prefer to have their case critiqued by these colleagues before taking it into the classroom. This chapter will explore various techniques for acquiring feedback and will offer recommendations on how to interpret what you learn about your case.

DEVELOPING A PRELIMINARY TEACHING PLAN

If you have been following the format of this book, you have already devoted time and thought to considering what your case is expected to accomplish and how it is likely to be used. What is needed now is to develop a plan for converting those objectives into actual student learning. You want to find out whether students can identify the key issues. You want to see whether they develop and apply the reasoning and skill levels that were your educational objective. You also want to make sure that the case includes enough information, and the right information, for the students to conduct their analysis.

Answers in these areas will not automatically flow from student discussion of the case. Even if you are the person who will be testing the case in class, you will need to set specific goals for the discussion. This means translating your key issues into questions, if you have not already done so in your draft of the IM (described in Chapter 5). You will need to go into class armed with a list of three to five questions (fewer for a focused case, more for one that is complex and interconnected). Writing the questions in advance, rather than "winging it" in class, enables you to direct the discussion. If it begins to stall or to move off course to other topics, you are prepared to refocus it in the areas that you feel are most important. Having the questions in writing will also make it easier for you to make notes on the discussion, as will be discussed later. These questions and your notes will form an important part of the IM for your case.

You may also want to plan your summary of the case, to be used at the end of the discussion. This would be a list of the important points that should have come up during class. Essentially, it is a list of the key issues. They may, however, be described in terms of significant details from the case. Instead of focusing on relevant theory, as you did in the Theoretical Linkages section of the IM, the summary should highlight how theory can be applied to the situation in the case. You may want to prepare an overhead with these summary points to take to class; perhaps more important than its use in the summary is its availability, lying there among your notes, to remind you and to make sure that nothing important is missed. Because this is your first experience teaching with this case, it is all too easy to stay too long on one point or to skip over something of importance in the excitement of the class discussion. Similarly, an overhead with the most relevant theories or models outlined or diagramed can serve as a reminder to you as well as a prompt for the class.

TESTING YOUR CASE IN CLASS

■ What to Tell the Class

One issue that has been raised concerning testing a new case is what to tell the class. When they assign the case, some case writers like to inform their students that it is new and to ask for their input. Others simply teach it like any other case and ask for feedback after class, if at all. There are arguments to be made on both sides. However, there are many other sources who can check your writing for clarity and completeness, but few others where you can test the case's effectiveness as a teaching tool. Generally, you will learn more about teaching the case by treating it like any other assignment.

A related question is whether to tell your students that you are the author. Students may be reluctant to critique you, the professor. If you feel that their input would not be as brutally honest as you would like, give them the case without any author identification. When you ask for their comments, tell them that the author has requested some feedback, so that he or she can include their reactions in improving the case.

If the reason for writing this case was to fill a gap in your syllabus, this will be the logical place in the course to assign it. Schedule it in, with the same type of advance assignment that you normally make and to which your students are accustomed. If your syllabus lists specific questions to consider, provide them. If you normally direct students verbally, follow your usual procedure. Your goal is to have the students treat the case with the same seriousness and thoroughness that they normally would apply. You will learn more about what students typically can learn from your case if you don't emphasize its importance or encourage your test class to work harder than usual.

If there is no obvious gap in your syllabus, you will have to decide when the case would be appropriate. You have already considered the prerequisite knowledge needed and, based on that, the most likely position for the case in the course. Testing this case may mean replacing an old favorite whose classroom effectiveness you know and appreciate. Only you can decide if this trade-off is worthwhile. Another possibility would be to use the new case for an exam or group project, where cases are seldom repeated from semester to semester. You will still learn a great deal about your case, although not necessarily the same things as if it were subject to students' discussion and interaction. If you are not currently teaching the course for which the case would be appropriate, you may want to have it tested by another instructor.

It is also OK to ask students for their feedback after the case has been used in class. If so, it is important to make the request immediately, while the case is still fresh in their memory and before they have gone on to another topic or situation. They may be more willing to offer feedback if it is anonymous, or they might lend you their copies of the case with whatever markings they made. They may be able to identify sections or sentences that were unclear or information that they would like to have had. There are other ways to find out these same points, however, without relying on the goodwill of the class.

An exceptional group of students may be able to handle both the case and its critique. This would be most likely if they are experienced in the case method and have demonstrated their ability and motivation in class. Students typically enjoy being included in the case-writing process. It makes them feel as though they have expertise to contribute—and, in fact, they do, because they are the ones who will be trying to analyze and learn from the case. However, if you ask the students in advance to provide feedback on the case itself, you are running the risk of distracting them from their regular preparation. You will learn about the case's readability and level of detail but may sacrifice some of the depth and intensity of the class's discussion of its issues.

■ The Mechanics of Class Testing

The first decision that you, the author, have to make concerning testing your case in a class is whether to teach the case yourself or have someone else test it for you. Again, there is a basic trade-off involved. If you teach the case yourself, you have the ability to direct the discussion where you want it to go, bringing it back on track or exploring a new area that the class uncovers. However, you are actively involved, which will mean that you can't be recording your observations. If another instructor teaches your case, you may have the opportunity to observe and note the class's responses; however, you will not be able to follow up on specific issues or test your ideas on how to teach the case. Although you will learn a great deal about some aspects of the case, they will not necessarily match your educational objectives and key issues for the case.

In this section, we will assume that you have decided to class test the case yourself. Teaching the case will give you the opportunity to test your key issues and see whether your educational objectives can be accomplished. There are a number of things you can do to overcome or minimize the difficulties of recording what you learned.

One approach is to tape the entire class period during which you first teach the case. Videotaping is not necessary, because you are primarily interested in the content of the discussion rather than making a record for future presentation. Video also requires a camera and a person to operate it. Unless you routinely videotape your class, this will be an intrusion that the students are sure to observe. If it makes them self-conscious, it may affect their willingness to talk about their analysis. An audiotape is less obtrusive. However, to be effective, the recorder must be positioned where it will pick up as many student responses as possible. This means that it must be centrally located and unobstructed and, once again, probably quite visible. There may also be privacy issues or university regulations concerned with either kind of taping. Check with your media department to determine if it is necessary to have the students sign consent forms.

Another alternative is to find someone to observe and make notes for you. Like taping, this involves having someone in class who is not part of the usual dynamics and who may affect the spontaneity of the discussion. However, this effect may wear off as the class gets involved; a human observer may be less threatening than a recorder.

The other alternative is to take notes yourself. You need to do this as soon after class as possible. Make sure to schedule a few minutes of free time immediately after the class, even if it means delaying lunch or the start of your office hours. It is very important to make your notes while the discussion is still fresh in your mind. Even stopping to talk to students after class, particularly if it is about next week's assignment rather than today's case, will allow other ideas to overlap with your recollections.

Find a quiet spot and write down the students' answers to the questions you asked. You may not remember everything, but write down as much as you can. What's important are the key points that students made in response to questions. Start with the last questions. They will be the clearest in your mind. If you structured your questions to build from simpler to more complex analyses, the last questions will also have been the most difficult, the best test of whether students can use your case to accomplish your educational objectives. It often happens that once you start to make notes, one point leads you to remember another, and you may find that you have recalled more details of the discussion than you thought possible.

If your questions did not already cover all of your key issues, you will also need to make notes about these additional issues. It would be helpful to make a copy of your key issues list before class, leaving room between them for your comments. Note also what issues were not covered. If any new ideas grew out of the discussion, write them down as well. These notes, both specific to the questions and more generally concerning discussion of the key issues, will be very helpful in determining what changes need to be made in the case, if any. They will also form the basis for the expanded discussion of teaching techniques for your IM.

Immediately after class, you should also make note of what is on the blackboard. The details that you've written there will help to jog your memory of students' responses to the case's issues. It's not just the words on the board that are important, however. The order in which you wrote down students' ideas and the way you grouped different ideas may suggest linkages among them that you will want to remember. The next chapter will describe "Board Layout" as one of the aids that you might give other teachers in the IM. Copy the blackboard, both words and their relative locations, as precisely as possible. Better yet, take a photograph of the board.

One additional source of observations may come from your students. After class or at the next class period, if you have someone in class who takes good notes, ask her or him if you may borrow and reproduce them. This may yield you additional details about students' responses to the questions you asked during class. It may even have notes about other issues that were discussed. Students' class notes should not be a substitute for your own immediate recollections, however. They are useful primarily as a back-up and enrichment to the notes that you yourself make. If you ask a student in advance to serve as a recorder, you will get more in-depth observations, but you have encouraged that student to step aside from becoming personally involved in the discussion. This could interfere with that student's learning from your case—and could eliminate the insights that she or he would have contributed.

■ What You Learned From Class Testing

Based on your notes and your recollections of the class's discussion of your case, you should be able to evaluate whether or not the case accomplishes the goals that you have set for it. You may need to make modifications in the case to improve its effectiveness. You may also have found that the case is richer or more complex than you had anticipated. If so, you may want to rethink your pedagogical objectives. It is possible that you may discover that the case is easier than you had planned. In that event, you should consider whether to modify the case, the objectives, or both.

It is easiest to begin with the key issues. Review your notes on students' responses to your questions and those you made concerning discussion of the key issues. Ask yourself about the students' ability to identify each issue and to find its relevant details and linkages. If the answer is "yes," your case has passed its first test of effectiveness. This does not mean that it is finished; as will be discussed later in the chapter, a case may be effective for you but not yet for other instructors.

If a key issue was not fully analyzed or not discussed at all, it is important to explore the reasons why. There are several possibilities. The issue may have been omitted because the class ran out of time. Analysis could also have been limited or inadequate because students were confused or because the case itself was too complex. Each of these possibilities has its own implications in terms of the teachability of the case.

If the class never discussed one or more key issues, one result is that you do not yet know whether the case will be effective for discussing them. This can be remedied when the case is next used in class or via one of the other techniques that will be discussed. However, you can learn much about your case from examining the reasons why the class never got to this issue. How did they spend the time during class? One interesting possibility is that they found things to talk about that were not part of your initial plan. One student's response may have inspired another student to come up with a linkage, or relationship, that led in a new direction that stimulated further discussion. This new direction may be worth exploring, particularly if it were one that appeared to be very interesting to the class in general. Did it lead to discussion of an important topic? Did it have the potential to lead to an important issue or to link with a theory? Because the case describes a real situation and reality contains many different forces, you may have included details that make the case much richer and more versatile than you had expected. This won't require any further changes in the case itself, but you may want to add the new topic to your list of key issues. If this unexpected discussion allowed students to go more deeply into the case and demonstrate more complex levels of skills, you may even want to include it in your educational objectives for the case.

The class may not have discussed one topic because they spent more time than expected on one or more of the other issues. Again, the reasons need to be explored. One reason why the class may have spent the extra time is that they had difficulty analyzing that issue. They may not have had enough information to complete the analysis. In the process of organizing the wealth of details you had collected, you had to make choices about what to include and what to omit. The missing piece may be a single detail whose importance you had underestimated or overlooked. In testing one case, the authors found that students repeatedly had difficulty with one of the key issues. The central character was the son of the company's founders; he had recently been put in charge of the company when his parents moved to Florida. Among other issues dealing with the change in management and future plans for the business, students should have been able to discuss problems that often occur in the transition between generations in a family-owned business. However, this part of the discussion never went as expected, until the authors added a detail that had been omitted: that the parents called him from Florida every day to see how the business was doing. Suddenly, the students could see that the son, although formally in charge of the company, was still having to run it under the close supervision of the older generation.

It is also possible that there is enough information to discuss a particular issue but that the information appears to point in conflicting directions. Although this is very characteristic of the real world, students may not know how to evaluate the divergent details. One way to deal with this confusion is to provide the case's readers with a way to weigh the conflicting items. Within the case, an impartial observer's opinion should be considered differently from that of someone who is highly involved in the situation, for example. The observer could be someone from outside of the situation: an industry analyst speaking about a company in the industry, an observer from another culture, or even a competitor. The social ranking of the different individuals within the situation might be another weighting tool. As noted in Chapter 6, any opinions should be those of the people involved in the situation, not those of the case author. Alternatively, you may feel that part of the challenge for the students is to determine for themselves how to weigh the conflicting evidence. This is a sophisticated skill that should be built into your educational objectives. In the IM, you should warn the instructor about the potential confusion and provide some guidance for helping students come to a conclusion.

Last, the class may not have analyzed all of your key issues in depth because there were too many of them. The case may be too complex and may present too many potential areas for discussion, more than can possibly be achieved during a single class session. You could, but probably don't want to, rewrite the case to make it more focused or simpler. This would require eliminating some of the issues and the information specific to them. The other alternatives involve reconsidering the pedagogy of the case. Consider whether the case would be effective later in the course. At that point, students might be able to move more quickly through some of the simpler issues. They could then focus on the case's complexities and interrelationships. Another possibility would be to tell future instructors how to segment the case, either by using it over several class periods or by focusing on a more limited set of issues. The IM would need to include a breakdown of what topics should be covered during each class setting. Alternatively, it could divide the key issues and the corresponding questions into groups, with each group focusing on a different set of key issues. One author finds that she frequently writes a very detailed, complex case, regardless of the topic. Although this is appropriate for an advanced, integrative course, she has learned to provide a more limited set of questions that allow the case to be used in other courses. When taking a course dealing with ethics, the students probably do not need to consider the full implications of the company's financial survival, including performing a complete financial analysis. However, if they are studying strategic management, it is important that they do a complete analysis of the company's situation, including its finances as well as its ethics.

Any theory or model that could be applied to your case should undergo the same type of analysis as you devoted to your other key issues. You are looking for feedback on whether the case provides an effective means of discussing the theory or applying the model. If students never reached the theory or model during class, as with the key issues, this would usually be interpreted that they spent too much time on other aspects of the case. However, sometimes the class may be resistant to applying theory. They may be more interested in practical problem solving or feel that the situation in the case is more real or relevant than any theory. Although they may uncover important issues themselves through the flow of discussion, it may be necessary to lead them to making associations with more abstract concepts. Look at your questions: Did you ask the class about the theory, whether or how it applied? Did you ask questions that led them to the relevant details in the case and expect them to make their own connections to their other readings? Or did you wait for them to discover those connections without your explicit guidance? If you did not explicitly ask or provide strong guidance, students who are inclined to segment their knowledge ("that was in the text, not the case") may have succeeded in avoiding the topic entirely. If the relevant theory would have led them to a better conclusion or suggestion for management, the case has demonstrated the value of that theory. This is an excellent—and uncommon—teaching point! When you revise your IM, you may want to include it as an explicit part of your key issues and pedagogy.

If you did ask the question and received only a partial analysis, there are several possible explanations. Either the students did not see the connection with a theory as vividly as you did or they were uncertain as to how to apply it. You are the best judge of your students' theoretical background. If they have not been asked to match abstract models with real situations, they may not know how to decide for themselves whether there is a theory that could be applied. Your question in class may be the first time they thought about this connection. As a result, they wouldn't be likely to come up with a full set of case details that could be applied.

There is also the possibility of confusion. As with the key issues, students may find information in the case that can be applied to the model or theory in more than one way. They may also feel that they don't have enough information to make complete theoretical connections. Look carefully to see if the case includes enough of the details about the situation to make the theoretical linkages that you had proposed. They may be widely scattered throughout the case, which places the burden on the students. However, if the necessary details must be drawn from different sections of the case, it is possible that one or more of them was left out when the case was written. If there are important details that can be used in more than one way or that contradict each other, note how you handled this during class. If your objective was to have students evaluate and make a judgment, you probably let them argue with each other. However, you may have given them more background or some other way to resolve the conflict. If some of the "problem" facts are not crucial to the case, it may be easiest to drop them. If the discrepancies disappeared once you provided more information, make sure that information is included in the case. Otherwise, in the IM, you will need to prepare other instructors for the potential for contradictions. When describing the theoretical linkages or providing sample responses to your discussion questions, include a short section that indicates why the difference in opinions will occur and your recommendation on how to handle them.

The success of the case's educational objectives is less directly observable. You will have to reconstruct the types of learning displayed by the class, based on your recollections and your notes. One place to start is to examine the type of learning that is embodied in each of your discussion questions. A question that asks students to show how a theory applies to the case's situation calls for a lower level of skills than one that asks them what theories might apply. The first question calls for matching specific details, whereas the second calls for more abstract reasoning. If students were asked for their recommendations or their judgment, a still higher level of skills and attitudes would be needed. If they successfully responded to these questions, they were able to demonstrate the appropriate level of learning. You may also have observed skills beyond those specifically asked for: students integrating facts, drawing comparisons, searching for linkages on their own. Your case is truly effective if these match the educational objectives that you set for the case. If you wanted these higher levels of learning skills but didn't observe them, as with key issues and linkages, you will need to determine whether students were confused or otherwise unable to accomplish your goals or whether the questions and discussion didn't probe deeply enough.

As noted earlier, a discussion that ran too long for the time available may indicate that the case is more complex or more difficult than appropriate for this position in this course. The reverse, a discussion that finishes easily in the time allowed, may also have several causes. The questions that you developed for class testing may have proved to be too easy or too obvious. Were there issues that were not explored in class? If so, then revising the questions may be all that is needed to bring the case to the level of learning you anticipated. But it is also possible that the case itself is less complex, the linkages straightforward. There may be additional information that you can add that is relevant but that will give students the opportunity to decide for themselves what is important. The alternative is to reposition the case earlier in the course, when students are still developing the relevant skills.

Last, testing the case in a classroom setting will have told you a great deal about its pedagogy. You will have a greater appreciation for the nuances of the case, how students will respond to your questions or whether new questions are needed, how to tell the "A" students from the average, how to lay out the board for maximum effectiveness. All of these will be important aids that you can provide to future instructors, as will be discussed in the next chapter.

DOUBLE CHECK FOR DATA

Several times in the previous section you were asked to take a critical look at the information in your case. This is a technique that you can use even if you are not able to test the case in a class. Start with your list of key issues. For each of them, go through the case and note the details that you would expect students to associate with that issue. This is not as easy as it seems. Because you collected the data and wrote the case, you have a wealth of information about the situation, but students will have access only to that part of the information that is in the written case. You are checking the case against the list of key issues to be sure that students do have all of the details that they will need. The same is true for any theoretical linkages. If students will be expected to apply a model, either theoretical or quantitative, work through the model yourself, using only the data in the case. Then go back to the case and include any information that your double check discovered to be missing.

GETTING A SECOND OPINION
(AND A THIRD . . .)

At this point, you have gone as far as you can go in testing the effectiveness of your own case. As already noted, you know too much about the situation; it is difficult not to mentally supply any missing information. There are a number of possibilities for additional feedback, each offering different inputs and having different advantages. Other readers who know nothing about the situation can help to identify any topics—or sentences—that are not clear. If those other readers are also case writers, you will receive more than just editorial feedback. Another possibility is to give the case to a colleague to teach, to find how her or his experience in the classroom compares with yours. The most intensive, but often very exciting and motivating, is to take the case to a workshop or other collaborative format, in which a number of other case writers work with you to improve your case, as you work with them on theirs. It is not necessary to use all of these techniques. However, you will probably find it helpful to use at least some of them. You may even prefer to have colleagues critique the case before it reaches the classroom. This would help to ensure that it is clearly written and contains all the information that students will need, before they have the opportunity to become frustrated by it.

When should you enlist these other forms of assistance? It depends on what you want to learn, as well as which of these resources you have available. It is not required to have a completed IM to benefit from other readers' or teachers' input on the case. However, if you have at least a draft of your IM to offer other teachers, they will be able to build on your ideas and techniques, rather than starting from zero. Another case writer would be able to give you feedback on the IM as well as the case. And most, if not all, of the collaborative formats require the draft of an IM as well as the case. For eventual publication, both the case and the IM will be subject to extensive reviews. The next chapter will cover the rest of the IM in detail.

■ Other Readers, Other Case Writers

Even a purely editorial reader has value in the case-writing process. Your students didn't tell you which sentences were unclear or which transitions were poor; their feedback was in the areas of content and teaching effectiveness. An editorial reader can help you to polish your style and improve the flow of your case from one paragraph or topic to the next. The only sentences that should not be open to modification are direct quotes from the principal figures in the case.

A reader who is also an experienced case writer brings another dimension to the process. He or she does not need to be an expert in your area of expertise but should be familiar enough with the subject to offer more than just a stylistic critique. Even if you have a draft of your IM, this type of case reader will most likely go over the case first. Because the case is the only document that students will see, it must stand on its own. The case writer reader will check for flow and clarity of expression. In addition, essentially "playing student," this reader will try to identify the critical points, the questions, and the key issues that a student would be asked to find. Only after carefully going through the case itself will this reader turn to the IM, if one is available. Then, he or she will be able to compare his or her impressions with your expectations concerning key issues and educational objectives. This reader will also look critically at whether there is enough information, and the right information, in the case for students to be able to do what you would assign.

A reader whose background differs somewhat from yours can sometimes provide unexpected insights. She or he may see linkages to theories or concepts that you would not have been looking for. You had in mind a particular student background and set of theoretical or pedagogical objectives in mind when you wrote the case. Reading the case without knowing them, she or he will make connections of her or his own. The case may or may not contain enough data to be able to explore these new ideas thoroughly. If it does, you may want to include a reference, at least, to these new perspectives when you write the IM. If the case does not have all the details needed to analyze these new concepts thoroughly, you will have to consider whether to add to your case to accommodate this new, additional direction or to maintain its focus on your objectives and issues.

One rather unusual example of the impact of diverse backgrounds was experienced by one of the authors. She was reading a case that described the problems being experienced by a social service agency. Each department had different information needs. These were complicated by the fact that each department had been responsible for tracking its own data and had developed its own system, hardware and programming, to manage that data. The agency realized that it had outgrown its current systems but was uncertain as to what type of system to buy. Management of information services is not this author's area of expertise, but she was immediately struck by the degree to which each department had been allowed to go its own way and wondered whether simply purchasing a common data system would solve the agency's communications problems. With the same case information but a different set of questions and key issues in the IM, the case has had an additional life for discussion of issues of designing a more effective organizational structure.

There is one category of readers that can offer a very intensive critique. It is the group of reviewers for the journals that publish cases and for conferences where cases are presented or discussed. By submitting your case for either of these, you are opening it to intensive scrutiny. Both publications and conferences typically use a blind review process. The reviewers receive your case without any indication of who the author is nor will you know who were the reviewers of your case. Reviewers, either for a conference or a journal, are experienced case readers and usually also case writers. This means that you will receive knowledgeable, intensive, feedback. Journal reviewers in particular, however, being experienced, have read other, possibly better, cases and will be very demanding. A reviewer may also disagree with you about the importance of your case's situation or even the need for another case on this issue. The price you may pay for this form of intensive critique is discouragement. It may also present a challenge or even encouragement. If you agree with and are able to follow through on their recommendations, the result may be publication in an academically reputable publication.

The readers who review submissions for case-related conferences are usually more likely to look at your case as a work in process. Although their critiques may be intensive, they will not only provide feedback but also (we hope) provide you the opportunity to present your case. Conferences provide the opportunity to talk about your case in an interactive, collaborative environment. We will talk about conferences in a separate section.

■ Other Teachers

Although class testing your own case yields many benefits, it also may have one significant problem. One of the authors had written a case about a small company that constructed replicas of classic cars. The company's founders were as interesting as the products they made for a select group of customers, and the case was accompanied by film clips of an interview with one of the founders and of one of the cars that was used in a made-for-TV movie. However, the discussion did not flow, despite the students' experience with the case method. The author found that he was having to feed the class additional pieces of information. Some were details that he had not felt were crucial enough to include in the written case, but some were facts that he thought he had in fact included. Because he knew so much about the situation, he was able to achieve his teaching objectives—but another instructor, without that detailed knowledge, would not have been able to use the case successfully. The hazard of testing the case yourself is that you may, consciously or unconsciously, feed the class the extra information that they need to complete their analysis.

If you were able to tape yourself when you tested the case in class, you will be able to see if you had to offer additional information to the class. Listen carefully to your role in the discussion. When you talk about details from the case, usually you will be summarizing students' observations. However, if these facts were not introduced by the students, you are most likely feeding them additional information that is not in the case but that they seem to need. If you spot this on the tape, check your written case to make sure these details were included and, if not, add them. Having someone observe and take notes while you teach the case does not work as well for this purpose, because these additional bits of information are often not obvious and are slipped into the discussion in the course of accomplishing some other pedagogical aim.

The ultimate test of whether your case is effective is whether someone other than you can teach it successfully. By now, you have done whatever you can to find missing information and improve the case's clarity. Now, ask a colleague to test the case for you. You will have to provide at least basic information about the case's objectives and key issues, so that he or she knows where and how the case will fit into his or her course. This is also an opportunity to get feedback on your preliminary IM. Your colleague may also want to know about your experiences with the case, what questions you asked, even how the class responded. What you need to know, in return, is how the case worked in his or her class, with these students and this set of teaching skills.

It would be ideal if you could observe the class without being a distraction. In this ideal situation, you would learn a great deal about your case's effectiveness. You would be able to see whether more information is needed, more clearly than when you taught the case, because this instructor does not have that information readily available. You will also observe other teaching techniques, follow up questions, even blackboard layout. All of these can add depth to your IM. Most of all, you will be reassured that your case will be effective for others, not just for you. And because every class finds something different in every case, you may well find that there are ideas and linkages in your case that even surprise you.

It is often not possible to observe the case in action, particularly if the colleague is testing it at another institution. In this situation, you will have to rely on your colleague to provide feedback on the case's performance in class. Make this request as specific as possible, preferably in writing before the case is taught. The best time to record impressions from a class discussion is immediately after that class. It is all too easy for a teacher to become occupied with students, preparations for another class, or any of academia's other distractions. By asking for information on specific aspects of the class testing, you are giving your request more importance than if you say, "Let me know what happened," or "Any feedback would be appreciated." She or he also has something specific to focus on, rather than having to try to reconstruct the entire discussion (a lengthy process) or to guess what you would like to know. Potential requests could include what other information would have been useful in the discussion, whether the teacher had to ask additional questions to lead students, what was the most surprising aspect of the discussion, or any other aspect of teaching the case that you would like to know more about. This can also be accomplished by a phone call to the instructor within a few days of the class's discussion. This does not mean that you won't get any useful feedback if you don't have the opportunity for immediate follow-up. However, it is up to you to take the initiative—your colleague is, after all, doing a favor for you, even if she or he is also making use of a potentially effective new case.

■ Workshops and Other Collaborative Formats

There are a number of workshops and even conferences devoted to case writing. They typically provide a wealth of feedback in a supportive, inter-active climate. The concept behind a workshop is that almost any case can be improved. Workshops typically require that your case be accompanied by an IM, at least in draft form. Each participant reads all the cases in his or her session, in advance. The IM helps the other participants to understand your objectives and to prepare their critiques. When your case is the topic of discussion, you hear these critiques (and often receive written versions) but also have the opportunity to respond. Sometimes, this takes the form of explaining why you wrote this case or how you use it. You can also ask for input on specific aspects of the case or IM. Because your readers are also participants whose cases will undergo the same process, the atmosphere is mutually supportive: "how to improve" rather than "what's wrong."

When possible, workshop organizers will generally mix new case writers with more experienced ones. Those who have written cases and participated in workshops before will be comfortable with the process and will have useful insights for the novice. But beginning case writers can also contribute their input on the case's clarity and style and whether there is sufficient information to achieve the author's objectives. Participants who are experienced case teachers can visualize how they would use the case, and they often come up with new perspectives.

The workshop format is used extensively by several of the associations of case writers, including the North American Case Research Association (NACRA), the Society for Case Research (SCR), the World Association for Case Research & Case Method Application (usually referred to as the World Case Association or WACRA), and various regional associations. These organizations, although predominately made up of business school faculty, are open to anyone who is interested in case writing and have included workshop sessions for cases in the fields of education, agriculture, hospitality and tourism, and engineering. Several publish their own journals, notably the *Case Research Journal* (NACRA) and *The Business Case Journal* (SCR). The Ivey School at the University of Western Ontario also offers workshops for new and experienced case writers.

Other professional organizations also may have sessions or tracks related to case writing. As the acceptance of cases as a teaching tool increases, more professional organizations are including sessions relating to case writing at their annual meetings. The broadest (covering virtually all business disciplines) and oldest of these sessions may be found at the annual meeting of the Decision Sciences Institute. Another type of case session that is increasing in frequency of use is the panel or "VIP" session. This features a team of experienced case writers, often including individuals who have also been journal editors, text writers, or are acknowledged master teachers, who can share their perspectives. The panel reviews several cases and presents its critiques, typically allowing the cases' authors the opportunity to respond briefly. At some professional meetings, there are case sessions where the author presents the case, as he or she would any research paper, with a discussant given only a few minutes to respond with a critique. In these authors' opinion, these are the least effective for the case writer, because of the limited opportunity to collect feedback to improve the case. However, presenting your case in this format may inspire a member of the audience to ask for your case to use in his or her course, enabling you to find "other readers" or "other teachers."

The advantage of a workshop or even a panel session goes beyond the specifics of the feedback that you will receive on your case. A collaborative format, such as a workshop, is an exercise in creative thinking. As issues are raised, you have an entire session with people who will interact and brainstorm to find potential solutions. They may see potential in your case beyond the issues and concepts you had included. They may recommend new approaches, perhaps an industry note or a series of cases on the same organization. When you don't agree with their critique, which does happen, you have the opportunity to explore the reasons why, both theirs and yours. The authors have experienced this on more than one occasion. There are not enough cases that have a decision focus in the area of business-government-society (BGS), so they have written several to be used in their own courses. However, their feeling is that, to make an informed decision, the student must understand the company's financial position. Consequently, their cases include more background about the company and particularly its profitability than is normal in the BGS field. This has caused intense discussions in several workshop sessions. Sometimes, we have conceded to the other participants' views, but sometimes we disagree—and have to acknowledge that we are probably going to be the primary users of that case. And, it is worth noting, the other participants have included some of our very good friends.

If your professional organization doesn't currently have any sessions devoted to cases, think about the possibility of organizing one yourself. If you can think of two or three colleagues who are also interested in cases, you could submit a workshop proposal together. The logical conference track would be any dealing with teaching issues, because your case is intended as a teaching tool. If accepted for the conference, you exchange cases in advance, as you would for a session with research papers. Each develops a critique for the other cases; you meet at the conference at the appointed time, and exchange notes. And, as noted earlier, you brainstorm . . . about what other information would be useful, what other teaching paths you could follow, and so forth. Once it is listed in the program for the conference, you will probably find that other people drop in to see what is happening. Get their names for next year's session. Once you have shown that your session adds value to the conference, you may be able to get your workshop preapproved for next year and send out a call for cases as part of the organization's preliminary materials for the next annual meeting.

PRACTICE SESSION

The case draft in Appendix 1 was critiqued extensively in the practice session for Chapter 6. Table 7.1 contains a checklist of questions that are commonly asked by workshop and journal reviewers. All of these topics were covered in the analysis of the draft case, although not necessarily in the same order. This time, we will concentrate on the final version of the case (Appendix 3), which was published by *The Case Research Journal,* a highly regarded, peer-reviewed journal.

TABLE 7.1 Elements of a Well-Written Case

This is not an all-inclusive checklist but is intended to help you identify some of the most common trouble spots in case writing. Depending on your objectives for the case, not all of these questions may apply.

Message
Is there a hook?
What are the key issues or learning objectives that students should identify?
Are there linkages to theory or models in your field?
Do the case characteristics match your chosen educational objective? (See Table 2.1)

Details
Is there sufficient information for students to carry out your desired analysis?
Is there more information than needed? If so, is its purpose to lend realistic complexity? to add interesting details? to allow students to follow red herrings and make judgments?
Are there characters with whom students can identify?
Do the characters speak in their own words, when possible?
Is the material organized in a logical fashion?
Are there exhibits, with detailed explanatory material? If not, should there be exhibits?
Is the timing of events clear?

Style
Is the case entirely in past tense (except for direct quotes)?
Is the tone objective? (i.e., no value judgments, such as "obviously," "excellent manager," etc., unless they are in direct quotes)
Does the case have "life"?

The message of the case is much clearer than in the previous version. There is a hook, in which two of the central characters, the decision makers, introduce both the third character, Mr. Adams, and the issues, both ethical and interpersonal. Students should be able to identify professional ethics as one of the key issues. It should also be obvious from the hook that the accounting firm has a human resource problem. However, only careful analysis of the partners' and Mr. Adams's expectations will identify the source of that problem. This sets up the potential for an A student/C student split, as described in Chapter 5.

There are no explicit linkages to theory. However, the case does contain an appendix on professional ethics in accounting, drawn from the professional association's Code of Conduct. The stakeholder model (described in the practice session in Chapter 5) can be used to determine who will be affected by Mr. Adams's actions and the partners' decision. The hook ends with a question that indicates one level of educational objectives chosen by the authors: "What do we do now?" According to Table 2.1, this is asking the students to build on their analyses and develop a recommendation (Category VI). When students debate the ethical question of whether Mr. Adams is acting unprofessionally, they are learning to evaluate according to the values of the partners and the accounting profession, using skills that are developed in Category VII. Although quite short, the case contains enough information to speculate on Mr. Adams's expectations and motives, as well as the types of discussions that were involved in recruiting and hiring him. However, these are not clearly spelled out, so students must judge for themselves what is important. This is appropriate for a case in the higher categories of educational objectives.

There is sufficient information for students to analyze the probable cause of Mr. Adams's behavior. This should give them a basis to discuss whether he deliberately acted unethically. We have background on the firm, which includes its reputation and the services it offers, and also a copy of the letter sent by Mr. Adams to M & M clients (Exhibit B). This should be sufficient for students to develop recommendations for Mr. Meyers and Mr. Morrison. There is very little, if any, extra information.

The case has three principal characters. For each, there is enough information about his background that a student should also be able to determine his values. Mr. Meyers and Mr. Morrison are allowed to speak in their own words, not only in the hook but throughout the case. Mr. Adams is seen primarily through their eyes, except for the letter, which is in his own words. However, the description of his chewing his fingers should give students a very vivid picture of his state of mind.

After the hook, the case is organized in a logical sequence, first describing events as they had occurred prior to the phone call in the hook. The case then provides additional background on the industry's norms and the company's philosophy, both important to understanding Mr. Adams's and the partners' points of view. The case ends with a confrontation between the partners and Mr. Adams over his future with the firm and returns to the phone call and Mr. Adams's letter. Except for the industry and company philosophy sections, the organization is chronological. Although there are few specific dates, the timing of events should be relatively clear. "In his second year," "before the end of tax season," and "a few days after the meeting" give a good indication of how much time has elapsed between events. The two exhibits, as already discussed, provide additional details that the students will need in their analysis.

Except for direct quotes, the case is written entirely in the past tense. The tone is objective in most sections: notably, company philosophy and the sections on competition and the industry. Parts of the Background section may not seem entirely objective. It is clear whose point of view is represented, however. Sometimes, it is stated to be that of coworkers. More often, as in the hook and the final section, the case is told from the point of view of Mr. Meyers and Mr. Morrison, often in their own words. These quotes are part of what gives the case reality, as though they were telling their story to the student. The vivid descriptions of Mr. Adams's behavior and the letter itself add to this feeling of immediacy and reality and give the case life.

SUMMARY AND CONCLUSIONS

As with any document, the first draft of your case is not the final one. On your own, you can work on the organization and style and check to make sure that there is sufficient information to answer the questions you would ask. Table 7.1 is a checklist that should be helpful for this purpose. However, if the case is to have a life of its own, apart from your own classroom, it must be subjected to outside scrutiny. There are many different possible sources of feedback, ranging from having the case taught by colleagues, to editorial review, to critique by experienced case writers through a workshop or even a journal's review process. You will want to know more about how well your case can be read and how complete the information is. You will also want to make sure that it is an effective teaching tool, first for yourself and then for other instructors. You will also want to collect as much information as possible for the IM, which will be discussed more thoroughly in the next chapter.

There are two important things to remember about the whole case revision process. One is that no one enjoys revising her or his own work. Rewriting is never fun. It is hard to forget the implicit assumption that you didn't do it right the first time, but you need to focus on the fact that rewriting is intended to perfect your creation. The second thing to remember is that all case writers face similar problems. As a result, they are always looking for collaborative, rather than critical, sources of feedback concerning their efforts. Working with other case writers is immensely satisfying and stimulating. In the words of an Indonesian colleague who was exposed to the process, "Once you get started, everything looks like a case!"

8

■

The Instructor's Manual
(Part 2)

■

Now that you have actually written the case and exposed it to other people, especially students, you can complete the IM with confidence. This includes making any necessary revisions in the sections that you have already written: the Summary, Objectives of the Case, Key Issues, Basic Pedagogy, Theoretical Links, Methodology, and Questions. Based on your experiences with class testing the case, you will now be ready to provide much more information for the instructor, both in terms of how to teach the case effectively and in terms of how to evaluate students' responses. In this chapter, we will discuss the remaining sections that are typically included in an IM. As shown earlier, in Table 5.1, these include Suggested Responses for the discussion questions, Teaching Tips, Further References, an Epilogue, and Exhibits for the instructor's use.

REFINING THE DISCUSSION QUESTIONS

When you tested your case in class, as described in Chapter 7, you were also testing your draft of the questions for discussion. Trying out the questions showed you how well your case worked for students and how the case might need to be revised. The same process also gave you insights into the questions themselves and whether they help to guide students through the case to achieve your educational objectives.

Based on what you observed in class, you may have discovered that your questions did not lead to the responses you expected. If the case contained all the necessary information, the class probably did not answer incorrectly. Their responses may have been incomplete, however. First, check your case, as described in Chapter 7. If it did contain the information they needed, then you may need to revise or add to your list of questions for student preparation and discussion.

One sign that an additional question may be needed is a discussion that simply fails to move on to new points. Students may not be ready to make the leap to the next concept, based on the analysis so far. A question that bridges this gap or gives them more guidance as to how to approach the new idea would be helpful. The instructor is always free to skip the bridging question if her or his class does not need the extra assistance.

Sometimes, the problem may be that students did not understand the question as it was originally asked. Some wordings work better than others; a question that may be clear when read may be difficult for students to follow when it is spoken. In general, a simple sentence structure works better. If the issue involved in the question can't be simply expressed, it should be broken into two questions. Another alternative would be to offer a back-up question that the instructor could use if the first version did not generate the right kind of discussion.

If the students didn't fully answer one of the questions or took a long time to get through their analysis, the question may be too broad, allowing them to go in a variety of directions. The question, or the analysis it requests, may be too complex for most students to answer without more guidance. A more specific question might be more effective. Sometimes, however, the point is to encourage students to wrestle with complex, unstructured issues. Rather than simplifying the question, you may want to offer the instructor some ideas for structuring the discussion, either in a section on Teaching Tips (to be discussed later in this chapter) or in your sample responses. An instructor can always omit or adapt the question if it is too directive for that particular class.

When students are having difficulty relating the case to its theoretical linkages, the problem may be similar to questions that are too broad. Cases with more limited educational objectives may be relatively easy for students to match with an appropriate theory or model, particularly if that theory is well known or in most texts. However, cases designed for more complex objectives may be more difficult for students to unravel.

Review the types of learning that your questions use. Do the questions ask for students to apply different skills, or are they simply variations on the same types of learning? If many of your questions start with the same words, such as "why" or "analyze," they are likely to be asking students to use the same techniques repeatedly. This may also be true if their responses are very short. Class testing may have given you ideas of other types of questions to ask. You can also go back to Bloom's Taxonomy (Chapter 2) to identify other types of learning that may be appropriate.

The text of the case may also raise explicit questions, particularly in the introduction or hook or in the concluding paragraphs. These questions arise out of the description of the situation in the case itself. They are the concerns of the case's characters, particularly its decision maker. Generally, they require a high level of student skills; they jump straight to "What should I do?" They are also extremely unlikely to call for any type of theoretical discussion. They are part of the description of the case's decision maker and his or her frame of mind, rather than intended as instructional tools. Students should be encouraged to think about these issues in one or more of the instructional questions included in the IM. However, students should also be helped to realize that the decision maker does not always ask the right questions. He or she may be thinking primarily of short-term, immediate problems, when it is also necessary to consider the broader picture, or may be focused entirely on the long run, when there are immediate issues that must be dealt with.

New questions may also be needed, to take advantage of new directions that were uncovered during the class discussion. If you decide to change the key issues or teaching objectives, there should also be new questions to correspond to these new class directions. In situations where the new issues are quite different from the old ones but both are potential directions for the case, it is possible to include a second set of questions for the new focus. These should be clearly identified and matched with their key issues. Using the example of the management information systems/organizational structure case (the social services case mentioned in Chapter 7), these would be labeled "Questions for use concerning information systems" and "Questions for use in management or organizational behavior." Some of the questions, particularly those covering basic analysis, may be on both lists. There should also be suggested responses for the new questions. The key issues could also be divided into two lists, but this is usually not necessary as the list is short and, based on the case, the students may potentially bring up any of them.

ANSWERS: SAMPLE OR SUGGESTED RESPONSES

The IM should also contain a section of suggested or sample responses to the list of questions. This represents a kindness to the instructor, as well as an opportunity to demonstrate the research that the case writer has done. Any instructor teaching a course in which the case would be used should be capable of answering the questions. However, sample responses will remind him or her of the important points. This section will be particularly valuable to the harried instructor who teaches under less than ideal conditions. As noted before, teachers may have multiple course preparations in the same semester, including one or more that are unfamiliar. They are even sometimes assigned to the course at the last minute, as late as the first day of classes. Both of these situations have been experienced by the authors. The time pressure to select and prepare cases for class is intense. Suggested responses from the case writer give these harried instructors the opportunity to teach the case with authority and with an idea of what kinds of issues will most likely be raised by a particular question. The students still benefit from being exposed to the full educational richness of the case.

It is also very helpful for the instructor if the question is repeated at the beginning of each response. The first response will typically be on the same page as the questions, but subsequent answers would otherwise require flipping pages repeatedly back to the question list. These responses should be specific and detailed and in a format that makes it easy for the instructor to find the most important points. The answer could take the form of a table or an outline, if that would provide sufficient detail. However, it is always appropriate to answer in complete sentences and paragraphs. The response may be brief if the question can be answered in a short, straightforward manner. It should not be kept short merely for the sake of brevity, however. It should be as long as is needed to answer the question thoroughly. In some situations, the responses may be so complex that the IM is longer than the case! A good example is the published version of the Meyers & Morrison case (Naumes et al., 1995, also found in Appendixes 3 and 4), which has a 10-page IM (single spaced) for a case that is six pages long, including two full-page exhibits.

If the question pertains to a theory, the linkages between the theory and the case should be explained in detail in the sample response. The suggested response may be very similar to what you have already discussed in the Theoretical Linkages section (Chapter 5) because both the theory and the situation's details are the same, but the intent of this discussion is different. The focus in this section is on helping the instructor to identify relationships that the students should be able to uncover. It is quite possible that the theoretical discussion in the sample response section will be longer than in the section of the IM specifically devoted to theory. In the Theoretical Linkages section, it can be assumed that the reader understands the theory itself. When you are writing for the instructor, it is more useful to assume that most students will have only a very basic knowledge of the theory and that this will be their first attempt to apply it in a so-called real setting.

If the students are being asked to apply a particular model—for example, a statistical technique or a framework for organizing data—the sample response should work out the model completely. The steps should be given in order. Along with each step, there should be a brief discussion of what information from the case should be used in connection with this stage of the analysis. Again, this is not to replace preparation by the instructor. However, it will serve as an aid for the instructor who is teaching an unfamiliar course or topic. It can also be used during class as a reference, if the students' discussion does not seem to be coming up with the "right" answer, or to check for the completeness of their data.

Questions that ask students to analyze cannot possibly be fully answered in the IM. Students frequently make connections and uncover relationships that even the case author had not anticipated. Even in a typical class, there may be diverse opinions concerning the weights to be given to different factors in the analysis. If there are a limited number of usual, but competing responses, it may be possible to include the basic points of each, together with a brief discussion of the students' assumptions that cause them to differ. It would not be realistic to include all possible interpretations or variables when writing a sample response for a question of this type. Instead, concentrate on the points that need to be covered for students to be ready for the next level of the learning process.

One problem with using cases that is often raised by students is that there doesn't seem to be a right answer. Not true! There are often a number of answers that are possible for a question of this type, depending on the weights given to different factors and perhaps the assumptions that students make. The students are being asked to do more than simply state relevant facts, a relatively low-level educational objective. They are being asked to make judgments about those facts, to form opinions about them. As a result, members of the class are likely to come up with more than one right answer, possibly including some that surprise even the author. Although the suggested responses in the IM cannot anticipate all of these, it should identify any likely wrong answers. These would be based on assumptions that are unworkable or unrealistic. Sometimes, as described in Chapter 6, "Organizing the Case," the case writer will deliberately include red herrings, facts, or ideas that could mislead the student into making these assumptions. It is only fair to warn the instructor of these potential student pitfalls.

The most difficult suggested responses are those for questions that ask the students to build on their analysis. These include those questions that call for them to "recommend" or "develop." The specific weights and assumptions of the analysis are the starting point for that recommendation and may therefore vary considerably from class to class. Here, however, students are then being asked to develop a complex solution, using their insights and creativity. The result is the possibility of an even wider variation in responses to this type of question. This is a situation in which class testing becomes extremely valuable. You do, in fact, have a sample of typical responses. Although repeated class tests may produce a few new ideas, there will usually be a limited number of proposals that appeal to the students. These should at least be identified in the suggested response to the question. If there are comparatively few "usual" recommendations, it should be possible to outline the important points of all of them. Where students become more creative and diverse in their ideas, one, or preferably more, should be worked out with the level of detail that is appropriate for the case's course level and objectives.

In situations in which there will be as many recommendations and ideas as there are students, it would still be useful to attempt to categorize the types of responses that might be anticipated. For example, a student who is asked to recommend a new strategy for a business could come up with a universe of ideas, including new products, new markets, whole new lines of business that could be investigated, and so forth. In this situation, it would be easiest to discuss the ideas by category. The sample response could identify the advantages and concerns for the business of developing a new product (of any type) and compare them with the advantages and concerns raised instead by moving into a new market or looking for a new group of customers for its current products.

One approach to providing the instructor with useful insight into questions of this type is to include actual student responses. This approach is not intended to replace the case writer's own response but rather to supplement it. If the case's class test involved a written assignment, one or more of these papers may be suitable to illustrate what can be expected of students. Rather than being incorporated directly into this section of the IM, such papers are usually attached as exhibits at the end of the IM, with the instructor being referred to the pertinent exhibit to see what might realistically be expected from a student. It would be appropriate to ask the student writers for their permission. They will be happy to oblige, knowing that you think enough of their answers to use them as examples for others. It is also appropriate to include the comments that you wrote on the student papers.

REFINING THE TEACHING OBJECTIVES
AND KEY ISSUES

Sometimes, after class testing or input from other readers, you begin to think about whether the case can be used in other ways or whether it perhaps can't be used exactly as expected. In either situation, you should consider whether to revise the case to achieve the original objectives or to change the objectives that you originally had stated. Case revisions based on the results of class testing and other readers' comments were discussed in the last chapter. How do you decide whether the case or the original teaching objectives need to be changed?

One way is to ask yourself, When the case was used in class, did it accomplish what I had intended? This can refer to either the key issues or the types of skills that students demonstrated. If students were prepared and eager to discuss the case but did not talk about one or more of the key issues that you had identified, the case may not contain the right information to make that issue seem important. It may also be that the issue was too obvious for much discussion. The case writer then has several options. One is to add information that will help the students understand the relevance of this issue. A quote from someone who is involved with the situation is a particularly powerful way to stress the idea's importance. The issue could be repositioned within the case to receive emphasis from being one of the first—or last—sections read by the student. It could even be given a subheading of its own, if the need seems strong enough.

The case may also be either too complex or not complex enough for the types of learning for which it had been written. If the case is not complex enough to fit your objectives, students will quickly complete discussion of your topics, finding the information easy to locate and analyze or the recommendations obvious. If your objectives are not dependent on having studied a particular theory or model that will be introduced later in the course, the simplest solution is to recommend repositioning the case. If the position cannot easily be changed, then the teaching objectives should be revised to reflect this more straightforward analysis, perhaps Level IV in Table 2.1 (a structured business problem) rather than V or VI (which are more complex), or VI (relatively unstructured but with a clear emphasis on action) rather than Level VII (complex, realistic, unstructured, and with a variety of different value systems within the case).

If a case is too complex, students will most likely react by being confused. They have too much information, given their background or their expectations as to how they are to use this case. In this situation, the case may be positioned too early in the course. Students may have studied the necessary theories but still lack the sophistication that comes with practicing analysis. Your objectives are more likely to be achieved if the case is taught later in the course or in a more advanced level of that course. Another option is to modify the teaching objectives to call for a higher level of student skills. The case may be more than a "complex, unstructured slice of life," as described in Level V (Table 2.1). It may be more appropriate for use in Level VII or VIII, where the student must display the judgment to decide which facts and which problems are most important.

A third option is to revise the teaching objectives to explicitly include several levels of analysis. In a case about a simpler situation, this two-step process would not be necessary. However, if the case is too complex for the students to handle as a whole, it may be necessary to make sure that they have successfully completed the analysis phase before attempting the more advanced objectives.

The original key issues may also have been less interesting than other topics that the students found in the case. This may have led to unexpected insights when the instructor asked for relevant theories or concepts and the class identified linkages or issues that had not been anticipated. If the case has sufficient information to support these new ideas, they should be added to the list of key issues. They should also be incorporated into the teaching objectives, particularly because the case is now richer and more complex and potentially more flexible than in the original description.

One of us coauthored a case on a small company that was having trouble getting orders. The CEO knew that one of his primary competitors was pricing its products very low because it was not making social security or tax payments for its workers. He wondered if he should blow the whistle and report his competitor. The case was initially written for a discussion of ethics or for use in a course on the relationship between Business and Society— What would be the ethical course of action for the CEO, and why? Financial information had been included in the case only to give an idea of the pressures that the CEO was facing. However, in class, the discussion of ethics rapidly gave way to concern as to whether this company could survive at all, even if the competitor were eliminated (Naumes & Oyaas, 1995). This completely changed how the case could be used. It turned out to be more appropriate for a course in Entrepreneurship or Strategic Management, where it raised the issue of survival and, secondarily, ethics. The type of learning had also changed from consideration of the ethical pros and cons of different courses of action (Level IV) to in-depth analysis of the firm's current financial situation and predictions for the future (Levels V and VI).

One of us, when reviewing a case for a journal, found herself out of her area of expertise. As written, the IM described the case's objectives in terms of U.S. laws on employment discrimination. The manager of a restaurant was "involved" with a teenaged employee; although the nature of that involvement was not made clear, the issue was being raised, primarily by the employee's mother. Not being an expert in legal matters, the reviewer could not determine whether the case could be used to meet its author's objectives. However, the case also contained a description of how the employee and her friends behaved: not doing the work they were told to do and hanging around with teenaged customers. There was enough information, in fact, to have a good discussion on the employees' motivation and on the leadership implications of manager-employee "involvement." The case could still potentially be used as the author had intended, but it had an abundance of additional topics that have consistently led to lively discussions in other classes. The case, untouched but with the IM radically revised to reflect these new issues and objectives, was accepted for publication in one of the leading case journals and has been reprinted in several texts.

WHAT YOU'VE LEARNED
FROM CLASS TESTING

Even if students' discussion revealed precisely the teaching objectives and key issues that the case writer had anticipated, class testing should have provided more detailed information concerning the pedagogy of the case. It may be necessary to add additional questions to have the discussion go smoothly. You have also learned something about how students are likely to answer your questions and can offer the instructor insights into evaluating their responses. You will also be able to make recommendations on several other aspects of using the case in class. These should be incorporated in a section of their own, which could be called "Teaching Tips" or "Pedagogical Suggestions."

■ The "A Student/C Student Split"

Sometimes, in class discussion, it becomes apparent that there are one or more questions that are more difficult for some students to answer. They may see relationships that are relatively obvious or conduct the first steps of an analysis but miss the more complex points. Better students, however, make the connections or understand how to complete the analysis. As mentioned earlier, case teachers call this the "A student/C student split." It is very useful for an instructor to know in advance when this might occur in class. How will the student with minimal preparation respond, compared with the person who has done a careful analysis? A properly structured set of questions should be able to bring virtually everyone along with the discussion, but if class testing has revealed a concept or question that could be used to discriminate between levels of understanding, it should be highlighted in the suggested response to that question.

In the whistle-blowing case example, which has already been discussed, a "C" student would be likely to focus only on the ethical question that was raised by the manager in the case and would respond in terms of its impact on his company. However, an "A" student would realize that the company does not have enough money to survive, even if the competitor were eliminated. In the Gustafson farm case, discussed in Chapter 5, the "C" student would look at the combinations of cost and effectiveness and recommend a grasshopper control treatment plan on that basis. The "A" student will also look at the implications of each choice in terms of its impact on the farmer's neighbors and his reputation in the community.

■ Timing

An important part of using a case effectively is knowing how long a discussion it is likely to generate. Few cases can stand up to intense scrutiny for the full length of a 3-hour, once-a-week class. However, many cases are too complex to be covered completely in a 50-minute or 1-hour class. Thus, matching the case to the class's length is a potential problem for the instructor.

Generally, the author will test the case in only one class format, whatever length is most common at her or his school. The case should work well in that length of class, because you will most likely have written a case similar in length and complexity to those that you already use. Based on the discussion, it should be possible to predict whether the case would work in a class of a different length. If there are points that could have been explored more fully, then the case could also be used in a longer class. If the discussion felt stretched or was completed very thoroughly in the time available, the case could potentially be used in classes shorter than the ones in which it was tested. The IM should include these estimates about teaching time. If the discussion of a longer case could be divided into two parts, tell the prospective instructor which questions or parts of the analysis fall into each group and give the estimated teaching time for each. This gives the instructor the potential to divide the case and use it over several class periods.

■ Board Layout

Many instructors like to plan out their discussion in advance. This does not mean that they can predict exactly what will be said or by whom. They know what key issues they wish to emphasize and what case facts will reveal or will be significant in these discussions. Chris Christiansen of Harvard University, a master teacher, likes to think through exactly how the blackboard will look at the end of class, perhaps even at intermediate points, as part of his preparation for teaching a case (M. Taylor, personal communication, August, 1990).

If the discussion flows freely, important points may come in any order, with the supporting details revealed over a period of time. If you are the one who class tested the case, you have a good idea of which points will be revealed and which are likely to come most easily, as already noted. How should those ideas be organized as they are independently presented? One effective way is to determine in advance how they will be grouped on the blackboard, once the discussion is complete. Then, as each important issue is identified or supporting fact is given, it can take its place in its proper location. This may create a random or patchwork effect early in the discussion, when only a few of the items have been mentioned. However, as the discussion progresses, the board will fill up and the pattern will become apparent. Having developed the teaching objectives and the questions, you are in the best position to know what the student should be able to take away from the discussion and how to organize the board to make the final summary easier.

This section of the IM can be very brief or very detailed. The brief version would be a list of headings that could be written across the board, either to direct the discussion or, afterwards, to identify the groupings that have been created. A more detailed version might include a table or graphic showing not only headings but also the expected relevant details. It could also include any circles, arrows, or other markings used to demonstrate relationships between points in different columns or locations. The board layout need not be rectangular, left to right. It might be more striking if, perhaps, the key points could be laid out in a circular pattern or a grid. Because many models are designed to structure information for comparison—for example, on a continuum of ethical behavior from "unethical" to "law abiding" to "extremely ethical"—this could serve as one axis of a grid into which case facts could be placed.

■ Other Techniques

A general class discussion is not the only way to use a case. Cases may also be used as the basis for written analyses, either by an exam or a paper, or for presentation. Some are not complex enough to form the basis of a major group project. Although a case is most likely to be class tested in the general discussion format, you may have some opinions as to other ways in which it could be used. Only a very short, relatively straightforward case should be considered for an examination in which the student receives the case in class to read and evaluate, because time is limited and students' reading speeds vary. However, if the case is to be handed out in advance, students have time to study its facts thoroughly and prepare for whatever questions are asked on the exam itself. For this use, a case could be longer and more complex, similar to those used for class discussion or for the assignment of an individual paper.

A good case for presentation might be one that has multiple issues or several points of view. Class discussion might be able to cover everything, but many times, the instructor will be constrained by the length of the class period to focus on only some of the topics. Assigning the case to a group, either as a written assignment or for presentation, allows it to be thoroughly analyzed. Presentation has the additional benefit that the group members are forced to coordinate their activities and hear each other's analysis, and the class is exposed to the possibility of multiple interpretations or competing views.

The discussion during class testing of the case may give an idea as to whether the case might be useful in these other class formats. It is probably also suitable for an exam, if the key issues were identified and fully discussed during the class period. If, on the other hand, the class was productively involved in discussion throughout the entire period and still had issues to cover or more supporting details to develop, the case would be a likely candidate for a group project. A sentence in the pedagogy section of the IM is probably sufficient to identify either of these possibilities.

In a case where there are multiple points of view, the class could be asked to role-play the leading characters. In this technique, the instructor assigns an individual (or group) to each major viewpoint. That individual then analyzes and discusses the case as if he or she were that character and held those views and values. The class learns to understand the different impacts that these diverse stakeholders and values can have. Students also generally enjoy this change of approach to a case. The case writer can identify whether the case has potential to be used in this way and whether there are less obvious stakeholders or viewpoints that should be represented. If the case is suitable for role playing, you should sketch out the main characters or viewpoints and whether the roles can be assigned during class or students need to prepare in advance.

One of your educational objectives might be to have students determine for themselves what other information they need and where to find it. Alternatively, the case might be extremely long if it included all relevant information. In either of these situations, you should provide a paragraph for the instructor on recommendations for students' further research. This should identify the types of information that students would need to look for. It should also give an idea of where the information could be found. Students, left to their own devices, will often accept the first information they find, whether on the Internet, in the popular press, or in their own textbook. Where else would you expect them to look? This is particularly important if the sources are not usual ones.

At a recent workshop, a case author presented a case based on personal experience. She described the process that a relative had undertaken in making a career decision. The case included details about his background and experience but not much information about the companies he was considering. One was a division of a large, publicly held corporation; the other was a regional, privately owned company. Students were expected to search out information about both companies as if they were the person looking for the job. This was relatively easy to do for the corporation, as there are many sources that analyze and provide statistics for publicly held companies; in fact, the company itself is required to provide a wide range of information to the stock market's regulatory agency and to the stockholders. The other workshop participants raised the question of whether students could also find the necessary information on the smaller company. However, the author demonstrated that it was possible to locate information on the company through regional newspapers and press releases via listings on the Internet and searches of computerized data bases. Her Instructor's Note was revised to include a description of these types of sources and how to locate them.

Not every IM has information about these alternative uses. Many times, class testing will not provide clues as obvious as those just described. If not, then just omit this topic from the pedagogical section of the IM.

DOUBLE-CHECKING FOR
THE CASE'S COMPLETENESS

When writing sample responses for the IM, the case writer often tries to make the answers as complete as possible. You, as the writer, have full knowledge of the facts of the situation and are able to make a thorough analysis. However, it is quite common that the answer may be more complete than the case. This occurs when a complete answer requires facts that are not in the case.

When new facts appear for the first time in the suggested responses, the instructor is faced with a problem. It will be impossible for the students to fully answer the question because the case they read does not contain all of the necessary information. The instructor must settle for a lower-quality response or must provide the extra information during the class discussion. This puts him or her in the position of "playing God," having superior knowledge about the company or the situation.

Class testing should have revealed any major gaps in the information in the case, as discussed in Chapter 7. However, it is a good practice to go over the case as though you were a student. This is particularly important if you have not been able to test the case in an actual class. Can you find all the information? Can you make the connection with the theory or model and support it with all of the relevant details? When you look at a case as a student would, do you come up with the answers that you, as the case writer, had expected? If not, then you will need to do one of two things. If the missing information is important to the case's learning objectives, then add it to the case. Otherwise, rewrite your sample responses to contain only information that the students would already know.

There are two exceptions to this general principle. As already discussed, sometimes the students will be expected to search out their own additional information. If this is the situation, it would be friendly to divide the suggested response to separate the part of the answer based on material in the case from the part based on student research. The other exception, an epilogue, is discussed later.

THE ROLE OF OPINION

Throughout our discussion, we have repeatedly stressed that the case itself should be written objectively. The only opinions in the case should be those of its characters, preferably expressed in their own words. However, as an outsider, you may very well have formed opinions about what you have observed. Sometimes, this can be incorporated into your sample response to a question. For example, you have observed that there is an inconsistency between what people in the situation are saying and what they actually do. If this information is in the case, students should also be able to spot the inconsistency. However, if it is subtle (perhaps the kind of issue that would constitute an "A student/C student split"), you might want to include your opinion in the form of your observations in the sample response.

If you have a strong opinion relating to the case or to the situation or people it describes, it is not inappropriate to include it in the IM. It should be a brief paragraph in a separate section of the IM, preferably after the pedagogical material. Be careful in writing this section. It should not be a diatribe or an occasion for venting your feelings. If you include a section on your opinions, it should be a reasoned explanation of how you feel about the situation and why. This lets the instructor know about your viewpoint, which could represent a bias that he or she may or may not share and which might affect his or her interpretation of the case.

EXHIBITS FOR INSTRUCTORS' USE

In addition to sample responses and teaching suggestions, there are a number of items that can be added to the IM to make life easier for the eventual instructor. These range from materials designed to aid preparation for class, to ideas for further reading and research for either the instructor or the student, to "what happened next." They may be written as separate sections of the IM, or they may take the form of exhibits. In general, these materials are very focused and specific and are located at the end of the IM. They may even be labeled as "Teaching Note Exhibit 1," and so forth.

■ Transparency Masters

These should be located on separate sheets at the very end of the IM, to make them easy to remove. For instructors who like to use an overhead projector to supplement blackboard work, the transparency masters provide the sheets to be copied. The most likely subject for a transparency master would be any model or theory that will be linked to the case. It could be a simple statement or outline of the main points of the theory. If it can be laid out to be more visually interesting—a diagram with a diamond or star shape, for example—this would be an effective use of the overhead projector. It is not possible to anticipate all the twists and turns of a class discussion, so it is probably not worthwhile to make an exhibit summarizing the case; leave this for the blackboard, which is more flexible, or for the instructor to write on the overhead. Another good subject for a transparency master is any relevant mathematical or statistical analysis. In a strategic management or finance case, this could be an exhibit of financial ratios.

Some cases present unique problems for which a transparency would be useful. A complex case might benefit from a time line. For example, a study of the issues surrounding silicon breast implants involves the developers' research, marketing, management decisions, medical discoveries, changes in the regulation of implants, and a series of lawsuits. Each of these headings has multiple events, many of which overlap. A major emphasis on research and development at one company followed the introduction of a new type of implant by competitors. Unlike most medical products, regulation by the Food and Drug Administration (FDA) came later. Tales of medical problems led to further research, as well as to the FDA threat and lawsuits. The story becomes quite tangled, even if the emphasis is on ethics, unless the reader constructs a time line so as to see the precise chronology and what was known at what time. The instructor would be able to use an overhead of the time line when the class discussion becomes confused between events or timing. Essentially, the transparency serves as a resource to be used primarily to refocus class discussion if necessary, but the time to prepare it is in advance. The transparency master reminds the instructor of this possibility; he can either take the prepared time line to class or assign the students to prepare one for themselves. A similar resource might be a chart of the key individuals and their relationship to each other—for example, a corporation's organization chart of top management or a government agency's levels of authority and responsibility. Either the time line or the organization chart should, of course, be constructed only from information that is in the case itself.

Alternatively, the same exhibit could also be duplicated as a class handout. The time line might be particularly useful for this purpose. Another potential handout for some cases would be a glossary or definition of terms. Every business or organization has its own special terms that serve as a shorthand for the people who understand it but that may be difficult for outsiders to follow. Students typically can't picture a "flexible folder-gluer," which, in its industry, is the machine that folds and glues sheets of cardboard to make boxes. A case set in another culture may contain words or concepts that are unfamiliar. If the terminology is particularly confusing, this exhibit should probably be an appendix to the case itself rather than being reserved for the

IM. Case sequels and industry notes that are intended as supplemental handouts will be discussed in Chapter 9.

■ Data Workouts

If the case has mathematical or statistical computations that are necessary to achieving its educational objective, it would be helpful to the instructor to provide a work sheet of these calculations. This has two potential benefits. For the harried instructor who has been thrust into a course that is not his or her specialty, such a detailed workout ensures that he or she is able to help students through the computations and reach the educational objectives of the case. Even for the experienced instructor, this provides a resource to take to class as a reference. It is not necessary to do simple arithmetic, because every student seems to have a calculator. However, if there is a sequence of calculations, as for example, in the financial analysis of the health of a company or in the application of a forecasting model, the case writer should provide a carefully worked out set of numbers. When students work through complex calculations, it is easy for an error to creep in, which then can be multiplied (or divided) throughout the remainder of the problem. Two common sources of errors are mistakes in multiplication (one of the authors has a particular problem with 8×7) and the student's inability to read his or her own handwriting ("1" mistaken for "7," or "4" confused with "9," for example). It is also easy to misplace a decimal point. Although the instructor should be familiar with the model or process, your clearly presented set of computations makes it easy to check the steps of the calculation for these little, but deadly, errors.

Another situation in which data workouts are useful is when the students are asked to compare alternatives, whether for cost, efficiency, scheduling, or other criteria that involve some mathematics. Because the quality of their recommendations will be greatly affected by the specific numbers they generate for each alternative, it is very important that the calculations be correct. Here, again, it will help the instructor to have a complete set of calculations carefully worked out and presented so that the different alternatives can be readily compared, and students' computational problems can be found and corrected easily.

A data workout could also be used as a master copy to make an overhead or handouts, if the instructor desires. It should be placed on a separate page at the end of the IM for ease in copying. If the information in this exhibit is needed earlier, for example, as part of one of the suggested responses, summarize the conclusions in the response and refer the instructor to the worksheet ("Exhibit TN-2") for the detailed computations. If the question's focus is on the model or computations, use the answer to discuss how the computation meets your learning objective, outline the steps in the process, then refer to the exhibit.

BIBLIOGRAPHY, RECOMMENDED READINGS, AND OTHER RESOURCES

Another useful addition to the IM is a section of recommendations for further reading. These could be intended either for the instructor, to increase his or her depth of knowledge about some aspect of the case, or as suggestions for supplemental readings to be assigned to students. This is also a good place to include other sources of materials that could be used to supplement the case.

A reading list for the instructor is particularly useful in situations where the main theoretical link or model is not yet well known or where one of the key issues of the case is not sufficiently covered in textbooks. One example mentioned earlier was the case involving a competitor's illegal behavior and whether the subject of the case should blow the whistle to the Internal Revenue Service. Although corporate and even government whistle blowers are mentioned frequently on the evening news, there was very little literature discussing the ethical issues involved or even how to blow the whistle effectively. Consequently, the author included those few references in a list titled "For Further Reading" for the instructor.

For a library case or a field-researched case that also draws heavily on published sources, this section could contain a bibliography of the most important references used in researching the case. Although the specific sources should be cited in the case itself, a general listing here in the IM enables the instructor to evaluate the thoroughness or potential biases that may be embedded in the case. Although the case writer has an obligation to be as objective as possible, library research does limit the sources available, and every periodical has a particular viewpoint, whether it is pro-business, representing a stakeholder's interest, critical of the abuses of capitalism, or focused on a single industry's interests. For both library cases and those field cases that have a library research component, the bibliography also gives the instructor an opportunity to carry out further research on the topics. If students are to be assigned a research project later in the course, the case's bibliography also provides a basis to discuss issues of bias and appropriate sources.

Even for a case that was researched entirely in the field, a section titled "For Further Reading" may be helpful. One approach is to list readings or sources that would provide additional information related to the organization or situation in the case. This could include concise articles about competition in that industry, for a business case, or background about a particular geographic region or political system. It should not be an extensive or exhaustive list, only those items that would substantially aid the instructor's understanding should he or she wish to explore the case's environment further than the material in the case itself.

If you know of other cases that take place in the same industry or setting, it would be appropriate to list them, as some instructors like to assign related cases. This gives the student the chance to study several organizations in depth but economize on the time spent in learning about their shared background. Position this type of "Further Readings" section closer to the other teaching-related material, rather than at the end of the IM, or refer to it under one of the sections dealing with pedagogy, preferably in connection with your case's position in the course.

This earlier location or referral is also appropriate if your suggestions are for additional readings for the students. Students could either be given these references to seek out on their own, or the instructor might prefer to include these readings as part of the syllabus. Perhaps you know of an article that provides an interesting complement to the case by discussing one of its key individuals or describing a similar situation. A concise reading containing background on the organization's environment or the development of an issue could also be included in a list of this type. An article on the underlying theoretical concepts, particularly if it is also well written, would be very useful to those instructors who like to assign original readings rather than rely on textbook summaries.

The bibliography or "For Further Reading" list need not include only printed material. Increasingly, students are relying on the Internet when doing library research. You may be able to point them toward important Web sites that they could use. Ideally, this would be a balanced list, containing more than one point of view, for example, that of the organization itself and that of any major stakeholder. Because Web addresses are often long and their authors not specifically cited, it would be helpful if you were to annotate this list with notes on the actual source and its interests or point of view. One author had students who were writing their own case and recommendations about a company and the allegations that it was exploiting workers in Third World countries. The students rapidly found a source on the World Wide Web that gave detailed information about working conditions, hours, and other aspects of making the company's products in Indonesia and Vietnam. They referenced only the Web address and did not know what organization or individual had posted that information, much less whether it was an impartial observer or someone with a strong viewpoint. It was with great difficulty that the author even persuaded them to look for the company's own point of view in response to these statements. "If it's on the Internet, it must be true," appeared to be their philosophy.

Other types of resources may be available for the instructor. If you know of any videos that could be used in connection with the case, this is a good place to list them. Many organizations will provide brief film clips that describe themselves or give their points of view on issues that affect them. During the intense controversy over preserving the endangered spotted owl, one of the companies that had been involved in logging the owl's old-growth forest habitat made a short film. It showed the company's positive impact on the environment, including its role in planting new forests and the ways in which it attempted to log selectively, so as to limit its impact on the spotted owl and other endangered species. Television news programs will often study an issue and for a fee, sometimes quite substantial, will make transcripts or video clips available. Public broadcasting stations may be another good source of shows that relate to your case. They may provide lists of videos that are available or can refer you to the producers or distributors. There are also organizations that produce short films for educational or training purposes. Examples include documentaries on particular regions, training films on topics such as how to negotiate with your boss in another culture, and shows about science or animal life. If you have found a video that could be used with your case, briefly describe how it could be used in class, including its length and whether it should be used in segments or run all at one time, with appropriate linkages to the case itself. Also, include the information that the instructor will need to obtain the video, including address, phone number and price, if applicable.

Do you know of other interesting sources? Are there government agencies that might publish documents related to your topic—for example, a report on educational testing at the preschool level or standards for testing the quality of different products? If you include items of this type in your Further Readings list, be sure to identify the name of the government agency or bureau and the publication's identifying number. Every state has libraries that are designated as U.S. government depositories, which receive copies of all federal publications; however, it would also be useful to include an address so the instructor can send for the publication directly.

An instructor is likely to look only at the early part of your IM when developing the syllabus for his or her course. As a result, the Recommended Readings section may not be read until she or he is actually preparing for class. This is too late to order materials or make additional assignments to the students. If there are readings that *should* be considered in advance, be sure to mention them earlier, rather than in a section close to the end. One way to do this is to footnote the key articles in your section on Theoretical Linkages, as well as in connection with the section on Position of Course. If they are designed for optional understanding or research only, leave them near the end of the IM so the harried instructor can focus first on those sections necessary to decide whether and how to use your case.

THE EPILOGUE

In a case that focuses on decision making, students often ask, "What happened next?" or "What did they decide?" If you know what actually occurred, help the instructor who wants to answer these questions. Write a brief summary of the actual events and include it at the end of the IM under the heading of "Epilogue." Not all instructors want to tell students about the actual outcome, because students might interpret this as the "correct answer." However, if there has been a thorough class discussion, they are more apt to be curious about how closely their reasoning and analysis matched those of the decision makers.

An epilogue is particularly useful when there is an element of the unexpected. If the decision maker chose an alternative that is not one of those you have developed through your analysis and suggested responses, you should explain not only the decision but also the reasoning behind it, to the best of your ability (in a library case, the decision maker's own thought process may not be available). Sometimes, outside events affected the actual outcome, and these should also be noted, particularly if they were unforeseen by the people in your case. If both are true or if there were several outside event, each with its own impact, you might want to label each separately, for instance, "Epilogue #1" and "Epilogue #2." In the whistle-blowing case, the first epilogue explained the manager's actual decision, which was not to report his competitor, based on the small number of companies in his area and the likelihood that someone would be able to identify him as the whistle blower. The second epilogue reported that the competitor had gone out of business a few months later.

In addition to satisfying the students' curiosity, the epilogue can also be a valuable teaching tool. It can demonstrate the complexities of the real-world situation and the need to be prepared for the unexpected, as well as illustrating the impact of different value judgments concerning the importance of various factors involved in the situation.

PRACTICE SESSION

This practice session continues the analysis that was begun in Chapter 5. In that chapter, we looked at the draft IM (Appendix 2) and the final version (Appendix 4) and talked about the sections on objectives, the case summary, basic pedagogy, key issues, theoretical links, methodology, and questions. In this chapter, we will discuss the remaining sections of the IM: suggested responses to the questions, refining the teaching objectives and key issues, what you learned from class testing, opinions, exhibits for instructors' use, further readings, and the epilogue. A typical IM will probably not contain all of these sections, but you should think about which of them are appropriate for your case.

There are potential responses in the draft (Appendix 2), but they are very brief. The response to Question 1 contains a useful analogy for explaining symptoms and problems. It does not follow through in terms of the case, however, merely citing two possible issues for discussion. The response to Question 2 is a list with no further discussion, exactly as the question asks. However, if the students understand stakeholder analysis, this may be all that is needed. Response 3 is short and relatively obvious, probably adding little to students' appreciation of professional ethics. The response to Question 4 is, again, in the form of lists with no discussion; in fact, the second list has been mislabeled as #5. There are no notes for Question 5, probably because it asks students to come up with their own ideas, which could be very diverse.

For several of these questions, there is not sufficient information in the case. However, Question 3 assumes a clear time sequence, which is information not available in the case.

Contrast these responses with those in the final version (Appendix 4). The response to Question 1 now contains an extensive discussion of the symptoms, in terms of Mr. Adams's behavior and other facts from the case, that have led to the situation in which the partners now find themselves. It has also been revised, probably based on class testing, to include an "A student/C student split," between average students recognizing symptoms and above-average students who will be able to identify the underlying problems. Question 2 has been reformulated to ask for an analysis of the stakeholders, rather than a list, and the response reflects this change. The response to Question 3 has been expanded; it now elaborates on both professional and ethical conduct. The response to Question 4 still contains the criteria, but they are now explained, rather than listed; several alternatives (probably not an exhaustive list) are now included, each with a brief list of advantages and disadvantages. There is now an answer to Question 5. Students may or may not agree with the choice of this alternative. However, the response gives the instructor an idea of the level of detail that he or she should expect.

The sections on teaching objectives and key issues have been substantially revised from the draft to the final version. In fact, as discussed in Chapter 5, the draft IM combined them into a very brief introductory paragraph. The draft IM does not have any hints learned from class testing, such as a blackboard plan or the time to teach the case, probably because it has not yet been tested. There is no summary of key issues; because the focus of the case was not clear, a summary would have been hard to develop at this point. There are no data workouts or exhibits and no epilogue. In short, aside from the questions and some sketchy responses, this version of the IM offers very little support for the instructor.

The IM in Appendix 4 contains much more information for the instructor. There are now separate sections on the case's purpose and key issues. After a brief discussion of basic pedagogy (courses for which the case would be appropriate and where the case should be positioned), the section on "Teaching Methods" continues with the time needed to teach the case effectively. The author then describes the flow of the class, including probable student responses ("Many students will feel uneasy with this question," for example). Key points are identified that could be converted into a blackboard plan by the instructor: for example, matching the expectations of Mr. Adams and the partners. The author provides a wrap-up for the class, noting that students should not be allowed to end by treating symptoms only.

The revised IM does not include several of the subjects covered in this chapter. There are no other techniques given, although the case is possibly short enough to be used for an exam and has characters that might make for effective role-playing. However, if the author has not tested these alternatives, he or she may not feel comfortable including them as possibilities. A section on the author's opinion is rarely necessary. This case does not have a wealth of technical details or numerical data to be analyzed, and the timing of events is clear, so exhibits for the instructor are probably not needed.

Students are expected to be familiar with some form of basic ethical analysis, as is indicated in the sections, Purpose and Teaching Methods. The case provides an exhibit with quotes from the relevant professional code of conduct. This should be sufficient background for the students, without the need for a Further Readings list, although additional references on professional ethics or codes of conduct might be useful. An epilogue is also optional; because the author does not provide one, it is probably safe to assume that the obvious happened: Mr. Adams went into business for himself, and the partners did not make any major changes in their practice. The authors have used this case in class, and students have never asked, "What really happened?"

SUMMARY AND CONCLUSIONS

The sections of the IM that have been discussed in this chapter are all concerned with helping teachers use your case effectively. They are not intended to do the instructor's work for her or him. Their intent is to enable him or her to go into class knowing what to expect from the discussion and how to help students make the connections to theory or develop the skills that you intended. As the authors of one IM described it, "These notes represent our best efforts with the case—what we'd tell you, were you to turn up in our offices, about our experiences with it" (Hatten & Hatten, 1987).

At the end of this chapter, you will find a check list of points to consider when writing an IM (Table 8.1). It does not cover every possible situation that you could encounter but should serve as a reminder of the important points from this chapter and Chapter 5. Use it as a reminder when you write your own notes. But don't forget to continue to learn about your case. When other people use your case in class, ask for their feedback. In our experience, we have learned something new about a case almost every time we have used it. Your IM should continue to evolve to reflect these new ideas.

TABLE 8.1 Checklist for a Well-Written Instructor's Manual

This is not necessarily an all-inclusive list that will catch every possible problem. Use it as a guide to help you identify areas where your IM could be strengthened. Not all items will apply to every IM.

Does the IM include:

A brief description of the research methods employed?
Specification of the course or courses where the case fits?
Indication of the position of the case within that course or courses? The level of
    students targeted? Prerequisite concepts that students should have studied, if any?
Learning objectives—what students should gain by discussing this case?
Key issues on which students might take sides?
Links to theoretical frameworks of the field, including potential ancillary readings?
A brief summary of the case, including decisions to be made by key actors (if any)?
Assignment questions for student preparation? Do they flow logically?
Complete analyses and answers to the assigned questions, including points
    differentiating outstanding students from others (what should an "A" student see,
    that others might not)?
Information provided in the IM that is not in the case?
A plan for the flow of discussion, with sample discussion questions and expected
    classroom dynamics? (A blackboard plan is optional here but often useful.)
Indication of the time needed to teach the case effectively?
Time schedule for use of audiovisual materials, if any accompany the case?
Potential topics for summary remarks at the end of the case?
Data workouts or other explanatory exhibits?
An epilogue (what really happened, if known)?
At least one specimen of an outstanding student paper, from a written case analysis
    assignment (including assignment question)?

SOURCE: Adapted from an unpublished form developed by George Puia, editor, for the *Case Research Journal*.

9
■

Industry Notes, Case Series, and Other Supplements

■

There are times when a single, stand-alone case is insufficient to meet the objectives of the case writer. It is these times when additional material or information is needed. Too often, case writers simply expand the length of the case to include this additional material. In reality, there are a variety of ways that this information can be provided.

There are situations when the background data provided in the case is not sufficient to fully explain the interactions within an industry. The industry in which the company being studied belongs may have an impact on the situation being examined. An industry note may have to be developed, to fully explore the interaction between the organization and its industry. Similarly, there may be other environmental factors that affect the individuals or situations being studied. These could include economic, cultural, legal, or other factors. They also could be developed as appendices or even additional notes to accompany cases.

There are other times when a single case cannot bring out the full richness and details that were generated by the initial interviews and material. It is at these times that a series of cases needs to be developed. The series could either explore the issues in a time sequence or relate to different issues that were found during the exploration of the situation. A case series can better develop the material to meet these objectives than can be achieved in a single case.

155

WHEN AN INDUSTRY NOTE MAKES SENSE

The most common type of note is one that defines and describes a particular industry. These are typically developed to support a series of cases that are all found within the same or related industries. There are different purposes for writing an industry note.

The first is for purposes of efficiency, when writing each of the cases that the note is designed to support. Typically, the situations that are being studied in each of the individual cases are affected by a variety of factors within the industry. Rather than present industry information in each case, all of which would be quite similar, a single industry note can be prepared for the series of cases. In this manner, the individual cases are actually shorter than they would have to be if the industry information were presented in each one. Also, the readers are able to read the cases in a more efficient manner. They are not distracted by the inclusion of the external, industry material in the body of the case. If they are asked to read the industry note before the case, the readers then have the advantage of understanding the industry environ-ment and can relate the specific case to it. Overall, there is efficiency in preparation through use of the industry note, because it only has to be written once for all the cases that are developed based on the same, or related, industries. The efficiency extends to the readers, as well, because they only have to read the material once.

An example of such a note is one that was developed for the ice cream industry. Several case studies were developed on companies in this industry, including Ben and Jerry's and Häagen Dazs. The industry note includes information that describes the different market segments that companies can attempt to develop. Information on methods of manufacturing, marketing, and distributing the products was also included in the industry note (Thompson & Strickland, 1993). This allows the students to read the material once for two or more cases. The material can be applied to each of the cases in a balanced manner. The student can then develop a similar analysis specific to each of the company cases studied.

Another purpose in writing an industry note is to allow the case writers to include more material on the industry than would otherwise be appropriate in a stand-alone case. There are situations where a large amount of data and information is needed to be able to fully understand and analyze the situation and issues developed in the case. To provide all this material in the case itself would make it unwieldy and extremely long. The length, in itself, would make it unlikely that students would read it and, therefore unlikely that it would be adopted by other teachers. Writing a separate industry note would make it more likely that students would read both the case and the industry note. It is also more likely that the case and note would be adopted by other teachers.

An example of this type of industry note would be where one of the objectives of the case is to have the readers prepare what is referred to as a *Porter Five Forces Industry Analysis* for the company. This involves examining how the firm relates to its competitors, suppliers, customers, substitutes, and potential new entrants (Porter, 1979). To be able to perform this type of analysis effectively, the readers need to have sufficient information about all of these different factors. To place this information in the case would often make the case extremely long. Setting up a separate industry note helps the readers to better focus their attention on the information that is relevant to the desired analysis. A separate industry note also helps the case writers to be able to provide sufficient information so that the readers can achieve the objectives of the case.

Typically, an industry note would include information that helps to define and describe that industry. This would include data and information about the major, and potentially, the lesser, competitors involved in the industry. Information such as sales revenues, profits, and market shares held, as well as geographic and product markets served would be included here. This would help readers to understand the degree of competition within the industry, especially as they are trying to analyze specific cases dealing with individual companies in the industry. Using this information, the readers could determine the relative position of that company in the industry.

Other information could include production and service procedures used. If there were special factors that were evident in the industry, these would be defined. In the previous example of the ice cream industry note, the process by which ice cream is produced was described. This included an explanation of how differences in the ingredients and the production process used helped to determine in what niche a company would be placed. Similarly, price levels, demand patterns, and historical growth patterns for the different segments would then help readers to be able to analyze past strategies, as well as develop future directions for the firm to take. As part of this information, constraints such as supply shortages and limited sources for inputs would be included, to help readers to determine the effectiveness of potential strategies. Other topics discussed might include methods of distributing the products or services, legal guidelines, issues or regulations peculiar to the industry, or patent or brand name strength. All of these factors would provide useful insights to readers as they try to analyze the total environment facing any one firm that is operating within the industry.

■ Technical and Other Notes

Notes may be written describing topics other than industries. One such topic would be a technical note. This type of note would be appropriate where there are issues and information that are peculiar to a type of product that make it difficult to fully comprehend that product without an extensive explanation of the issues surrounding it.

Information in a technical note usually includes the specific language used in the development and production of that product or service. This might take the form of a couple of paragraphs of prose or a glossary, placed as an exhibit or appendix to the case or note. In any industry or area, there is always language—sometimes, simply jargon—whose definition is specific to that area. Some of this language may involve commonly used words that have taken a different definition from the standard, dictionary definitions. To a financier, *leverage* involves the use of debt versus equity in the financing of the purchase of an asset. To a physicist or engineer, leverage means the use of a lever to decrease the power needed to move an object. To a physician, *OB* means *obstetrics.* To a management professor, OB means *organizational behavior.* We have used the lack of understanding of that distinction to some success when our two children were born, because the delivery room was staffed with OB (Obstetrics) nurses and we have taught OB (Organizational Behavior) in a university with a medical school. There are many other, similar examples of terms that are used by two groups having different meanings. These distinctions have to be defined so that readers will understand what is being said in a case.

In other situations, there are terms that are simply not defined as normal words. The people dealing with that product or service have invented words to better describe the various aspects of the functions surrounding or related to that product. Although most of these terms are related to the development or production of the product, they may also relate to marketing, personnel, or other functional areas.

One of the authors wrote a case on a company that manufactured box-making machinery. There are a variety of terms that are used in the industry to define the products and the manufacturing process. Terms such as *flexographic printing* have been used to define a process where flexible rubber printing plates and fast-drying inks are used in the printing process for shipping boxes. Also, we had to define the term *chip* as it is used in this industry, because it has several connotations in other industries. Most students would assume the term would refer to computer chips. In this industry, however, the term is used to designate paperboard that is made from waste papers. We included a glossary of key terms as an appendix to the case to help readers to better understand the case. The glossary was referenced early in the case. The reader was told to use the glossary to help to understand the technical terms that were used by the various principals and notes throughout the case. In this manner, we did not have to interrupt the flow of the case by including definitions within the body of the case. Instead, we were able to place all the definitions in the appendix. This placement also helped to tie the terms together. In this manner, the readers were also better able to put the development and production processes in a clearer light because the definitions were presented together. The definitions now became a coherent and cohesive whole (Merenda & Naumes, 1993).

■ Cultural and National Notes

There are times when there is the need to describe the culture, economy, or other aspects of a country or region for a reader to understand the intricacies of a case. Cases that take place in a foreign environment may require information about that environment for the readers to fully understand the issues that are the object of the case. Foreign environments frequently involve differences in culture, laws, economies, and physical environments that are not well understood by the readers of the case. An objective of this kind of case is to introduce the concept of decision making and behavior under different environmental circumstances. The objective cannot be achieved, however, without an understanding of environment surrounding those decisions and actions.

This would necessitate the development of a note to describe those factors. These would include factors such as cultural norms relating to the interaction between employers and employees in a job setting. In some countries, the cultural norms might indicate that a supervisor's decision is always accepted, regardless of its consequences, simply because of the superior relationship of the decision maker. In other cultures, the decision needs to be based on at least an appearance of consensus building by the supervisor. In yet other cultures, the background of the decision makers with respect to their caste, clan, education, or other factors may determine whether their decisions will be accepted. Similarly, some forms of advertising and promotion may be acceptable in some cultures but be unacceptable in other cultures. Also, similar to the discussion earlier, under industry notes, language can be a contributing factor to decisions and actions. General Motors realized too late when they named the Chevrolet Nova, that *nova* means roughly "no go" in Spanish. The name created a problem with promoting the car in southern California and southern Florida, as well as Spanish-speaking countries.

Other issues that may need to be defined include the weather and other environmental conditions. Climactic conditions can make a significant difference, especially in fields such as agriculture and leisure management.

Economic factors may also need to be described. The economic background surrounding the situation may have a significant impact on decisions that are made by individuals. Job decisions are frequently different when there is a recession and jobs are tight as opposed to when the economy is booming and jobs are plentiful. Similarly, investment decisions are different during periods of high consumer demand versus periods of low consumer demand. Also, the economic policies of the government have a significant impact on business-related decisions.

Other factors, such as regulatory and legal systems, may need to be defined as well. What many Americans do not realize is that there are different legal systems. In English-based countries, the legal system is based on the concept of common law. In other countries, where France had a dominant role at some point in its past, the Napoleonic Code is the basis for the legal system. The differences may be significant to individuals involved in situations in those countries.

Much of this data can be found through government sources. The U.S. Department of State frequently develops country reports detailing the culture aspects of countries, as well as a variety of demographic data. The Department of Commerce also offers reports and projections on different countries. Also, the Department of Defense prepares and publishes a small series of reports detailing the cultural as well as geographic aspects of countries where it expects to be involved or is actually involved. The governments of the countries themselves also publish a variety of reports. These are usually available through the embassies or consulates of these countries. All of these can be useful sources for developing a note to accompany a case study on a country or region about which most case readers would not be informed.

There was a time not long ago that use of this type of information required access to a library that was a repository for government documents. Most state universities are such repositories. However, much of this data and information is now available on the World Wide Web and can be accessed directly by anyone who can access the appropriate government agency Web site. Alternatively, most college and university libraries now can access these sites through their own dedicated computers.

One of the authors was involved in the writing of a case that took place on the island of Dominica, in the Caribbean. The case involved the attempts of two American entrepreneurs to set up a plantation to grow the aloe plant on part of the island. Critical factors in deciding how, when, and where to set up the plantation were dependent on the economy, regulations, and culture of the island nation. The facts that the country had high unemployment, support from the United States government due to the then-recent invasion of the island nation of Grenada, an almost unique set of weather characteristics of the island, as well as the cultural interaction between various groups on the island all had an impact on how the entrepreneurs should have made decisions, as well as what decisions should be made in the future. We included a country note that included information on all of these factors. The note was intended to be used by the readers of the case to help both in the analysis of the past actions as well as how, when, and why future decisions should be made. A cultural "trap" was included in the case and national note that indicated that groups on the island had different norms concerning how they lived and worked together. These factors should have been taken into consideration when developing the living and working conditions on the plantation. They also should have determined what actions the entrepreneurs needed to take to make the operation a success. Similar information was provided to help readers, who would not ordinarily understand the peculiarities of Dominica, to be able to analyze and make recommendations for the case. By including the national note, the case could then be used by readers in a wide variety of locations, regardless of whether they had access to information about the island nation of Dominica (Naumes, 1988).

■ Sources of Information for Notes

There are a variety of readily available sources for these types of information. Many of them come from the government document centers of major libraries. *The Annual Almanac of the United States* provides basic statistical data on the economy of the United States for any given year. This material can be used to provide background information on the economic climate and conditions in place at any given period of time. Other data, including population statistics, legislative agendas, and climatic conditions can also be developed from this source.

Industry information can also be developed from a variety of sources. Industry trade associations are a common source of information. Whenever there are several companies in an industry, they are likely to form a trade association. In the United States, this is due, partly, to the antitrust laws. Trade associations provide a convenient method of sharing information between companies without violating these laws. The trade association is the vehicle for collecting information from the companies, aggregating that information, and then feeding it back to the individual companies. In this manner, the companies can share information legally. Granted, the information is typically presented in the form of averages. However, this is often sufficient for purposes of comparative analysis. You can find these groups listed in the *Encyclopedia of Associations.* This gives the names, addresses, and other relevant information of these groups. An alternative source for this information is the *National Trade & Professional Associations of the United States.*

A particular association that provides relevant financial data on industries is Robert Morris Associates. It publishes the *RMA Annual Statements.* These annual compilations provide aggregated data on a wide variety of industries, separated by four-digit SIC codes. The data is in percentage format, by company size and historical base. The data is provided by Robert Morris Associates members, who are bank commercial loan officers. They send data on companies seeking loans to RMA, which aggregates and averages the data and sends it back to the loan officers who then use it to compare the data with companies seeking loans. Each column of the data indicates the number of firms reported in that category. The column also includes either total sales or total assets for all the companies reported. By simple arithmetic manipulation, average numbers can then be assigned to each of the categories within the columns. This source is especially effective when seeking data on industries with smaller, privately held companies. Because these companies do not have to provide data to the stock exchanges or the Securities and Exchange Commission, there may be no other way to secure this kind of information.

Other sources include *Standard and Poor's Industry Surveys* and *Moody's Investors Services Industry Review.* Both of these provide both quantitative and qualitative data on companies and industries. This information is mostly historic in nature. It provides a capsule of how the companies and industries have performed in the past. These sources also provide some forecasts for future activities through both internal as well as external research analysts' reports.

Further information of the future of a variety of industries can be found in the different reports of the *United States Industrial Outlook.* These are annual reports of different industries. Each year, a different series of industries was highlighted for analysis and forecasts. Unfortunately, due to budget cuts, this series ceased publication in 1994. For somewhat older cases, these forecasts could still be useful. DRI/McGraw-Hill has taken on a contract to provide similar forecasts through its publication of *United States Industry & Trade Outlook,* annual reports for a variety of industries, on a private basis. Although most reasonably sized libraries carried the former government series, many do not carry the latter series due to the subscription cost of these reports.

Where the companies in the industry are publicly traded, data can be secured from both the company and the regulatory bodies with which the companies have to deal. This data can then be provided for each of the major competitors in the industry. In this manner, readers can analyze the comparative financial strengths and weaknesses of many of the companies in the industry. Annual reports of most publicly traded companies can be found through libraries, as well as directly from the companies themselves. Annual reports tend to be filled with public relations pieces as well as historical financial data. The Securities and Exchange Commission also requires all companies that are publicly traded in the United States to publish a variety of other reports, including the 10 K. These reports provide more detailed information on these companies and are also frequently available through reasonably sized libraries. 10 K reports break down financial data by subsidiary groupings, where appropriate, as an example. These reports are also increasingly available through the World Wide Web and Internet searches. Company Web sites frequently use the company name with the add on of ".com." A competent search engine should provide appropriate Web sites in response to the company name being entered, as well.

More complete data on companies and industries can be found in *Business Information Sources,* as well as *Business Information Desk References.* Both are used by most business reference librarians as a first source for locating data for these purposes.

WHEN IT MAKES SENSE TO DIVIDE A CASE (CREATE A SERIES)

There are times when the information that has been developed through interviews becomes too confusing for the original purpose of the case. Although that purpose may well be developed effectively in one case on a particular company or situation, the subsequent events may open up the reader to other equally interesting and relevant situations and decisions. These can occur when there are multiple decision points presented through the material developed for the case.

■ Time Series Cases

Multiple decision points occur for a variety of reasons. The most common reason is that the decision maker simply makes an incorrect decision, for one reason or another. The first decision point, therefore, involves the original set of circumstances analyzed. Frequently, this is what initially drew you to the situation. You may then find that the circumstances that led to this decision were actually a series of decisions, each leading to another, sometimes even worse, set of circumstances. The question then becomes one of whether to present all of the decisions as part of a single case or to split them up into a case series.

If the decision is to present them as one case, then the case becomes a combination of an evaluative and a decision-focus case. The events leading up to the final decision provide an opportunity for students to analyze why and how the events and decisions occurred. You could also build questions into the Instructor's Note asking what could have been done to keep the situation from getting worse. The problem with a case where there are a series of sequential decision points is that the readers can readily determine what happens after each point by simply reading the next section. They have the luxury of analyzing the situation with perfect hindsight. This usually limits the discussion and the analysis of the case.

By splitting the decisions into separate cases, the readers can be asked to evaluate each decision point, sequentially. As long as the subsequent cases can be kept from the readers until the previous decision has been analyzed and discussed, the full range of issues and decisions can be expected to be presented during the class discussion of the case. This requires that each subsequent case be distributed to the students after the previous decision point has been discussed. This can often create problems.

A major problem is that the subsequent cases often need to be short enough that they can be read in class without detracting from the flow of discussion. This type of case series is best used in the analysis of relatively straightforward, qualitative situations. This would include cases dealing in subjects such as organization behavior and ethics. An example of this type of case would be the Fallon-McElligott case study (McDougall, 1991), dealing with management responses to a letter of complaint over the actions of one of its managers. A woman professor of marketing attended a seminar where a manager for the Fallon-McElligott advertising agency made what the professor felt were insensitive remarks. She wrote a letter to the founders of the firm objecting to these remarks. The first case ends with the initial letter of complaint. The second case presents the responses of the founders, which were viewed as even more insensitive. The third case describes the reaction of the professor, and others, to these responses. At the end of each case, the readers are asked to analyze what has occurred and what the various parties should do in response. Each subsequent case is brief enough that it can be read and discussed in the same class session as the first case, without detracting from the overall flow of the class.

The alternative is to discuss each case in a separate class session. At the end of the discussion and the class, the next case in the series would be distributed to the students. They would then use the time between classes to study and analyze the next case in the series. This type of series would allow longer cases and more careful reading and would best be used with complex decision-focus cases, such as those dealing with strategic management and policy-oriented issues and situations.

An example of this type of situation can be seen in some of the case series developed by Jeff Timmons (1990). He has written several case series designed to demonstrate the problems facing entrepreneurs as they proceed through various phases of the development of their ventures. One such series depicts the start, growth, and development of the Jiffy Lube chain of oil change centers. Timmons wanted to show different financing and marketing and the potential for strategic partnerships for a rapidly growing entrepreneurial enterprise. Because the entrepreneur involved had to proceed through a series of strategic financing changes during the development of the firm, Timmons wanted to present readers with all of these decisions sequentially. The purpose of the case series was to have the readers try to analyze the pros and cons of the potential alternative courses of action at each decision point and to develop their own solutions. Each case in the series looks at the issues during one time period.

A potential problem with such a series is that if, as Timmons desired, all of the cases in the series were to be used in a single text book, then readers could jump ahead to the next case in the series to determine what was actually done and the effects of that decision. In that manner, they could at least eliminate one set of possible actions, if the actions that were actually taken were not effective. Or if the decision were effective, even if only partially, the readers would have the ability to develop an effective solution set without having to perform a full analysis of the situation. Timmons overcame this problem in his book by giving each case in the series a different name. Instead of calling the cases *Jiffy Lube (A), (B),* and *(C),* he called them *Jiffy Lube, Hindman & Company,* and *Bridge Capital Investors, Inc.* In this manner, he was able to present all the cases in the series in the same text while reducing the likelihood that readers would be able to make their decisions about each situation without the use of perfect hindsight as to what actually happened.

■ Multiple-Approach Case Series

Another reason to develop material into a series might be to develop different types of focused decisions or analyses. As with the previous reason for a case series, the initial impetus to develop a case may have come from a specific incident, situation, or decision. You may start by looking at a managerial action, as an example, that is reasonably well defined. In business cases, this may start as an analysis of a production problem. While conducting interviews, you may find evidence of other types of decisions that also could be made, revolving around the same basic situation. The question that you are now faced with is whether all of the different actions should be wrapped together and the readers asked to resolve all of the problems in one proposal. This, after all, is what real life is like. It is often complex and confusing. There are rarely simple, unidimensional issues and solutions in actual settings. Adding all of the other material into the case may distort and distract the attention of the readers from the purpose you intended in starting to develop the case in the first place. Under these circumstances, you may decide to ignore all but that material that is necessary to develop that purpose.

Taking the approach of focusing on one issue would mean discarding potentially extremely valuable and interesting material, however. We have reviewed many case studies where we felt that the case might be used in a manner not originally intended by the author. We have, on occasion, recommended that if additional material could be secured, then a case series might be attempted. We have felt, on these occasions, that the material was sufficiently valuable and that the different aspects were all of sufficient interest that the case writer should split the material up and devote a separate case to each of the issues. The question then becomes one of determining whether each case should be self-sufficient or whether the material should be developed into a true case series, where each subsequent case draws on the material of the earlier case. The former approach allows for each case to be used separately for its own purpose. The latter approach provides more efficient use of the material from the perspective of the reader.

An example of the case series used to develop different objectives was found in a text by Pearce and Robinson (1994). They used a series of cases on the Coca Cola Company to present a variety of issues relating to the strategic management of the firm. Each case was designed to demonstrate and analyze a different aspect of strategic management. The cases go through different functional areas of management, such as accounting, finance, marketing, manufacturing, and research and development. There are also separate cases on leadership and organization structure and process, as well as the process of strategy development and implementation.

This series is often called a *cohesion case*. It is designed to present a way for the material in a particular chapter to be discussed through each subsequent segment in the case series. This means that the readers of the text could analyze a variety of issues dealing with strategic management without having to learn and read about a new company each time they read a case. There were clear efficiencies for the readers through use of the series. There were also efficiencies for instructors using the text, as well. It was easier to structure the course. It was also easier for them to prepare for the individual class sessions. Moreover, the students were able to track the various aspects of the concept of strategic management through one company, instead of having to piece them together from a group of cases dealing with different companies, competitive environments, and time frames. This is simply an addition in the case tool box, however. It does not preclude the need for more traditional or individual cases to integrate the various concepts of an area.

This has become of greater importance and interest as more business schools adopt a more integrative approach to teaching, especially in MBA programs. Many such programs have changed their courses to provide an interdisciplinary approach to their teaching. This often includes the use of team teaching. Where this includes case discussions and presentations, there is a need for cases that take a multidiscipline approach to the material. A case series can often help in this type of program.

In other situations, especially Executive MBA programs, there is a desire, and even a need, to provide more overall integration in the presentation of the material. This is due to the tighter time frame of such programs, where classes are frequently taught over a 2-day period or in a compressed manner. Having the students in such programs read one set of background material for a series of cases allows for better use of their limited time. This also shows that the faculty have given some thought to both the integration of the program, as well as the efficient use of the student's time. The integrative use of cases in this manner tends to develop a positive outlook on the part of the students.

PRACTICE SESSION

The final version of the Meyers and Morrison case, as written, is focused on a single topic and is self-contained; the information that students would need is contained in the case itself and its exhibits. However, in the original draft (Appendix 1), there is the potential for development of either of two cases: the ethics and professional standards case that was ultimately published or the case that was introduced in the first paragraph, dealing with the recruitment and hiring of Mr. Adams. Even the original IM doesn't seem certain which case is being written. Because the two events occur at very different times (Mr. Adams's hiring and his leaving the firm 2 years later), it might be possible to write that other case, creating a short series.

What would be the objectives of that (chronologically) first case? Its focus would appear to be on personnel decisions: how a new employee was recruited and hired and the nature of the contract he was offered. At this point, several years later, it is unlikely that the company still has records of any other, unsuccessful candidates. The limitations of available information most likely mean that this case will be evaluative, rather than decision-focused, perhaps Category V according to Table 2.1. Students should be given a description of the events, most easily organized by the order in which they occurred, and sufficient background to understand the accounting firm and its partners. It would be both vivid and revealing if one or both of the partners would personally describe his first impressions of Mr. Adams. They could be asked to explain in their own words why they decided at that point in time that it was time to look for a potential third partner. Their descriptions of the actual hiring process, particularly the offer that was made to Mr. Adams, would also be very useful. These quotes could be backed up by any relevant documents: the actual advertisement, the contract signed by Mr. Adams (which may be worded quite differently from the partners' views of his responsibilities and career opportunities), and any file notes to which the partners would allow access. Professional firms often issue a press release to announce a new employee; this would make an interesting addition, and perhaps a third view of his role.

Students would be expected to study the recruiting and hiring process in terms of the norms and models in their human resource management text. They should be encouraged to look for potential problems in the process itself (i.e., what the partners could have done better), as well as considering whether Mr. Adams was the right person for the job. The evaluation can be extended to a search for potential signs of trouble, by including a brief epilogue or referring students to the second M & M case (Appendix 3). The "A" students may be able to identify the difference in expectations from the new case alone; knowing the outcomes (Mr. Adams's unhappiness and eventual departure), even the "C" students should be able to find the potential for problems in the human resource case.

Could there be a third case in this series? It would certainly be interesting to discuss Mr. Adams's actions over time, from a behavioral perspective. What was driving him to become more and more unhappy, and what work-related implications might we expect to see? However, this case would require access to performance appraisals and much more detailed observations from other individuals, if not from Mr. Adams himself. The case writer is unlikely to be able to get this information, in part due to issues of privacy, but also due to the passage of time—people's recollections are likely to be colored by their knowledge of how he left the firm.

SUMMARY AND CONCLUSIONS

There are times when additional material is needed to provide sufficient information for students to complete the case. Frequently, this is due to the need for material that defines an industry, technology, political situation, or even a country. It may be appropriate to write a separate note to meet these needs. At times, the note may be attached as an appendix to the case itself. At other times, it may be developed as a freestanding and separate note to be used in conjunction with one or more case studies that relate to the material in the note.

Reasons for developing a note usually revolve around the need for sufficient information for readers to be able to fully analyze and develop potential solutions for the case. The specialized information about the industry in which a company operates may be difficult to incorporate within a typical case. Similarly, information about the culture, economy, religion, environment, and legal system in a country may be added, for the readers to be able to generate reasonable realistic alternatives for the problems presented in one or more cases.

A note may also be developed when there is more than one case dealing with the same overall environment. Instead of including the same basic material in each case, a separate note can be written that includes that material and is then available to the readers of any of the cases. Teachers can then use any or all of the cases dealing with this information while having the students analyze the material only once. The readers are presented with a more efficient way to prepare for the case analysis. Also, more information on the environment being studied can be included in a note than can typically be included within any single case. The information from these notes can be found in a variety of sources. Industry sources, government reports, and trade associations all provide ready sources for the kind of material that can be found in case notes.

There are times when it makes more sense to split up the material that has been gathered into more than one case, rather than trying to put it all in one case. It may make more sense to set up separate cases where there is more than one area where decisions have to be made. Writing a separate case for each of these different types of decision points may make more sense than trying to overload one case with all the relevant material necessary to develop all the points in the situation.

The main problem to be overcome with case series is keeping the readers from gaining perfect hindsight into what actually happened in the situation. There are a variety of ways to keep this from happening, from distributing subsequent cases after the previous case has been discussed to calling each case by a different name.

Last, an increasingly popular approach is to include video supplements to written cases. Although these can add interest and value to a case, care must be taken to ensure that the material is sufficiently well developed that it actually adds, not detracts, from the effectiveness of the case. They will be discussed in more detail in the next chapter.

10
■

Video and
Multimedia Case Studies

■

Technology has now caught up with the traditional, paper-bound, written case study. The availability of video and multimedia techniques have opened up new avenues for the development and presentation of case studies, especially for pedagogical purposes. Case studies using these technologies can offer an excitement and opportunity for exposure to a wider range of factors that affected the people wo felt the impact of the situation. As much as these technologies offer, they also need to be approached with caution. They are difficult to format. They also require skills with which many of us are unfamiliar.

These types of cases do more than simply use video and multimedia activities as visual supplements for what, in essence, is a written case. The focus of the case study is the video and multimedia aspects of the case. The difficulties, as well as the benefits, of these types of cases need to be carefully considered before undertaking to use these potentially valuable teaching tools.

VIDEO SUPPLEMENTS,
INCLUDING THE EXECUTIVE INTERVIEW

One supplement that has come into common use for cases is the addition of video material relating to the case. Frequently, this includes interviews or

171

presentations by key individuals involved in the situation described in the case. Often, this material is designed to be used after the case has been discussed in class, to show what has happened since the decision point presented in the case. Sometimes, the videos are designed as supplemental material for use during the discussion of the case, to provide added emphasis to the presentation of the material in the case. At times, the video material is simply a visual presentation of the same material described in the case. There are a variety of other video supplements that are meant either to present material that better demonstrates the situation as it occurred or to provide material that can be used as an epilogue for the decision and actions that actually were made and occurred. Although the format is different from the traditional printed supplements, the contents and uses are very similar to those supplements described in Chapter 8. However, they share many of the same benefits and problems as longer, more complex video cases.

VIDEO CASES[1]

The advent of video technology has made it possible to capture a further dimension of so-called realism in the classroom. A true video case is more than a series of camera shots of individuals discussing their views of the situation. It is a full compilation of all the factors involved in the case. When used appropriately, a video case can be an extremely effective teaching tool.

■ Benefits of Video Cases

In the experience of Kinnunen and Ramamurti (1987), seven principal benefits usually accrue from using videotapes:

1. One obvious benefit is that the videotapes serve as updates or elaborations of case issues that students have spent a lot of time thinking about and discussing. Essentially, this is using the tape as a video supplement or epilogue. It can be used very effectively as part of the wrap-up of the class's discussion. Students enjoy finding out "what really happened" or "why the company was doing that."

2. Students at all levels enjoy watching CEOs talk about their jobs and their companies, especially when they have read and analyzed a detailed case on that company. Most students do not have many opportunities to meet

CEOs or to get a good feel for them as individuals. Using taped interviews in a policy course also enables students to compare personal and possibly leadership styles of CEOs. In some ways, seeing and hearing CEOs through videotapes is better than having them live, because the students can be frank in judging or criticizing them. (One of the authors of this book remembers having a high-level insurance manager in his class shortly after a whistle-blowing scandal in another insurance company. The students were slow to ask critical questions about which of the people from the scandal-plagued company the manager would hire. When he was finally asked, the students would not criticize or even question his responses. When asked after the manager had left why they had not questioned his responses, the students said that they were nervous about criticizing him to his face.) Again, this is using taped material primarily as a supplement to the written case and class discussion.

3. The tapes add realism to the case; they truly breathe life into what is otherwise still just words on pieces of paper. The people develop faces and voices, and even complex processes become more understandable.

4. The tapes add credibility to themes that recur in the strategic-management literature but are not easily impressed on students, particularly those without managerial experience (e.g., implementation being as important as and often more difficult than formulation; human relations skills and other "soft" issues being critical factors from a general manager's viewpoint, etc.).

5. The tapes allow students to appreciate the importance of intangible aspects of general management, such as leadership styles, the impact of personal values on strategic choice or its implementation, how styles can affect organization culture, and so forth.

6. The tapes highlight the complexity inherent in a general manager's job: how they have to make decisions without all the necessary information, how they must be able to think across functional areas and the difficulties involved in maintaining consistency across functional strategies.

7. The tapes provide a basis for discussion of additional issues—often issues that are worrying the CEO but that are not captured or highlighted in the (traditional) case. This aspect is particularly valuable among executive students who find there is a lot in the CEO's comments that deserves discussion.

The first of the benefits serves as an addition to the IM. This type of video is really meant as a means for providing an update or epilogue, as mentioned in Chapter 8. It gives students the opportunity to hear the people who were involved explain what happened and why. Students can compare their own views with those of the principal players in the situations they have analyzed, discussed, and often tried to resolve. This use of videos is not limited to CEOs and heads of companies or divisions. There are several instances where case writers have included tapes of people other than those at the top. In this manner, the problems or effectiveness of implementation plans can be effectively presented.

The ability to see and hear the people talking adds another dimension than simply reading about the person. The written word rarely conveys the intent or intensity of the spoken word. Having the person present the comments in his or her own videotaped words helps to demonstrate the feelings behind those words. The trick here is to get the people who are being taped to really open up for the camera. The inflections, body language, and other visual and audio cues presented by the people being taped are often as valuable as the words themselves. These tapes are often used primarily as an epilogue. They can also be used effectively during class discussion, however, to allow the characters in the case to explain in their own words.

The use of videotapes also adds a living dimension to the case. The words are seen as coming from living, breathing people. No longer can there be a complaint that the case is dry and lifeless. Moreover, there is also no longer a complaint that the case writer has paraphrased the words or thoughts of the people involved in the case. They are speaking for themselves in their own words, tones, and inflections. This living dimension can be extended to issues and processes as well. A view of the air pollution in the skies over a refinery, a demonstration of how a traditional Norwegian bride would be helped to dress for her wedding, or a tour of the manufacturing plant all are richer and more memorable than a description in words alone.

There is far less likelihood that our students will question the reality of the events presented in the case. There have often been times when we were confronted by students who, on reading a case, remarked that this couldn't have happened; no one would possibly do something or say something like that. They have remarked that these words or actions are simply unbeliev-able. Having the people involved in the events relate their actions in their own words adds to the believability of the events.

Videotapes are much more likely to be used in more complex, decision-oriented case situations. As such, having the people who were involved present their own views in a visual manner helps our students to gain insight into why decisions were made. It also helps our students to understand what factors caused the people to act the way they did. This typically occurs because the students are able to gain insight into the values and beliefs of the people concerned. Their words and visual cues help to set the value-oriented parameters of the decisions and actions. This is often difficult to convey with written words. It also helps to bring together the complexity of the decisions surrounding the events.

It is difficult to convey through a written case the interactive effects of the events and environment surrounding a complex decision. Videotaped presentations or discussions often demonstrate in a far more graphic manner how the environment, both internal and external, added to the complexity of analysis and decisions surrounding a particular situation. The tapes also helped to demonstrate the anxiety and concern generated by the overall environment on the part of the people involved in the events. In the example of the Norwegian bride, the student sees also the dark, wooden interior of a traditional home and the costumes of those preparing her for her wedding and feels the pace of the process, which could take several hours. A video case dealing with pollution can show the sooty residue on buildings and on picnic tables in an otherwise pastoral park and can also show the poverty level of nearby residents, who may be willing to trade poor air quality (and health risks) for jobs.

Last, as Kinnunen and Ramamurti (1987) point out, the tapes bring out discussions that would not otherwise typically occur in class devoted to a traditional, written case. The demeanor of the people in the tapes may lead to discussions about the effectiveness of these people as leaders or decision makers or simply their believability. Style issues may come forward that would probably not have evolved in class discussions with a written case. As was noted earlier, this is especially true with students who have had significant experience in managerial situations. They can often relate the people on the tapes to managers and others with whom they have had dealings. This adds to the comparative nature of the subsequent discussions. Being able to use these comparisons adds immeasurably to the analysis and discussions that ensue. These types of students have a wealth of experience that they can bring to the class room. Moreover, they want to be able to draw comparisons and analogies from their professional and personal lives to what they learn in the class room. The use of video cases helps them to do just this.

■ Problems of Video Cases

A major problem associated with a video case is that many people simply do not do well in front of a camera. Many people tend to freeze up when they are videotaped. This leads to an unnatural look and feel in the resulting video. Similarly, many people, including seasoned managers, may be unwilling to make full disclosure of events on video, where they might be willing to discuss these same events in a traditional interview that would lead to a written case study. Both situations would lead to a very general video or one that appears poorly made. It may also create a bias or view of events that is misleading: for example, stage fright creating a negative impression of someone who may be a skilled interpersonal leader. This could lead our students to doubt the value and credibility of the entire case.

Another problem involves the cost and expertise required to develop a professional video. Trying to produce a video without the appropriate levels of expertise will rapidly show through in the resulting product. The problems start with preparing the setting of the video. The lighting must be set up in a manner that allows for effective taping of the people. Lighting and set design are often areas requiring a reasonable degree of experience to carry off well. The proper use of a video camera is an art in itself. One does not simply mount a camera on a tripod and begin taping a situation or person. This results in a "talking head" situation, a very static image with little visual impact. The settings have to be prepared and implemented carefully and professionally. Next, the equipment also has to be of a professional quality. Anyone who has tried to use a video camera soon realizes that the resulting tape is far from perfect when the person operating the camera is an amateur and is using the kinds of equipment that are available to the public.

Attempts to add other material to the interviews present more problems. This added material usually takes the form of video shots of items such as factories, stores, and office sites. These video pieces are even more difficult to produce than the interviews. These added pieces typically require moving shots. These require even more sophisticated equipment and expertise in setting the scene and operating the equipment. Moving sequences are simply far more complex to produce than stationary scenes.

What this all says is that the technical aspects of an effective video require the kind of expertise and experience that is absent at many college and university communications and multimedia groups. Even when the expertise is available, it may be expensive. The cost of using these groups where the expertise is available has to be covered by someone. Although the expenses are usually a transfer cost within the institution, they still must come out of someone's budget. In this era of tight budgets, that may create serious problems, especially when the cost can easily reach $10,000 for anything that is more than simply so-called talking heads.

This brings us to another problem. Simply putting the edited versions of interviews of the key individuals on tape is not sufficient to the development of an effective video case. A typical written case contains descriptions of places, as well as events. It may also contain a variety of exhibits and numerical statistics and data. This is often difficult to present in video form.

Talking heads can often be quite boring, even when used as video supplements to written cases. Unless the people who are speaking display some form of animation in their discussions, they have not added much, if anything, to the written version of the case. As noted earlier, however, these interview or speech-oriented presentations can be used effectively as supplements to written cases, as image portrayals of the key individuals in the case.

MULTIMEDIA CASES

A way to overcome some of these problems is to combine the best aspects of various media formats. Videotapes provide the clarity of presentation that is needed to maintain the interest of the students. Our students are accustomed to high-quality video productions, such as those presented on MTV. On the other hand, they are becoming more accustomed to the use of interactive, computer-based routines and programs in their education activities, as well as in the use of computer games.

■ Benefits of Multimedia Cases

Multimedia cases allow for these qualities to be combined in one package. Instead of opening a textbook or course packet and reading, the student calls up a case on his or her computer. The opening scenes, like those of a conventional case, set the scenario. The student can progress from topic to topic, as in a written version of the same situation. However, at many points, the student will also be offered the choice to jump ahead, changing the sequence. She or he can also ask for additional information, for example, a report on competitors in the industry. These links need not only be to written documents. Video clips, such as interviews with the CEO and various other managers, enable the student to hear first hand about their personalities and their concerns. A film tour of the plant would allow him or her to "walk through" the production process, or he or she could view the company's TV and radio ads, not just those intended for print media. All of these are possible because of the large memory available on a CD-ROM.

Multimedia cases are multisensory and can be used effectively by students with different learning styles. The student determines the pace at which he or she proceeds through the case. He or she also controls the quantity and types of information that he or she uses in the case analysis. Computer-based systems allow for more interaction between the student and the material. Used properly, multimedia cases can give the students a feeling of being more active participants in case method pedagogy. This can be seen in the ability to switch between text and graphics, video and static images, from one medium to another. It also is demonstrated by allowing students to decide how fast and with what degree of intensity to review any particular piece of information. The traditional, written case usually assumes a relatively linear learning style. The true multimedia case allows our students to follow nonlinear lines of thinking.

Models, formulas, spreadsheets, or other analytical tools can also be included among the resources on the CD and linked to the case or its supplemental materials. This may make the student more willing to use these tools to analyze and interpret what she or he is reading and viewing. Moving back and forth between theory and case does not require a physical move, a textbook to be retrieved from the shelf or a pencil located; it is as effortless as "point and click." For technically oriented material, this could even allow students to engage in creative thinking, such as "what if" scenarios or even simulations. In addition, the multimedia package may include more than the typical text, which may not include all of the models or tools that a student might want to apply, assuming that he or she brings a background of tools and theory from other courses. These tools and even theories can come from any discipline or functional area that is appropriate to the material it is linked to. Thus, a business case set in a foreign country could enable the student to explore the impact of currency changes (via financial spreadsheets and foreign exchange models), the likelihood of political change (via a written description or filmed expert's explanation), or cultural factors that might affect the demand for a new product or employees' behavior (via links to anthropological material). This type of cross-disciplinary learning is very difficult to achieve through conventional text-oriented means or even written cases.

Last, written material in the multimedia case also allows the student to have something to take home with them to study. This is necessary in the event that they do not have access to the full range of media when they are studying and analyzing the case to complete the educational assignment. Although CD-ROM drives and Web access are increasingly available, it is not safe to assume that all students will have these available even at home.

A multimedia case can be taught like a traditional written case, the main difference being that students prepared on computers rather than by reading a text. However, because each student may have chosen to pursue different information, there may be a wider dispersal of analyses and interpretations.

This is not unlike a written case that was designed for students to use with outside research, an option that was discussed in the chapter on organizing the case (Chapter 6) but with a wider range of information. Some students will be more adept at determining which information is most useful, whereas others may find themselves more sidetracked than enriched (a definite source of an "A student/C student split"). A multimedia case simulates the complexity of a real-world situation, which includes so-called noise, as well as facts of varying degrees of relevance. A valuable part of the learning process from a multimedia case may well be learning how to filter information, as the real-world decision maker must be able to do.

■ Problems of Multimedia Cases

There are also many problems with the development and use of multimedia cases, however. The research and data gathering that go into a multimedia case are just as time consuming as in any other case writing situation. In fact, due to the need to search out and select materials to be linked to the main subject line of the case, even more research time and effort may be needed. There is no point in offering the student a link to more in-depth information if that link doesn't really offer the student anything new. Thus, topics that you, the case writer, might eliminate from a written case as being unnecessary or adding too much to the length may have to be developed as if they were notes such as those described in Chapter 9.

Multimedia cases require a great deal of sophistication and expertise to produce. Because the multimedia case combines the best aspects of each of the different media, development of such a case requires a combination of skills in many areas. The video aspects of the multimedia case need to be of the same high quality as the professionally produced film clips that our students are accustomed to from such sources as MTV and the evening news. They want graphics that are as good as they encounter in their video games. And they want the ease of use that is always promised by software companies but rarely delivered. All this needs to be packaged in a format that provides for a high degree of interactivity. Last, as will be described in the next section, developing a multimedia case requires a reasonable degree of proficiency with programming skills. This is necessary to be able to tie all of the different media parts together. All of these factors add to the cost of the development of a multimedia case.

One of the biggest problems with a multimedia case is the assumption that all of our students and colleagues have easy access to a suitable computer. Although this may be true at some major institutions, this is not the situation at many smaller or less well-endowed schools. Preparation for discussion of a multimedia case takes time, which may not be possible in a situation where computers have to be shared. This may make it very difficult, if not impossible, for all of our colleagues and students to take advantage of these tools. As the cost of the multimedia hardware and software decrease and their availability increases, these problems should disappear. Until that occurs, however, the costs and benefits of such cases must be carefully evaluated before embarking on their development.

Like any other teaching case, a multimedia case requires an IM. In fact, the IM may be even more necessary, considering the wealth of information that is available to the student. This added information may substantially increase the time required for an instructor to prepare to teach a new multimedia case. In addition to its normal functions, the IM should provide summaries of the information in important linkages. It should contain exhibits and data workouts for linked information, where appropriate. Once class tested, it should also identify which links students are most likely to follow.

DEVELOPMENT OF INTERNET CASES[2]

Another case format that is being developed is that of the Internet case. The Internet is actually a global network of computer networks. Within the Internet is the World Wide Web, a system that connects information stored on Web servers situated around the world. Organizations, companies, educational and nonprofit institutions, governments, and even private individuals have their own sites on the Web, each with a unique address that enables it to be reached from other Web locations. Many of these Web sites contain information that is useful in case analysis; in fact, our students are increasingly turning to the Web, rather than the library, as their primary location for research. The Web is especially well suited for storing graphics. It not only handles text and the broad array of exhibits typically employed with cases; it can also accommodate colored photographs and illustrations in virtually unlimited quantities. Thus, in medical and agricultural cases, colored images that are of significant diagnostic value can be included with other case exhibits. As more libraries and government organizations provide on-line access to documents, students can be sent to read the original sources and determine for themselves what is important, rather than relying on a text's or case's summary. Access to additional, often original source, information can give students a more realistic experience, in which they are forced to take responsibility for acquiring and interpreting their own information. An

Internet-based case can, in turn, be linked with other study materials and with the course syllabus itself.

Many of the constraints are similar to those of a multimedia case. Students need to have extensive access to a computer that must be linked to the Web. As with multimedia cases, a student can proceed at his or her own pace and collect as much, or as little, information as he or she desires. This will have a similar impact in the classroom, except that students can go beyond the linkages built into the case and, with a Web browser, seek out sources beyond those that the instructor might anticipate.

■ Case Documents

Normally, case descriptions are presented in a linear fashion, with material organized under a series of headings and subheadings. Exhibits are inserted at appropriate locations within the body of the text or attached at the end of the document. Internet cases may be organized the same way; however, an alternative that takes fuller advantage of the way Web pages can be organized is to construct a case page and hyperlink other pages to it. For example, the case page (actually, the home page for the case) might include a general description of the case along with titles of subsidiary pages that provide more detailed information on several important aspects of the case. When these titles are constructed as anchors, linked to other Web sites or documents, they are usually highlighted to make them stand out from the rest of the case text. The links can be to existing Web sites of other organizations or developed specifically for the case. "Blue Course Green," an Internet case written for Pennsylvania State University's Turfgrass Management Course in the College of Agricultural Sciences, has a brief description of the sixth hole on the University's Blue Golf Course, a nightmare hole with everything but grass. The three subheadings are "Soil Conditions," "Shading," and "The Green." Clicking on the anchor for "The Green" brings up a subsidiary page on the computer screen. In this case, the page is a more detailed description of the condition of the green, including drainage, damage from foot traffic, composition of the turf, and other factors. This page has links to "turf," "no grass," "green," and "puddles," which students can use to obtain further information. This could include graphics, including pictures, illustrations, and charts—for example, a photograph of the green itself, showing the areas where water puddles and the large number of neighboring trees.

Thus, the case description and associated exhibits can be organized as an interconnected array of Web pages that can be accessed as needed with a click of the mouse. This hierarchical organization of documents enables the reader to grasp the essence of the case from the information presented in the case page and to obtain more detailed information from the subsidiary pages. Obvious advantages of Internet cases are (a) the virtually unlimited amount of material that can be included in the description; (b) the ease with which new information can be added or existing components modified by simply accessing the Web pages and making the changes at any time; and (c) the opportunity to use a broad array of graphics, including colored pictures and illustrations, as appropriate.

In addition to the case description, the case page can include other materials as well. For example, anchors that bring up interviews of some of the principals in the case can be organized under a separate heading following the description. These can include written or audio recordings of responses to questions, as well as quick-time movies of all or a portion of the interviews that can be downloaded and played on the computer screen. An obvious advantage to doing this is to provide students with opportunities to become better acquainted with the principals and, thus, to better understand the social aspects of the case.

Another component that could be included in the case page is a study materials section. This might be a set of articles or graphic-intensive instructional modules that provide students with opportunities to acquire relevant knowledge to better prepare them for analyzing the situation and developing solution strategies. It could also include analytical tools, such as the models and even simulations that were included in the discussion of multimedia cases. These could be custom developed for the course or could be linked to other software programs.

Specific assignments can be described in a subsidiary page that is hyperlinked to the case page. Students could be assigned to participate in a role-playing exercise, present an oral report to the class, or submit a written report to the instructor, just as with a conventional case. All of the cases used in a particular course can be accessed from a home page for the course. The cases may simply be listed by their respective titles as anchors or represented by hyperlinked pictures or illustrations emblematic of the case.

The Internet case and accompanying documents are written in the HTML language. Many software programs, including word-processing programs, contain features for directly converting word documents to hypertext documents and thus obviate or reduce the need to learn HTML. Creating a basic Web page is quite easy. What is more difficult is to set up the anchors and links. The most difficult aspect of writing an Internet case, the art in this type of case writing, is to make the case flow smoothly from one topic to another.

Much as the hard copy case needs to flow smoothly so that students will want to continue reading the case, a multimedia case needs to be able to draw the students from one form of the case to another. If the flow is too choppy, the students will become bored with the case. If the links are too slow or difficult to access, then the students may not follow the appropriate leads to the information necessary to complete the analysis or decision development required for the case. Simply using software to set up the case does not ensure that the various Web sites are developed in a manner that leads to the clear and readable flow necessary to maintain student interest and involvement in the case.

SUMMARY AND CONCLUSIONS

Written cases are limited by what can be presented on paper. There are often areas of information that do not lend themselves to presentation in this format. The use of video supplements can add realism, credibility, liveliness, and variety to the written case. They also help our students to gain a better perspective of the key players involved in the case situation. Video supplements also allow for the development of a wider variety of material in the case. They allow us to actually see the complete environment in which the case takes place. A complete video case, on the other hand, is designed to be used as a freestanding instrument. All of the material in the case is to be found in video format. The advantage here is that many of our students have become used to videos through MTV and computer games.

There are problems with video cases that can be overcome through the use of multimedia cases. This type of combined format allows for the development of material that enhances a straight video case. This includes the use of charts, graphs, exhibits, spreadsheets, and data sets that would not be available through the use of only the video format while providing the visual cues and experiences that are difficult to convey with the printed page. The use of a multimedia format, especially when combined with the Internet, also allows our students to proceed at their own paces and learning styles. As such, it allows them to feel more in charge of the learning process. This should enhance the overall educational experience.

There are significant problems that need to be overcome with the use of these various media, however. The greatest of these is that a large amount of experience and expense are required to successfully implement a case in any of these formats. Without these factors, the advantages described earlier can easily be lost and overcome whatever benefits that can be accrued by the use of these various media. The fact that many people do not come over as sincere or lifelike before a video camera simply makes the need for this expertise even more important to the success of a multimedia case. When the use of computers is added to the overall equation, both the value and the complexity of the cases are extended. The decision to use these formats, therefore, needs to be carefully evaluated before choosing to adopt their use.

One last note on the development and need for Internet and multimedia cases. As worldwide communications become even more integrated and students and decision makers world wide become technologically more sophisticated, the demand for cases in these formats will increase. Student demand for technology shouldn't be our only, or even our primary, reason for learning to write cases for multimedia or the Internet. Our students will increasingly go to work in environments that are rich in information, both useful and noise, and where much more is just a mouse click away. They will have to learn to filter and structure their environment. Cases have always been well suited to helping students develop their thinking skills, as well as their knowledge bases. Multimedia and Web-linked cases may be a logical step toward making the classroom environment even more similar to their future experiences in the real world.

NOTES

1. Much of the section on video cases is based on Kinnunen and Ramamurti (1987).

2. This section was coauthored by Prof. A. J. Turgeon, Professor and Director, Educational Technologies Program, College of Agricultural Sciences, Pennsylvania State University.

■

Appendix 1:
Early Draft of a Case

■

MEYERS & MORRISON:
A QUESTION OF PROFESSIONAL ETHICS

William Naumes,
University of New Hampshire

This case deals with the events surrounding the recruiting and subsequent hiring of a new associate at a public accounting firm in New Hampshire. Meyers & Morrison had been founded by Phillip Meyers in 1958. Michael Morrison was hired as an associate in 1972, after having served with KPMG Peat Marwick's Boston office for 5 years. He was promoted to partner by the end of the 1970s. Despite some setbacks, the firm continued to grow. The partners decided to hire another associate during the beginning of the 1980s. After a search, they hired Stephen Adams, an accountant with another small accounting firm. He was hired with the expectation that, if he successfully met current client needs and secured new clients, he would be promoted to partner.

At first, everything seemed to be going well. During the next tax season, in his second year with Meyers & Morrison, however, Mr. Adams appeared to all in the office to be irritable, nervous, and impatient, especially with his progress within the firm. He stated to the partners that his wife was unhappy with the Portsmouth area. His most visible symptom involved biting his nails and fingers until they were actually bleeding. The office staff became more uncomfortable around Mr. Adams. They stated that his appearance was even a concern to clients.

Mr. Adams, in a meeting with the partners, handed in his resignation, with only 2 weeks' notice. During the discussion that ensured, Mr. Adams stated that he needed a substantial raise and that he was frustrated at not having been offered a partnership yet. The partners were in a quandary, because they had been expecting to offer him a partnership later in the year. The partners asked for some time to consider their options, and Mr. Adams appeared to agree. Shortly after this meeting, Mr. Morrison was told by a long-standing client that he had received a letter from Mr. Adams stating that he was leaving Meyers & Morrison and was soliciting the business of many of the firm's clients at lower rates than those charged by the firm. After receiving a copy of the letter sent out by Mr. Adams, the partners are considering what response to take.

Appendix 2:
Early Draft of
the Instructor's Manual

MEYERS & MORRISON
INSTRUCTOR'S MANUAL

The case can be used to study the interactions between the hiring process, professional ethics and standards, personnel review procedures, and customer relations. The case can be used in accounting, ethics, human resources, and organization behavior courses.

QUESTIONS

1. Analyze the symptoms presented in the case and the underlying problems relating to these symptoms.

2. Who are the primary and secondary stakeholders in the Meyers & Morrison case?

3. Discuss the ethical considerations of the actions taken by Mr. Adams.

4. What alternatives are open to Meyers & Morrison? Evaluate these alternatives against a stated set of criteria to be met through any changes proposed.

5. What actions do you propose Mr. Meyers and Mr. Morrison take in response to the situation presented in the case? How should they be implemented?

POTENTIAL RESPONSES

1. Symptoms and underlying problems

All too often, students, and managers as well, confuse symptoms with the underlying problems in a given situation. It is helpful to relate this issue with a physical situation, such as an allergic reaction. We often state that our "problem" involves a runny nose, watering eyes, headaches, and sneezing. These are simply symptoms of the underlying problem of an allergic reaction to some environmental agent. Taking medication to reduce the symptoms may help, temporarily. The underlying problem remains, however. That will probably be the situation in this case, as well. The average student will be able to note the underlying problems and pose solutions for them. The issue of whether the actions of Mrs. Adams's actions are symptoms or problems should be discussed. Also a similar analysis of Mr. Adams's behavior and expectations should be developed.

2. Who are the primary and secondary stakeholders in the Meyers & Morrison case?

Primary Stakeholders	Secondary Stakeholders
The partners	Other employees
Mr. Adams	Clients of Meyers & Morrison
Mrs. Adams	

3. Ethical considerations

What Mr. Adams has done, to date, may well be considered unprofessional but is probably not considered to be technically unethical. He is leaving at the end of tax season, the busiest and most important time of year for an accounting firm. Moreover, after he had implied that the relationship could be salvaged, through a higher salary and a clear statement concerning the partnership, he had apparently already planned to solicit the business of the clients of the firm.

4. Criteria

    a. Maintain good client relations.

    b. Avoid negative publicity.

    c. Maintain dignity.

    d. Maintain client base.

   e. Maintain employee morale.

5. Alternatives

   a. Do nothing.

   b. Send letter to clients urging them to remain with Meyers & Morrison.

   c. Send letter to clients to inform them of Mr. Adams's departure from the firm and wishing him the best of luck in his endeavor.

■

Appendix 3:
Published Version of the Case

■

MEYERS & MORRISON:
A QUESTION OF PROFESSIONAL ETHICS

By William Naumes,
Whittemore School of Business and Economics,
University of New Hampshire,
and Michelle Wilson and Sherry Walters, students.

INTRODUCTION

Michael Morrison, partner in the accounting firm of Meyers & Morrison, didn't know what to think after the telephone conversation with one of his firm's oldest clients. The client had stated that he had received a letter from Stephen Adams, an associate with Meyers & Morrison, asking the client to switch to a new firm that he, Adams, was about to start. Morrison remarked to his partner, Phillip Meyers, "I can't

AUTHORS' NOTE: This case was written solely for the purpose of stimulating student discussion. All events are real, but names have been disguised at the company's request. The authors thank John Seeger and the anonymous reviewers of the *Case Research Journal* for their assistance and advice. This case was originally presented at the Casewriters Workshop, Decision Sciences Institute Annual Meeting, November 1993.

believe that Stephen would actually do this. He hasn't even left the firm yet. I thought he was going to wait to see what we could offer him to stay with the company." Meyers responded, "This isn't what I expected from someone in this office. We've always treated everyone like family here. This isn't a big impersonal, public accounting firm. I thought we all got along pretty well. This doesn't make a lot of sense."

Morrison paused and looked back at Meyers. "What do we do now?"

BACKGROUND

Phillip Meyers had started his own small, certified public accounting firm 30 years earlier, in the seacoast town of Portsmouth, New Hampshire. For several years, he worked independently, establishing a small, but loyal customer base. As the business continued to grow, Meyers realized that he would need to hire additional employees in order to capitalize effectively on his firm's excellent reputation.

Thus, after 10 years on his own, Meyers hired Michael Morrison, the son of one of his largest clients. Morrison was a graduate of the MBA program at Boston University. He had worked for 5 years for KPMG Peat Marwick in their Boston office, but even then he knew that he would prefer moving back to the Portsmouth area. He also preferred the style and feel of a small firm to that of a major international accounting firm. Together, Meyers & Morrison continued to expand their firm's client list, primarily by providing excellent customer service. Their focus was on small business and professional clients such as Michael Morrison's father.

As the firm continued to grow, Morrison was rewarded for his effort and dedication by becoming a partner in the new firm, Meyers & Morrison. The staff was gradually expanded until there were 10 employees, including a computer operator, a payroll specialist, staff accountants, and clerical workers. The only CPAs, however, were the two partners.

A few years after Morrison was made a partner, a client responsible for over 40 percent of the firm's revenues went into bankruptcy. The partners were forced to lay off some employees in an effort to keep the firm profitable. After this incident they vowed to never again become dependent on any one firm or client for a significant portion of their profits.

Due to the combined efforts of the partners and the remaining employees, Meyers & Morrison regained the profitability they had once enjoyed and eventually expanded the staff to its previous level. As a result of the continued expansion of the client base and workload, the partners decided to hire an additional CPA. Morrison stated,

Our intent was to find someone who was like us and who would be able to share some of our increased auditing and tax load as well as help us to continue expanding. Besides, my partner, Phillip, wanted to slowly start to withdraw from active involvement with the firm.

As a result the partners hired Stephen Adams, a Certified Public Accountant in his early thirties, to help service the firm's current and projected client base. Adams had an undergraduate degree in business from a local business school with a concentration in accounting. The partners, confident that Adams would prove his ability, offered him a position that was designed to lead to making him a partner in the firm. Morrison stated that "the process of bringing Mr. Adams in was somewhat loose and informal, much the way we do everything around here." The partners believed that their offer included an extremely generous salary and benefits package, compared to those of associates in other small firms in the region. They admitted that they had not done a full salary analysis of the local market, however.

Stephen Adams came to Meyers & Morrison from another small public accounting firm in Massachusetts. He was married, although he had no children. According to Morrison, the period of adjustment appeared to go very well. He stated, "Mr. Adams was looked upon very favorably by the office staff. He worked long hours serving the needs of his clients. He spent additional hours recruiting new business." Morrison added, "After the first 12 months, all in all, we were very happy with Mr. Adams's performance. Everyone in the office seemed to be getting along pretty well."

During Adams's first 9 months with the firm, he went through his first tax season, which gave him the chance to become acclimated to the area and to the policies and procedures of the firm. Adams's responsibilities increased until, by the end of his second year with the firm, he was responsible for almost one quarter of the firm's clients. Most of these clients were new, having been brought into the firm by Adams. Morrison noted that although Adams expressed confidence during his first year with the firm, Adams's wife seemed to be finding things a bit more difficult. Morrison recalled later that Adams confided that his wife was miserable in the area, and was not making new friends to ease the transition. Adams told Morrison that she spent her time shopping and renovating the house that the couple had purchased. Adams occasionally joked that she was trying to drive him into poverty, but added that this was nothing new.

Although the partners expressed their satisfaction with Adams's performance during his first year with the firm, they began noticing small changes in his behavior during his second year. Morrison remarked that

He became impatient with his progress within the firm. This was difficult for us to understand, as he was only in his early thirties and had a very promising future with the firm. We estimated that he would make partner within the next couple of years.

Staff members reported that by the end of his second year, Adams began having difficulties handling crisis situations in the daily operation of the firm. Later, they noticed that Adams had begun to chew at his fingers until they bled conspicuously. The other employees stated that they were uncomfortable looking at his fingers. They were worried that clients might feel slightly disgusted having to shake such disfigured hands. They told Morrison that when they questioned Adams about his habit, he told them that he bit his fingers to deal with the pressures of daily life. Morrison recalled that Adams hadn't seemed to be pressured during his first year at the firm. The partners wondered what had changed.

LOCAL COMPETITION

The accounting industry in the Portsmouth, New Hampshire, region was primarily comprised of small to medium-size firms. There were approximately 35 accounting firms or independent accountants listed in the area as certified public accountants. There were no major national firms in the immediate area, although there were several with offices in other parts of the state. The closest national firm was based in Manchester, the state's largest city, located 45 miles west of Portsmouth.

INDUSTRY NORMS

Industry sources noted that it was common for a firm the size of Meyers & Morrison to seek a third professional as the number of clients expanded. While there were no set standards for the time that it might take before a senior associate was offered a position as partner, in a small firm this would typically occur during the first three years with the firm, especially if the associate had held a senior position previously with another firm. The decision to offer an associate a partnership would depend not only on the professional results demonstrated by the associate, but also on the associate's people-oriented and interpersonal skills. In a small firm, such skills were a critical part of the partner decision.

There were also no industrywide standards concerning the amount of notice that an associate was required to give a firm before leaving. Typically, it was expected that a person leaving a firm would stay long enough to acquaint someone else within the firm with the departing person's clients.

There were no specific restrictions about who retains clients after an associate leaves a firm. Practically, however, it was recognized that clients brought into a firm by an associate would probably want to stay with that person, since the personal component of accountant-client relationships is as important as the professional component. There were restrictions in the AICPA Code of Conduct concerning advertising, however. Solicitation of clients while working for a firm would have to be handled very carefully so as not to violate the advertising prohibition. A summary statement of the Code of Conduct is presented in Exhibit 1.

COMPANY PHILOSOPHY

Meyers & Morrison was a small local firm that had to work hard to ensure a varied client base and avoid relying too heavily on one industry or client type. By developing such a client base, the firm had became one of the most successful in the area. Some of the accountants working for Meyers & Morrison had waiting lists to take on new clients. This was astonishing for a firm that did not have an advertising or promotion plan in place. Meyers & Morrison relied solely on word of mouth from satisfied clients to expand their customer base.

Although the firm claimed to be following a mid-range pricing policy, their average fees appeared to be on the upper side of most private firms in the area. The partners stated that they did not want to have a cost-conscious client base. They were more interested in doing complicated corporate returns than simple personal returns, which were jokingly referred to by Morrison as the "H&R Blockers." The partners' philosophy was that if no one was complaining, then the prices must be too low. On the other hand, if everyone was complaining, then the prices must be too high. The partners felt that somewhere in the middle was just right.

THE CONFRONTATION

One day before the end of his third tax season, Adams asked for a meeting with the partners. At the outset of the meeting, he stated that he wanted to give his notice of resignation. This was accompanied by a formal letter of resignation. He said that he would be available for only 2 more weeks, taking him just to the end of tax season. Michael Morrison felt that "while this may be customary for most industries, it is rather short notice for the accounting profession."

The partners were shocked. Adams had been well liked and respected. Morrison stated, "He had been given every advantage, with the hopes that eventually he would become a partner." In fact, the partners agreed that they would probably have offered him a partnership within the year. This would have entailed both greater responsibility and higher compensation. Basically, he would have been sharing, on an agreed upon basis, in the profits of the firm. In line with common practice, this would have required a financial commitment on Adams's part to buy into the partnership.

Morrison noted, however, that some form of long-term financial arrangement could have been developed to allow Adams to pay for his partnership with a portion of his expected earnings from the firm.

Morrison stated that when the partners asked Adams to explain why he was resigning his position with the firm, he said, "The decision finally came down to one of money." As Morrison reported, Adams

> claimed that he liked working at Meyers & Morrison, but he just couldn't afford it anymore. His wife was spending money faster than he could make it. He also stated that he had become frustrated that he hadn't been offered a partnership in the firm yet.

Morrison also noted,

> He said that he was not sure that he would be able to afford waiting much longer. However, he said that if the we (the partners) would give him a sizable raise and a partnership he would be willing to stay. We told him that we needed some time to think over this proposition.

After learning that Adams was planning to leave the firm, most of the staff, including the partners, wanted to ask what his plans were for the future, but they felt that if Adams had wanted people to know, he would have told them. Morrison noted that the staff had learned of Adams's resignation from Mr. Morrison's secretary, after she had filed Adams's resignation letter. The office staff also learned about Adams's request for more money and a partnership, but had no idea what the partners were going to do about the request.

It was a few days after the meeting with Adams, while the partners were considering their options, that Morrison received the phone call from his client. As Morrison explained, "The client had received a letter in the mail from Mr. Adams and was very upset about the contents [reproduced in Figure 1]. He thought that I should look it over immediately, and agreed to fax it to me." Morrison said,

> After contacting a few of our other most trusted clients, we realized that Mr. Adams had probably sent a similar letter to all of our clients. At that point, we felt that some kind of quick action was needed.

EXHIBIT 1 Summary of AICPA Code of Conduct

Responsibilities

In carrying out their responsibilities as professionals, members should exercise sensitive professional and moral judgments in all their activities.

The Public Interest

Members should accept the obligation to act in a way that will serve the public interest, honor the public trust, and demonstrate commitment to professionalism.

Integrity

To maintain and broaden public confidence, members should perform all professional responsibilities with the highest sense of integrity.

Objectivity and Independence

A member should maintain objectivity and be free of conflicts of interest in discharging professional responsibilities. A member in public practice should be independent in fact and appearance when providing auditing and other attestation services.

Due Care

A member should observe the profession's technical and ethical standards, strive continually to improve competence and the quality of services, and discharge professional responsibility to the best of the member's ability.

Scope and Nature of Services

A member in public practice should observe the Principles of the Code of Professional Conduct in determining the scope and nature of services to be provided. . . .

Rule 502—Advertising and Other Forms of Solicitation

A member in public practice shall not seek to obtain clients by advertising or other forms of solicitation in a manner that is false, misleading, or deceptive. Solicitation by the use of coercion, over-reaching, or harassing conduct is prohibited.

FIGURE 1 The Letter Sent by Adams to the Client of Meyers & Morrison

---

Dear Client:

I am writing this letter to inform you of my impending departure from the accounting firm of Meyers & Morrison. Upon resignation, I will be starting my own practice in Dover, NH.

The services which I will be offering include:

Preparation of Individual Tax Returns—My rate is $100.00 minimum with a charge of $50.00 per hour. Meyers & Morrison have a $150.00 minimum with a charge of $80.00.

Estate Planning—My rate will be contingent solely on my hourly rate stated above. This is true at Meyers & Morrison also.

Corporate Tax Returns—My rate will be a $500.00 minimum. Meyers & Morrison charge a $750.00 minimum.

At the present time I am not equipped to provide any auditing services. I hope to be adding them in the very near future.

As you can see, my rates are much more affordable than those of Meyers & Morrison. In addition, it is my belief that you will find my service to be much more efficient and of higher caliber than the service provided at Meyers & Morrison.

I would like to emphasize how pleasurable it has been to do business with you over the past three years. It is my hope and intention that you will follow my lead and bring your future business to my new office.

Sincerely,

Stephen Adams, C.P.A.

Appendix 4: Rewritten Instructor's Manual

MEYERS & MORRISON:
A QUESTION OF PROFESSIONAL ETHICS

Instructor's Manual

William Naumes,
Whittemore School of Business and Economics,
University of New Hampshire.

CASE OVERVIEW

This case deals with the events surrounding the recruiting and subsequent hiring of a new associate at a public accounting firm in New Hampshire. Meyers & Morrison had been founded by Phillip Meyers in 1958. Michael Morrison was hired as an associate in 1972, after having served with KPMG Peat Marwick's Boston office for 5 years. He was promoted to partner by the end of the 1970s. Despite some setbacks, the firm continued to grow. The partners decided to hire another associate during the beginning of the 1980s. After a search, they hired Stephen Adams, an accountant with another small accounting firm. He was hired with the expectation that if he successfully met current client needs and secured new clients, he would be promoted to partner.

At first, everything seemed to be going well. During the next tax season, in his second year with Meyers and Morrison, however, Mr. Adams appeared to all in the office to be irritable, nervous, and impatient, especially with his progress within the firm. He stated to the partners that his wife was unhappy with the Portsmouth area. His most visible symptom involved biting his nails and fingers, until they were actually bleeding. The office staff became more uncomfortable around Mr. Adams. They stated that his appearance was even a concern to clients.

Mr. Adams, in a meeting with the partners, handed in his resignation, with only 2 weeks' notice. During the discussion that ensued, Mr. Adams stated that he needed a substantial raise and that he was frustrated at not having been offered a partnership yet. The partners were in a quandary, because the had been expecting to offer him a partnership later in the year. The partners asked for some time to consider their options, and Mr. Adams appeared to agree. Shortly after this meeting, Mr. Morrison was told by a long-standing client that he had received a letter from Mr. Adams stating that he was leaving Meyers & Morrison and was soliciting the business of many of the firm's clients, at lower rates than those charged by the firm. After receiving a copy of the letter sent out by Mr. Adams, the partners are considering what response to take.

This case was prepared primarily from discussions with the partners of the accounting firm, with Mr. Morrison providing most of the detailed information. This case has been disguised at the request of the partners in the accounting firm.

PURPOSE

This case is designed to allow for the development of a discussion of definitions of professional ethics. Although this case deals specifically with an accounting firm, the issues presented here are generic enough to fit most similar situations involving a professional organization.

Students are also expected to be able to develop an appropriate response to the issues in the case. Because the question of ethics presented in the case is somewhat muddy, this case can be used to develop an understanding of various responses that students can prepare when confronted with ethical questions. Moreover, the effects of these actions can be related to a stakeholder analysis of the various groups interacting with the firm. To aid students in understanding the often murky aspects of defining professional ethics, an abbreviated version of the AICPA Code of Conduct has been included in the case.

The Meyers and Morrison case can also be used to explore issues dealing with the recruiting, selection, and orientation process for professionals and managers. The owners of the firm had hired an associate without going through a full evaluation of his background. Moreover, it is unclear as to what expectations were held by both sides of this recruiting process.

Finally, the case can be used to evaluate the exit process when a high-ranking employee decides to leave the firm. All too often, this critical aspect is ignored, leaving all concerned with bitter and confused feelings concerning the manner in which the relationship was severed.

KEY ISSUES

1. Ethics and professional standards
2. Stakeholder analysis
3. Recruiting standards in a professional firm
4. Motivation and expectations for professionals

TEACHING METHODS

This case is designed to be used in a course dealing with ethics or corporate social responsibility. Alternatively, it could be used in courses in human resource management, accounting, accounting ethics, and small business management. The comments presented here are primarily designed for a discussion focussing on the issue of professional ethics and managing in a professional organization.

The case is pretty straightforward. Aside from an understanding of behavioral techniques dealing with motivation, evaluation, and supervision, there is little background material that is required. The case could be set early in a course where ethics is discussed. Although MBA students might be able to relate best to this case, it could also be used in an undergraduate course, particularly with accounting students.

The case could be presented early in a course on corporate social responsibility or ethics. The case is designed to be discussed in one class session of 1- to 1½-hour duration. The class could begin with a simple question as to whether the students feel that Mr. Adams had violated any norms or ethical standards through his actions while leaving the firm. Many students will fell uneasy with this question. They will have a feeling that something is wrong here but cannot verbalize precisely what is the problem. This should be followed with a description of just what happened. During the analysis of everyone's roles in the case, a better understanding of the culture and environment of Meyers & Morrison should come out.

It should become clear that the firm is loosely managed. The perception of the two partners is that everyone understands the expectations of the partners. Moreover, it should also be brought out that the partners expected their associate to be self-motivated and require little supervision.

Students can be asked what they feel were Mr. Adams's expectations as he entered and progressed with the firm. These expectations should then be matched with those of the partners.

Students can be asked to list the stakeholders in the case and note how they were affected by the events that have taken place. Students should then be asked to evaluate the actions of the three main principals in the case. The evaluation should be based on the concept of fairness to all those involved, including Mr. Adams's wife. A definition of what is fair, in these circumstances, will lead to different and often conflicting conclusions, especially when taking into consideration the various stake-holders. The advantage to using this case for a stakeholder analysis is the relatively concise list of stakeholders involved (presented later in this note), as well as the relatively clear view of the stakes held by the different groups.

The session should end with a presentation by the students as to what actions the partners should take at the end of the case. They have been presented with informa-tion concerning Mr. Adams's intentions. Some type of reaction is now expected. The responses will probably range from suing Mr. Adams to doing nothing. An appropri-ate response is probably somewhere in between.

Students should not be allowed to end with a response to Mr. Adams, however. That only resolves the immediate problem. They should be asked how the partners should change their actions and behavior in the future, because they will undoubtedly seek to replace Mr. Adams at this point. It should be pointed out that if they do not change, the partners will be doomed to repeat their past mistakes. This situation must also be viewed as a learning experience.

QUESTIONS

1. Analyze the symptoms presented in the case and the underlying problems relating to those symptoms.
2. Develop a stakeholder analysis relevant to the issues of the Meyers & Morrison case and firm.
3. Discuss the ethical considerations of the actions taken by Mr. Adams.
4. What alternatives are open to the Meyers & Morrison? Evaluate these alternatives against a stated set of criteria to be met through any changes proposed.
5. What actions do you propose Mr. Meyers and Mr. Morrison take in response to the situation presented in the case? How should they be implemented?

POTENTIAL RESPONSES

1. Symptoms and underlying problems

All too often, students, and managers as well, confuse symptoms with the underlying problems in a given situation. It is helpful to relate this issue with a physical situation, such as an allergic reaction. We often state that our "problem" involves a runny nose, watering eyes, headaches, and sneezing. These are simply symptoms of the underlying problem of an allergic reaction to some environmental agent. Taking medication to reduce the symptoms may help temporarily. The underlying problem remains, however. That will probably be the situation in this case, as well. The average student will be able to readily define the symptoms. The above-average student will be able to note the underlying problems and pose solutions for them.

One of the underlying problems involved Mr. Adams's wife. Adams stated that she is unhappy in the Portsmouth area and had few, if any, outlets for her energy, other than shopping and fixing their house. Because the partners claim that this was supposed to be a close-knit group, why was she not considered during the recruiting process? Also, why wasn't she included in any other aspects of the operations of the firm? At the very least, she could have been included in social events by the two partners. Also, in this day of two-worker families, the partners could have inquired if they could be of help in resettling her, as well as offering Mr. Adams the new position. They would have to be careful, however, because this can only be asked after the offer has been made. It could be considered discrimination if they ask about his wife's occupation or even about Mr. Adams's marital status. At the very least, once Adams made it known that his wife was having trouble adjusting to life in the seacoast area, the partners should have responded in a positive and helpful manner. It has long been felt that if the spouse of an employee is unhappy, some of that unhappiness will soon be reflected in the work of the employee. This was definitely the case in this situation. As Mrs. Adams became vocal about her difficulties, Mr. Adams's performance and attention began suffering. His focus was not centered entirely on performing his job well but only on his advancement within the firm.

Another obvious symptom was the out-of-control spending that was being done by Mrs. Adams. Adams stated that she was spending a great deal of money; more than he earned. A question that could have been asked was whether this had happened in the past or whether this was new behavior. One can infer from Mr. Adams comments in the case that this behavior may have occurred in the past, as well. This indicates that not all is right at home, however. The partners knew the income that Mr. Adams was receiving and should have known that unless there were mitigating circumstances, the couple couldn't afford her hobby much longer. This would lead most people to wonder about an unhappy home life or dissatisfaction with some realm of the couple's current situation.

Also, Mr. Adams started to become impatient with his progress within the firm. The partners had told him that if his good work continued, he would eventually become a partner. Yet Mr. Adams could no longer wait for that. He wanted to be a partner now, not in the future. This, however, was not addressed directly by the partners. It was almost as if they thought that it was a phase that would soon pass. There did not appear to be any formal evaluation process. The partners noted to each other that they were planning to offer Adams a partnership later that year, if everything continued to progress well. Yet they do not seem to have told him of that decision. There was clearly a communication problem between the partners and Adams. Moreover, Adams did not approach the partners until he was ready to leave. Once again, this implies that there was no real communication going on among the professionals in the firm.

Although Mr. Adams had once been able to successfully cope with the daily trials and tribulations of life in an accounting firm, he started to become a victim of stress. Other employees began to notice symptoms such as that Mr. Adams's hands were bitten raw in several areas. Sometimes, they bled openly at work. Although people handle stress differently, this is definitely not the most healthy way to do it. One might have questioned the stability of Mr. Adams at that point. Clearly, Adams was suffering. The employees even mentioned this to the partners, yet they did nothing. The partners were not controlling their work place or maintaining a stable environment. These factors were affecting the entire office.

Also, the partners didn't seem to be curious about the length of Mr. Adams's notice. Although most professions require only 2 weeks' notice, it is accepted procedure for professionals to give at least 1 month, generally more. This is due to the difficulty of transferring clients to other accountants, as well as the seasonality of the profession. And Mr. Adams's resignation came right at the end of tax season. This would not be an ideal time for someone to leave who was responsible for the preparation of the tax returns of one quarter of the firm's clients. This indicates a lack of planning on the part of the owners. They are not thinking ahead and of the best interests of the other stakeholders in this organization.

Perhaps, if the partners had paid more attention to these symptoms, they would not have been faced with having their clients solicited by Mr. Adams. What made the situation even worse is that the letters were sent out while Mr. Adams was still serving out his notice with Meyers & Morrison. Although it might be expected that the clients he had brought into the firm might leave, the partners were not prepared to have some of their oldest and best clients solicited, clients that had been brought in by other accountants and that Mr. Adams apparently had not even worked with. Clients who had no need to know that there had been any turnover in the firm were now exposed to the fact that there was a serious conflict going on between the partners and Mr. Adams. This leads to a question and problem of professional ethics and standards. The partners should have been asking why Adams was taking such a radical and questionable step.

2. Stakeholder analysis

The Partners

The partners need to be concerned about the reputation of the firm. Should they decide to challenge Mr. Adams and his ethics, they might cause a public scandal that could irrevocably affect the firm. Also, clients now must wonder about the judgment of the partners for having hired such a troublemaker in the first place. In addition to these issues, some clients may leave, causing the revenues of the firm, and thus the partners, to decrease.

Mr. Adams

Mr. Adams obviously wants the partners to let him go quietly. He is hoping that his firm will be very successful so that he might deal with his wife's spending. On the other hand, he doesn't want to irritate the partners, as his firm might fail, and he may need them at some point in the future. He is hoping that a significant portion of his clients will leave Meyers & Morrison to become his personal clients.

Other Employees

Should Mr. Adams successfully obtain a significant portion of Meyers & Morrison's clients, their jobs might be affected. There might no longer be a need for such a large office staff. Also, all the employees who remain might be looked at more carefully and with less trust, making the workplace less enjoyable. Should the environment change, the quality of their work might be affected, without their having any control over the situation.

Clients of Meyers & Morrison

The clients of Meyers & Morrison have much at stake. Should the partners perceive Mr. Adams to be a threat, they might lower their fees, making services much more affordable. On the other hand, if the firm does lower its fees, then they might feel that they have been overcharged in the past. Also, some of the larger clients that Mr. Adams worked with may find it inconvenient that he can no longer provide the full range of services he had when with Meyers & Morrison. Although they might consider staying with the firm to be able to continue receiving these services, they might wonder what kind of a firm Meyers & Morrison is if such a problem developed. All of the clients are probably wondering how they should respond to both the partners and Mr. Adams, at this point.

Mrs. Adams

Mrs. Adams is now in a very difficult situation. Starting up a new firm requires tremendous resources. She must curtail her spending so that Mr. Adams has available the resources he needs to make a fruitful attempt at starting his own firm. Also, she now must maintain a certain image. Her behavior will reflect on her husband who, starting a new business, needs all the help that he can get.

3. Ethical considerations

What Mr. Adams has done to date may well be considered unprofessional, but according to the accounting profession, it is not considered to be technically unethical. The problem is that the partners never set clear standards for Adams to follow concerning the amount of notice required before leaving, as well as approaching clients when leaving. Moreover, the partners' failure to maintain communications with Adams concerning his future with the firm, as well as problems he appeared to be having with the move and his new position, fits in here.

As noted, however, Mr. Adams's actions do appear to be unprofessional, at the very least. He is leaving at the end of tax season, the busiest and most important time of the year for an accounting firm. Moreover, after he had implied that the relationship could be salvaged, through a higher salary and a clear statement concerning his partnership, he had apparently already planned to solicit the business of the clients of the firm. None of this could be considered to be likely to enhance his reputation if it became widely known. A standard that could be applied here would be to ask Adams if he would be willing to state publicly all the details of his actions. One would question his response. Moreover, this question should be asked of those students who take either side in this situation. One could question whether this would instill trust and confidence in his abilities and services as required by the AICPA Code of Conduct. A reading of that Code, however, leads the reader to realize how vague many such codes are when it comes to reacting to a situation such as this.

4. Criteria and alternatives

Criteria

Maintain good client relations. It is very important to the partners that, no matter what, they maintain good relations with their existing clients. Infighting within an accounting firm is not looked on favorably, as accountants have access to confidential information.

Avoid negative publicity. The partners don't want any negative publicity because they rely on word of mouth to gain new clients. If the reputation of the firm were to suffer, the partners might find it difficult to lead the firm toward growth.

Maintain dignity. The partners don't want to look like they are being petty. Obviously, they expect some of the clients that Mr. Adams brought into the firm to follow him to his private practice. Should they decide to take any action, they must be careful not to seem unreasonable. Also, the partners don't want to look as if they are afraid that Mr. Adams could take away a significant portion of their business.

Maintain the client base. Although the partners recognize that losing some clients is unavoidable, their ideal goal would be to lose as few as possible. The partners have made sure that they are not dependent on any one client for a significant portion of the firm's revenue, but if they lost enough, it could seriously damage the firm.

Maintain employee morale. The partners don't want the other employees to feel as if they are being judged because of what happened with Mr. Adams. Happy employees are the most productive, and right now, the firm needs all that they can get from their employees. Mr. Adams produced a significant amount of the work within the firm, and now his services are gone. Through a combined effort, the other employees must make up this difference.

Make sure that this doesn't happen again. The partners have never had to deal with a situation like this before and definitely won't want to again. Gradually, this could erode their reputation, as well as their client base. Also, they would be ineffectual business people if they couldn't even control their own business.

One possible action could be to require a noncompete clause in any contract with a new associate. In this manner, if a subsequent hire decides to leave the firm, the ability of that person to take clients from the firm would be severely limited. Although these clauses cannot be all encompassing, they can reduce the negative impact of such an occurrence.

As noted in the case, most senior associates coming into a firm such as this would expect to be evaluated for partner status earlier and more formally than was done here. Moreover, some of these expectations would have been outlined in a contract between the firm and the associate. Although this was not done in this circumstance, it should be included in future negotiations.

Alternatives

a. Do Nothing

Advantages	Disadvantages
Causes no friction	Doesn't maintain employee morale
Maintains good client relations	Doesn't maintain client base
Avoids negative publicity	Partners might look weak and afraid

| The partners maintain their dignity | Does nothing to prevent same situation from happening again with the next professional-level CPA employed. Maintains pricing strategy |

b. Send Letter to Clients Urging Them to Remain With Meyers & Morrison

Advantages	Disadvantages
Maintains pricing strategy	Doesn't maintain good client relations
Might maintain client base	Might not avoid negative publicity
Might avoid negative publicity	Might not maintain client base
	Doesn't maintain partner dignity
	Doesn't prevent situation from happening again
	Firm might appear weak and afraid

c. Send Letter to Clients to Inform Them of Mr. Adams's Departure From the Firm and Wishing Him the Best of Luck in His Endeavor

Advantages	Disadvantages
Maintains good client relations	Doesn't prevent situation from happening again
Avoids negative publicity	Might not maintain client base
Maintains dignity	
Might maintain client base	
Don't look weak and afraid	
Maintains employee morale	
Maintains pricing strategy	

5. Recommended actions and implementation

After carefully considering all of the options available, the following appears to be a reasonable way out of the predicament faced by the firm. It is in the firm's best interest to implement a combination of the alternatives described earlier. By doing this, they have the potential to satisfy as many of their criteria, as possible.

As for implementation, it must be very precise. A lawyer should be contacted to have a legally binding contract drawn up for the employees to sign. This should be checked for viability in different states but does seem to be effective in most states.

The partners need to become more communicative with their employees. They must explain to their current employees why they feel the contract is necessary. When doing so, they must be sure to stress that any clients they bring into the firm are exempt from the contract. The employees should be told that the partners recognize that they work hard to gain these clients and don't want to do anything to hinder their progress.

As for the letter, it must be extremely diplomatic, with no undertones. The following sample letter may be considered adequate. You may choose to modify it some.

Dear Client:

We regret to inform you that we recently received notice of resignation from Stephen Adams. He has been with this firm for three years, and we know that many of you have worked closely with him.

Phillip and myself are currently in the process of interviewing applicants to replace Mr. Adams. When we have decided upon a candidate, we will have a reception for you all to meet him or her. We want to make the transition of working with a new accountant as easy as possible for all of you. Should there be any other way to smooth the transition, please call either one of us at your convenience.

Please be assured that your tax returns have been and are continuing to be completed in the thorough manner with which we hope you have been accustomed while being served by Meyers & Morrison.

We would like to wish Mr. Adams the best of luck in his new endeavor.

Sincerely,

Michael Morrison & Phillip Meyers

Meyers & Morrison, CPAs

This will, hopefully, reduce the immediate fallout from the problems with Mr. Adams. The partners need to revamp their hiring procedures for his eventual replacement, however. If the firm is able to retain most of their clients, as is likely, it will need another associate rather quickly. Although the partners will have to put in extra hours, as well as hire part- time people to complete the tax work this season, they will have to recruit a new person.

They need to set up and follow clear procedures during this next hire. First, they need to set clear expectations. These should include a clear time line concerning expectations as to both that person's role and results. These expectations should be an outgrowth of a well-thought-out set of objectives and plan of action for the firm to follow.

The partners also need to determine why the person wants to work in a small firm, especially because they would be looking for someone with experience in securing new business as well as meeting the needs of existing clients. The partners should be ready and able to check each applicant's credentials. The partners may even want to hire a search firm to help them, given their lack of success when hiring Adams.

The partners also should invite the applicant's spouse to join in the interview process. If appropriate, they should try to learn what the spouse's expectations and needs are concerning the position and, potentially, the move to the Portsmouth area.

The partners also need to set up a clear policy for evaluating the new associate, on a formal basis. Moreover, they need to commit themselves to maintaining open lines of communication with the new associate, as well as the rest of the office staff. At least for the short term, they might want to have a regular time set aside for open staff meetings. These could be potentially held either at the beginning or end of the week.

Basically, the partners need to set in motion a plan to overcome their shortcomings in the areas of planning, communication, recruiting, hiring, and orientation.

References

Baker, A., & Green, E. (1987). *Storytelling: Art and technique* (2nd ed.). New York: Bowker.

Bloom, B. S., Hastings, J. T., & Madaus, G. F. (1971). *Handbook on formative and summative evaluation of student learning.* New York: McGraw-Hill.

Bock, E. A. (1970). *Improving the usefulness of the case study in political science* (Working paper). Syracuse, NY: Inter-University Case Program.

Chandler, A. D., Jr. (1962). *Strategy and structure: Chapters in the history of the industrial enterprise.* Garden City, NY: Doubleday.

Feagin, J. R., Orum, A. M., & Sjoberg, G. (Eds.). (1991). *A case for the case study.* Chapel Hill, NC: University of North Carolina Press.

Hatten, K. J. (1987). Mark Whitcomb. In K. J. Hatten & M. L. Hatten, *Strategic management: Analysis and action* (p. 694). Englewood Cliffs, NJ: Prentice Hall.

Hatten, K. J., & Hatten, M. L. (1987). *Instructor's guide: Strategic management: Analysis and action.* Englewood Cliffs, NJ: Prentice Hall.

Hofer, C. W. (1973, August). *Some preliminary research on patterns of strategic behavior.* Paper presented at the annual meeting of the Academy of Management, Boston, MA.

Hulpach, V. (Ed.). (1965). Who brought the sun? In *American Indian tales and legends* (pp. 17-22). London: Paul Hamlyn.

Katz, R. (1970). Burns Corporation. In R. Katz, *Cases and concepts in corporate strategy* (pp. 152-193). Englewood Cliffs, NJ: Prentice Hall.

Kazdin, A. E. (1982). *Single-case research designs: Methods for clinical and applied settings.* New York: Oxford University Press.

Kinnunen, R., & Ramamurti, R. (1987). Making cases more "real": The use of videotapes to enhance business policy cases. *Case Research Journal, 7,* 1-5.

Kolb, D. A., Osland, J. S., & Rubin, I. M. (1995). *Organizational behavior: An experiential approach.* Englewood Cliffs, NJ: Prentice Hall.

211

Lawrence, P., & Lorsch, J. W. (1967). *Organizational structure and design.* Homewood, IL: Irwin.

Marzano, R. J., Brandt, R. S., Hughes, C. S., Jones, B. F., Presseisen, B. Z., Rankin, S. C., & Suhor, C. (1988). *Dimensions of thinking: A framework for curriculum and instruction* (Ch. 4). Alexandria, VA: Association for Supervision and Curriculum Development.

Maslow, A. H. (1943). A theory of human motivation. *Psychological Review, 50,* 370-371, 394-396.

McDougall, P. P. (1991, Summer). The Fallon-McElligott Advertising Agency: Image making by image makers. *Case Research Journal,* 91-102.

Merenda, M., & Naumes, W. (1993, Summer). Post Manufacturing Company. *The Case Research Journal,* 1-26.

Miller, D., & Friesen, P. H. (1980). Momentum and revolution in organizational adaptation. *Academy of Management Journal, 23*(4), 591-614.

Naumes, M. (1988, August). Toward a theory of the case note. In *Expanding case horizons.* Proceedings of the 5th Annual NACRA Symposium on Case Development and Research, Anaheim, CA.

Naumes, M. J., & Oyaas, A. C. (1995). The Possum connection: An ethical dilemma. In A. A. Thompson, Jr., & A. J. Strickland, III (Eds.), *Strategic management: Concepts and cases* (8th ed.). New York: McGraw-Hill.

Naumes, W. (1982a). Clemens Super Market, Inc. In F. T. Paine & W. Naumes (Eds.), *Organizational strategy and policy: Text and cases* (3rd ed.; pp. 502-519). Chicago: Dryden.

Naumes, W. (1982b). Gulf and Western Industries, Inc. In F. T. Paine & W. Naumes (Eds.), *Organizational strategy and policy: Text and cases* (3rd ed.; pp. 473-485). Chicago: Dryden.

Naumes, W., & Naumes, M. J. (1995). The Merck-Medco merger proposal. In J. E. Post, W. C. Frederick, A. T. Lawrence, & J. Weber (Eds.), *Business and society* (8th ed.). New York: McGraw-Hill.

Naumes, W., & Schellenberger, R. (1983). Vail Industries, Inc. In R. Schellenberger & G. Boseman (Eds.), *Policy formulation and strategy mangement* (2nd ed.; pp. 282-297). New York: John Wiley.

Naumes, W., Wilson, M., & Walters, S. (1995, Winter). Meyers & Morrison: A question of professional ethics. *The Case Research Journal,* 41-47.

Noetzel, D. M., & Stanford, M. J. (1992, Summer). The Gustavson farm. *Case Research Journal, 12,* 121-129.

Ó Cinnéide, B. (1997, October). *The need to re-consider the teaching note's contribution to the case writing process.* Paper presented at the annual meeting of the North American Case Research Association, Cincinnati, OH.

Pavan, R. J. (1988, November). The case research note. *Proceedings of the North American Case Research Association, 2,* 1-6.

Pearce, J. A., II, & Robinson, R. B., Jr. (1994). *Strategic management: Formulation, implementation & control.* Chicago: Irwin.

Porter, M. (1979, March/April). How competitive forces shape strategy. *Harvard Business Review,* 137-145.

Porter, M. E. (1990). *The competitive advantage of nations.* New York: Free Press.

Prawat, R. S. (1991). The value of ideas: The immersion approach to the development of thinking. *Educational Researcher, 20,* p. 8.

Resnick, R., & Klopfer, L. E. (1989). Toward the thinking curriculum: An overview. In R. Resnick & L. E. Klopfer (Eds.), *Toward the thinking curriculum: Current cognitive research* (Yearbook of the Association for Supervision & Curriculum Development, pp. 1-18).

Reynolds, J. (1978, January). There's method in cases. *Academy of Management Review, 3*(1), 129-133.

Sawyer, R. (1962). *The way of the storyteller.* New York: Penguin.

Scott, C. R., Jr. (1980). The case teaching note. *Case Research Journal, 1,*39-44.

Scott, W. (1808). *Marmion,* Canto Six, Stanza 17.

Schatzman, L., & Strauss, A. L. (1973). *Field research strategies for a natural sociology.* Englewood Cliffs, NJ: Prentice Hall.

Shedlock, M. L. (1951). *The art of the story-teller.* New York: Dover.

Stake, R. E. (1995). *The art of case study research.* Thousand Oaks, CA: Sage.

Thompson, A. A., Jr. (1993). Turner Broadcasting System—1992. In A. A. Thompson, Jr., & A. J. Strickland, III (Eds.), *Strategic management: Concepts & cases* (7th ed.; pp. 321-344). Boston: Irwin.

Thompson, A. A., Jr., & Strickland, A. J. (1993). Competition in the U.S. frozen dairy dessert industry. In A. A. Thompson, Jr., & A. J. Strickland, III, (Eds.), *Strategic management: Concepts & cases* (7th ed.). Boston: Irwin.

Timmons, J. A. (1990). *New venture creation* (3rd ed.). Chicago: Irwin.

Towl, A. C. (1969). *To study administration by cases.* Cambridge, MA: Harvard University Graduate School of Business Administration.

Whyte, W. F. (1984). *Learning from the field: A guide from experience.* Beverly Hills, CA: Sage.

Wood, C., Kaufman, A., & Merenda, M. (1996, Winter). How HADCO became a problem-solving supplier. *Sloan Management Review,* 77-88.

Yin, R. K. (1989). *Case study research: Designs and methods* (Rev. ed.). Newbury Park, CA: Sage.

Recommended Reading:
A Resource List by Topic

CASE TEACHING

Applegate, L. M. (1988). *Case teaching at HBS: Some thoughts for new faculty* (ICCH 90189-062). Boston, MA: Harvard Business School.

Argyris, C. (1980). Some limitations of the case method: Experiences in a management development program. *Academy of Management Review, 5,* 291-298.

Baker, A., & Green, E. (1987). *Storytelling: Art and technique* (2nd ed.). New York: Bowker.

Berger, M. A. (1983). In defense of the case method. *Academy of Management Review, 8,* 329-333.

Bloom, B. S., Hastings, J. T., & Madaus, G. F. (1971). *Handbook on formative and summative evaluation of student learning.* New York: McGraw-Hill.

Bludent, R. G. (1993). The real case method: A response to critics of business education. *Case Research Journal, 13,*106-119.

Bower, D. D., Lewicki, R. J., Hall, D. T, & Hall, F. S. (1997). *Experiences in management and organizational behavior* (4th ed.). New York: John Wiley.

Charan, R. (1976). Classroom techniques in teaching by the case method. *Academy of Mangement Review, 1,* 116-123.

Christensen, C. R., Garvin, D. A., & Sweet, A. (Eds.). (1991). *Education for judgement: The artistry of discussion leadership.* Boston, MA: Harvard Business School Press.

Christensen, C. R. (1987). *Teaching and the case method.* Boston, MA: Harvard Business School Press.

Coleman, D. R., & Edge, A. G. (1978). *The guide to case analysis and reporting.* Honolulu, HI: System Logistice.

Comerford, R. A., & Callaghan, D. W. (1985). Strategic management: Case, casebook and course preferences of business policy professors. *Case Research Journal, 5,* 25-38.

Corey, E. R. (1982). Case method teaching. *Case Research Journal, 2,*1-21.

Dooley, A. F., & Skinner, W. (1977). Casing case method methods. *Academy of Management Review, 2,* 277-289.

Enrick, N. L., & Myers, B. L. (1971). A structured approach for case methodology in the business policy course. *Decision Sciences, 2,* 111-122.

Erskine, J. A., Leenders, M. R., & Mauffette-Leenders, L. A. (1981). *Teaching with cases.* London, Ontario, Canada: University of Western Ontario.

Feder, B. (1973, April). Case studies: A flexible approach to knowledge building. *The Social Studies,* 171-178.

Feeney, H. M., & Stenzel, A. K. (1970). *Learning by the case method.* New York: Seabury.

Finch, B. J. (1993). A modeling enhancement to teaching with cases. *Journal of Management Education, 17,* 228-235.

Fiol, M., & Lyles, M. (1985). Organizational learning. *Academy of Management Review, 10,* 803-813.

Gragg, C. I. (1940). *Because wisdom can't be told* (ICCH 451-05). Boston, MA: Harvard Business School, HBS Case Services.

Greenwood, R. (1983). The case method at Harvard: A short history. *Case Research Journal, 3,* 3-10.

Hay, R. D. (1982). Management theory and practice: Implications for case research and teaching. *Case Research Journal, 2,* 27-31.

Hazen, M. A. (1987-88). Learning how to learn: An experiment in dialogue. *The Organizational Behavior Teaching Review, 12,* 72-85.

Hendry, C. (1996). Understanding and creating whole organizational change through learning theory. *Human Relations, 49,* 621-641.

Kolb, D. A., Osland, J. S., & Rubin, I. M. (1995). *Organizational behavior: An experiential approach.* Englewood Cliffs, NJ: Prentice Hall.

Levinthal, D. A., & March, J. G. (1993). The myopia of learning. *Strategic Management Journal, 14,* 95-112.

Marzano, R. J., Brandt, R. S., Hughes, C. S., Jones, B. F., Presseisen, B. Z., Rankin, S. C., & Suhor, C. (1988). *Dimensions of thinking: A framework for curriculum and instruction* (Ch. 4). Alexandria, VA: Association for Supervision and Curriculum Development.

Matejka, J. K., & Cosse, T. *The business case method: An introduction.* Reston, VA: Reston Publishing.

Pavan, R. J. (1988, November). The case research note. *Proceedings of the North American Case Research Association, 2,* 1-6.

Prawat, R. S. (1991). The value of ideas: The immersion approach to the development of thinking. *Educational Researcher, 20,* 8.

Rappaport, A., & Cawelti, G. S. (1993). Using peer review to improve the writing of case analyses: Requirements and experience. *Journal of Management Education, 17,* 485-489.

Resnick, R., & Klopfer, L. E. (1989). Toward the thinking curriculum: An overview. In R. Resnick & L. E. Klopfer (Eds.), *Toward the thinking curriculum: Current cognitive research* (Yearbook of the Association for Supervision & Curriculum Development, pp. 1-18).

Reynolds, J. I. (1980). *Case method in mangement development* (Management Development Series No. 17). Geneva, Switzerland: International Labour Office.

Ronstadt, R. (1977). *The art of case analysis: A student guide to the diagnosis of business situations.* Needham, MA: Lord.

Safavi, F. (1978). Informatice: The complete information approach to case administration. *Management International Review, 19,* 99-107.

Sawyer, R. (1962). *The way of the story-teller.* New York: Penguin.

Schiro, S. F. (1994). Introducing case analysis by telling real cases. *Journal of Management Education, 18,* 484-489.

Schoon, D. A. (1984). Education for reflection-in-action. *Case Research Journal, 4,* 3-24.

Shedlock, M. L. (1951). *The way of the storyteller.* New York: Dover.

Stewart, K. A., & Winn, J. (1996). The case debate: A new approach to case teaching. *Journal of Mangement Education, 20,* 48-59.

Thomsen, C. J. ((1980). Changing technology and the future of business education. *Case Research Journal, 1,* 45-52.

Towl, A. C. (1969). *To study administration by cases.* Cambridge, MA: Harvard University Graduate School of Business Administration.

Vesper, K. H. (1985). *Entrepreneurial education, 1985.* Wellesley, MA: Babson Center for Entrepreneurial Studies.

Waltz, L. E. (1981). Establishing objectives, evaluating accomplishment, and assigning grades in a case-oriented course. In R. A. Ajami (Ed.), *The state of the art in teaching business policy* (pp. 128-141). Columbus: Ohio State University, College of Administrative Science.

Wernette, P. J. (1965). The theory of the case method. *Michigan Business Review, 7,* 47-52.

CASE WRITING

Anyansi-Archibong, C. (1987). Problems and challenges in using the case study method in a foreign based field research project. *Case Research Journal, 7,* 1-18.

Barach, J. A. (1985). Creating publishable cases: Using MBA student case writers. *Case Research Journal, 5,* 15-24.

Chrisman, J. J. (1990). Writing a publishable case. *Case Research Journal, 10,* 4-9.

Clinton, J. W., & Camerius, J. W. (1997). Casewriting caveats: Bugaboos and boo-boos. In. G. Lindstrom (Ed.), *1997 Proceedings of the Society For Case Research,* 15-24.

Culliton, J. W. (1973). *Handbook on case writing.* Makiti, Philippines: Asian Institute of Management.

Erskine, J. A., & Leenders, M. R. (1989). *Case research: The case writing process* (Rev. ed.). London, Ontario, Canada: University of Western Ontario.

Gebhard, C. (1980). Overview of the case workshop. *Case Research Journal, 1,* 19-21.

Gentile, M. (1991). *Field interviewing tips for the case researcher* (ICCH 9-391-041). Boston, MA: Harvard Business School, Publishing Division.

Gold, B. A. ((1993). The construction of business cases: Reframing the debate. *Case Research Journal, 13,* 120-125.

Kinnunen, R., & Ramamurti, R. (1987). Making cases more "real": The use of videotapes to enhance business policy cases. *Case Research Journal, 7,* 1-5.

Lane, H. W., & Burgoyne, D. G. (1988). The case of developing country cases. *Case Research Journal, 8,* 9-22.

Marzano, R. J., Brandt, R. S., Hughes, C. S., Jones, B. F., Presseisen, B. Z., Rankin, S. C., & Suhor, C. (1988). *Dimensions of thinking: A framework for curriculum and instruc-*

tion (Ch. 4). Alexandria, VA: Association for Supervision and Curriculum Development.

Mager, R. F. (1962). *Preparing instructional objectives.* Belmont, CA: Fearon.

Megginson, L. C. (1980). The case method as both a research technique and a pedagogical method. *Case Research Journal, 1,* 10-18.

Naumes, M. (1988, August). Toward a theory of the case note. In *Expanding case horizons.* Proceedings of the 5th Annual NACRA Symposium on Case Development and Research, Anaheim, CA.

Naumes, W. (1989). Editorial: Case writing, professional development, and publishing standards for the case research journal. *Case Research Journal, 9,* 1-8.

Naumes, W. (1997, September). Writing effective cases: A methodological approach. *Asian Case Research Journal, 1,* 223-236.

Ó Cinnéide, B. (1997, October). *The need to re-consider the teaching note's contribution to the case writing process.* Paper presented at the annual meeting of the North American Case Research Association, Cincinnati, OH.

Reynolds, J. (1978, January). There's method in cases. *Academy of Management Review, 3*(1), 129-133.

Ross, R. H., & Headley, E. (1997). The role of refereed cases in the new AACSB environment. In G. Lindstrom (Ed.), *1997 Proceedings of the Society For Case Research,* 10-14.

Scott, C. R., Jr. (1980). The case teaching note. *Case Research Journal, 1,*39-44.

Sharplin, A. (1990). Toward reasonable standards for publishable cases. *Case Research Journal, 10,*10-16.

Stanford, M. J. (1972). *Case development and the teaching note* ICCH 9-373-733). Boston, MA: Harvard Graduate School of Business.

Tate, C. E., Flewellen, W. C., & Phillips, D. (1980). The state of the case arts: Teaching, research and writing. *Case Research Journal, 1,* 1-9.

Towl, A. C. (1969). *To study administration by cases.* Cambridge, MA: Harvard University Graduate School of Business Administration.

Towl, A. C. (1980). Discovering the natural habitat of cases. *Case Research Journal, 1,* 26-38.

Towl, A. C. (1990, Spring). Case development—A cooperative effort. *Case Research Journal, 10,* 1-3.

CASE RESEARCH

Beukenkamp, P. A., & Boverhoff, G. J. (1972). Case method and case research in European marketing education. *Management International Review, 6,* 115.

Bock, E. A. (1970). *Improving the usefulness of the case study in political science* (Working paper). Syracuse, NY: Inter-University Case Program.

Boulton, W. R. (1985). Case study as a research methodology. *Case Research Journal, 5,* 3-14.

Brigley, S. (1995). Business ethics in context: Researching with case studies. *Journal of Business Ethics, 14,* 219-226.

Chandler, A. D., Jr. (1962). *Strategy and structure: Chapters in the history of the industrial enterprise.* Garden City, NY: Doubleday.

Crombie, A. (1969, October). The case study method and the theory of organizations. *Australian and New Zealand Journal of Sociology, 5,* 111-120.

Feagin, J. R., Orum, A. M., & Sjoberg, G. (Eds.). (1991). *A case for the case study.* Chapel Hill: University of North Carolina Press.

Heald, K. A., & Yin, R. K. (1982, September). Using the case survey method to analyze policy studies. *Administrative Science Quarterly, 20,* 371-381.

Herron, D. J. (1975). The case study method. *Journal of Chemical Education, 1* (July), 460.

Hofer, C. W. (1973, August). *Some preliminary research on patterns of strategic behavior.* Paper presented at the annual meeting of the Academy of Management, Boston, MA.

Jauch, L. R., Osborn, R., & Martin, T. N. (1980). Structured content analysis: A complementary method for organizational research. *The Academy of Management Review, 5,* 517-526.

Kazdin, A. E. (1982). *Single-case research designs: Methods for clinical and applied settings.* New York: Oxford University Press.

Lawrence, P., & Lorsch, J. W. (1967). *Organizational structure and design.* Homewood, IL: Irwin.

Miller, D., & Friesen, P. H. (1980). Momentum and revolution in organizational adaptation. *Academy of Management Journal, 23*(4), 591-614.

Moussavi, F. (1989, Spring). Capturing the politics of organizational life: An organizational analysis approach. *Case Research Journal, 9,* 9-18.

Naumes, W., & Merenda, M. J. (1998, July). *The use of case-base research: A typology-based example.* Paper presented at the annual meeting of the World Case Research Association (WACRA), Marseilles, France.

Porter, M. (1979, March/April). How competitive forces shape strategy. *Harvard Business Review,* 137-145.

Porter, M. E. (1990). *The competitive advantage of nations.* New York: Free Press.

Ratliff, R. L. (1990, Autumn). An argument for case research. *Case Research Journal, 10,* 1-15.

Schatzman, L., & Strauss, A. L. (1973). *Field research strategies for a natural sociology.* Englewood Cliffs, NJ: Prentice Hall.

Stake, R. E. (1995). *The art of case study research.* Thousand Oaks, CA: Sage.

Stanford, M. J. (1988). Current issues in case research. *Case Research Journal, 8,* 1-8.

Vesper, K. H. (1985). *Entrepreneurship education, 1985.* Wellesly, MA: Babson Center for Entrepreneurial Studies.

Whyte, W. F. (1984). *Learning from the field: A guide from experience.* Beverly Hills, CA: Sage.

Wood, C., Kaufman, A., & Merenda, M. (1996, Winter). How HADCO became a problem-solving supplier. *Sloan Management Review,* 77-88.

Yin, R. K. (1989). *Case study research: Designs and methods* (Rev. ed.). Newbury Park, CA: Sage.

CASES CITED

Hatten, K. J. (1987). Mark Whitcomb. In K. J. Hatten & M. L. Hatten (Eds.), *Strategic management: Analysis and action* (p. 694). Englewood Cliffs, NJ: Prentice Hall.

Katz, R. (1970). Burns Corporation. In R. Katz, *Cases and concepts in corporate strategy* (pp. 152-193). Englewood Cliffs, NJ: Prentice Hall.

McDougall, P. P. (1991, Summer). The Fallon-McElligott Advertising Agency: Image making by image makers. *Case Research Journal,* 91-102.

Merenda, M., & Naumes, W. (1993, Summer). Post Manufacturing Company. *The Case Research Journal,* 1-26.

Naumes, M. J., & Oyaas, A. C. (1995). The Possum connection: An ethical dilemma. In A. A. Thompson, Jr., & A. J. Strickland, III (Eds.), *Strategic management: Concepts and cases* (8th ed.). New York: McGraw-Hill.

Naumes, W. (1982a). Clemens Super Market, Inc. In F. T. Paine & W. Naumes (Eds.), *Organizational strategy and policy: Text and cases* (3rd ed.; pp. 502-519). Chicago: Dryden.

Naumes, W. (1982b). Gulf and Western Industries, Inc. In F. T. Paine & W. Naumes (Eds.), *Organizational strategy and policy: Text and cases* (3rd ed.; pp. 473-485). Chicago: Dryden.

Naumes, W., & Kane, K. (1988). Windward Islands aloe. *International Journal of Value Based Management, 1,* 113-132.

Naumes, W., & Naumes, M. J. (1995). The Merck-Medco merger proposal. In J. E. Post, W. C. Frederick, A. T. Lawrence, & J. Weber (Eds.), *Business and society* (8th ed.). New York: McGraw-Hill.

Naumes, W., & Schellenberger, R. (1983). Vail Industries, Inc. In R. Schellenberger & G. Boseman (Eds.), *Policy formulation and strategy mangement* (2nd ed.; pp. 282-297). New York: John Wiley.

Naumes, W., Wilson, M., & Walters, S. (1995, Winter). Meyers & Morrison: A question of professional ethics. *The Case Research Journal,* 41-47.

Noetzel, D. M., & Stanford, M. J. (1992, Summer). The Gustavson farm. *Case Research Journal, 12,* 121-129.

Pearce, J. A., II, & Robinson, R. B., Jr. (1994). *Strategic management: Formulation, implementation & control.* Chicago: Irwin.

Scott, W. (1808). *Marmion,* Canto Six, Stanza 17.

Thompson, A. A., Jr. (1993). Turner Broadcasting System—1992. In A. A. Thompson, Jr., & A. J. Strickland, III, (Eds.), *Strategic management: Concepts & cases* (7th ed.; pp. 321-344). Boston: Irwin.

Thompson, A. A., Jr., & Strickland, A. J. (1993). Competition in the U.S. frozen dairy dessert industry. In A. A. Thompson, Jr., & A. J. Strickland, III, (Eds.), *Strategic management: Concepts & cases* (7th ed.). Boston: Irwin.

Timmons, J. A. (1990). *New venture creation* (3rd ed.). Chicago: Irwin.

Author Index

Subject Index

About the Authors

William Naumes, PhD, is Associate Professor of Management at the Whittemore School of Business and Economics at the University of New Hampshire. He received a BS in Industrial and Labor Relations and a master's degree in Business Administration from Cornell University and a PhD in Business from Stanford University. He has written over 100 cases and instructor's notes, many of which have been published in journals and texts; seven of these are books he has authored. The cases span the areas of entrepreneurship, strategic management, corporate social responsibility, and organization behavior. He has participated in numerous case workshops and case review panels at regional and national professional meetings throughout the United States and in Europe and has taught and worked with faculty in Europe and Indonesia, as well as the United States. He has served twice as the Program Chair for the North American Case Research Association (NACRA) and as president in 1996-1997. He was editor of the *Case Research Journal* from 1988 through 1991 and has acted as one of the coordinators of the New Case Writers panel and Case Writers Workshops at the Decision Sciences Institute for many years.

Margaret J. Naumes, PhD, is Adjunct Assistant Professor of Strategic Management at the Whittemore School of Business and Economics at the University of New Hampshire, where she teaches Strategic Management and Business, Government, and Society. She received a BS in Economics from Connecticut College, an MA and PhD in Economics from Stanford University, and an MBA from Clark University. She has published articles and case studies dealing with cross-cultural management, entrepreneurship, management decision making, and ethics, and she has written several books on management and case writing. She has presented papers and

233

from Connecticut College, an MA and PhD in Economics from Stanford University, and an MBA from Clark University. She has published articles and case studies dealing with cross-cultural management, entrepreneurship, management decision making, and ethics, and she has written several books on management and case writing. She has presented papers and workshops throughout the United States and in Europe and has taught and worked with faculty in Europe and Indonesia, as well as the United States. She has been active in the Decision Sciences Institute and the North American Case Research Association (NACRA) at the regional and national levels and has served as an officer in both organizations.